Signposts in Adoption
Policy, practice, and
research issues

Acknowledgements

We would like to thank the authors of all the papers contained in this collection for their kind permission to reproduce them. Although every effort has been made to trace each of the authors, we have not been able to do so in every case and have selected and included their paper on the assumption that the author would have willingly given permission if we had been able to reach them.

We are also very grateful to Malcolm Hill and Martin Shaw, both of whom have had a long association with *Adoption & Fostering* including its editorship, for their work in selecting and introducing the papers in this anthology.

Finally, thanks are also due to Miranda Davies, the Production Editor of *Adoption & Fostering*, for her help with the preparation of this book.

Note about the Editors

Malcolm Hill is Director of the Centre for the Child & Society, University of Glasgow, and has authored several studies and journal articles. He is the Commissioning Editor of *Adoption & Fostering*.

Martin Shaw was Senior Lecturer in Social Work at University of Leicester until retirement and the author of several books and journal articles. He was Commissioning Editor of *Adoption & Fostering* from 1994 to 1995.

Signposts in Adoption

Policy, practice, and
research issues

Edited by Malcolm Hill and
Martin Shaw

British
Agencies
for **A**doption
and **F**ostering

362.
7340
941
Sig

Published by
British Agencies for Adoption & Fostering
(BAAF)
Skyline House
200 Union Street
London SE1 0LX

© BAAF 1998

Charity registration 275689

British Library Cataloguing in Publication Data
A catalogue record for this book is available
from the British Library

ISBN 1 873868 53 7

Designed by Andrew Haig & Associates
Cover photographs (posed by models):
John Birdsall Photography
Cover illustration by Andrew Haig
Typeset by Avon Dataset Ltd, Bidford on Avon
Printed by Russell Press Ltd. (TU),
Nottingham

This collection is dedicated to Margaret Kornitzer (−1996)
Founder Editor of the Bulletin
of the Standing Conference of Societies Registered for Adoption,
later Child Adoption, and
Tony Rampton (1915–1993)
Honorary Secretary and Treasurer to the Standing Conference.

Contents

Preface

What we know today as "The Journal" began life as "The Bulletin" of the Standing Conference of Societies Registered for Adoption. The first edition was published in October 1951 and was available for member societies only – membership was then open to all registered adoption societies on payment of an annual affiliation fee of £2 and 2 shillings! It was edited by its founder, Margaret Kornitzer, who was also the Press Officer of the Standing Conference; Tony Rampton was Honorary Secretary and Treasurer. It was all of 14 pages long and typed with only a few errors, clearly at a time when Tippex was not invented.

This first edition introduced readers to the purpose of the Bulletin. It promised that it would tell members "what the Standing Conference is doing as an organisation, with your money, to further the cause of adoption, whether by approach to official bodies or otherwise. It will contain general items of news, advance notices of meetings, information on special points that have presented difficulties to member societies, and anything else likely to be interesting . . .

. . . In large measure we must depend on you to make this Bulletin your own, both by reading it and commenting on its contents, and by contributing to it yourselves when you have something worth saying. From time to time we hope also to print short articles by experts. Let us know what you would like to see in these pages . . ." (p 2)

That edition included short "newsy" items on family allowances, the filing of adoption applications, the difficulties of defining domicile and residence, adoption by US citizens stationed in Britain, problems posed in passport applications by/for adopted children, and the concerns of member agencies about the numbers of mothers of illegitimate children who were driven to adoption not because they wanted to give up their children but because they could not find accommodation. One item related to intercountry adoption, but this was about children adopted *from* Britain. The book reviews section kicked off with Dr Bowlby's *Maternal Care and Mental Health*, a study that has since been cited frequently in the pages of the journal.

By January 1953 the Bulletin had acquired a name – *Child Adoption*. Two years later *Child Adoption* took on a different garb – it was professionally printed with the titles of the articles appearing on the front cover. In keeping with this change of status, it stopped describing itself as a "Bulletin" and became the more scholarly "Journal". It carried on like this until 1970 with a gradual increase in the number of pages.

By 1970, *Child Adoption* was published by the Association of British Adoption Agencies. A sizeable 52 pages long, the journal cost five shillings. It was in 1976 that it rechristened itself and became *Adoption & Fostering*, the journal of the Association of British Adoption and Fostering Agencies (ABAFA) – a further change of status bringing it into line with journals published by professional and learned societies. Now 72 pages long, it also had a new Editor, Sarah Curtis, following the retirement of its founder Editor, Margaret Kornitzer, after 25 years in post.

The journal was to go through still more changes. ABAFA changed its name and became British Agencies for Adoption & Fostering (BAAF) and the first *Adoption & Fostering* published by BAAF in 1980 had further improved its presentation. In 1987, a brand identity in the shape of BAAF's logo was introduced on the cover. A single copy then cost £3.00 and the first revamped edition contained an article on adoption allowances co-authored by John Triseliotis and Malcolm Hill, the latter then a Research Fellow and Lecturer at Edinburgh University and today, the Journal's Commissioning Editor.

In 1997, to coincide with *Adoption & Fostering's* 21st birthday, the Journal was relaunched yet again, now 80 pages and with a spine to hold it together (to the delight of Felicity Collier, Director of BAAF, who had agitated for a spine ever since she joined us) and an impressive peer review panel in place assuring quality standards of papers submitted to the journal for publication. The first relaunched issue, published on the eve of the 1997 General Election, attracted statements from the key health spokespeople of the Liberal Democrat, Conservative and Labour parties who commented on the Draft Adoption Bill – a coup for the journal. Alongside the well established tradition of practice-based and accessibly written academic articles, this provided testament to the confirmed status of *Adoption & Fostering* as *the* authoritative journal on adoption and fostering matters in *the* UK.

Leigh Chambers and Shaila Shah,
BAAF

Introduction
Adoption in the UK

The nature of adoption policy and practice has altered
dramatically over the last 20 years. The numbers and types of
children needing adoptive families are quite different, since far
fewer babies are now placed for adoption. Partly as a result, the
experiences of adoptive families are likely to be significantly
different from those of a generation ago. In this volume we have
sought to represent some of the more recent changes by selecting
from the journal *Adoption & Fostering* articles which reflect and
analyse key trends in the UK in the last ten years. We hope that
the reader will find in the range of materials food for thought and
indications of some of the major issues and controversies which
have been taking place in the UK as we approach the millennium.

There was so much rich and relevant material in the journal that it
was necessary to set limits around our choices. With some regret,
we have decided to focus on material related to the UK, so that
some very interesting articles from and about other parts of the
world are not included.

In this chapter we aim to discuss briefly what we see as the main
issues which have involved and affected adoption over this period.
In doing so we shall provide brief summaries of the articles which
make up the chapters to follow, while also drawing attention to
other relevant publications, including a few other articles from the
journal that space did not allow us to include. References to
chapters in this book will be indicated in bold to distinguish them
from other references (e.g. **Triseliotis, 1991**). Details of these
references are placed at the end of the book (see p 291).

The order in which this chapter deals with different issues related to adoption corresponds with the structure for the rest of the book. It seemed helpful to begin with an overview of recent changes in adoption and its context. Then we review some of the key principles which underpin practice and discuss trends in policy and law. Next attention is turned to evidence about experiences and outcomes of adoption. A major development of the last ten years has been the move towards greater "openness", whereby adoptive families and adult adoptees may have some kind of information exchange or contact with the original families to which the child was born. Openness is a fluid and at times misunderstood concept, but it is undoubtedly having an important impact on all aspects of adoption, so we present some indications of its application in this country.

Among the most important debates about adoption (and fostering) in recent years has concerned the significance of taking account of children's ethnic and racial background when making placements. While there has been broad support for actively seeking to match children and adopters in domestic adoption, this principle has not usually applied to the growing number of adoptions from overseas. Hence our next section discusses ethnic and cultural issues in adoption.

The final sections of this chapter and correspondingly the last part of the book deal with post-adoption issues. Both changing placement patterns and the tendency towards greater openness have highlighted the fact that many adopted children and adults, adopters and birth relatives have needs for information, support and other services after adoption – in some cases many years after.

Changing patterns of adoption

Adoption statistics indicate some of the enormous changes which have occurred over the past 20 years. They reveal patterns which reflect social and policy changes. These evolving patterns have themselves prompted some alterations in practice and attitudes.

A well-known development has been the overall steady decline in the total number of adoptions. In England and Wales the peak year for adoptions was in 1974 when 22,502 adoptions took place. By 1992, the total had fallen to 7,342, just about one-third of the 1974 figure. Scottish figures show a similar decrease, with the number of adoptions halving between 1985 and 1995 (ignoring adoptions by step-parents) (Scottish Office, 1997).

The overall decline conceals differences among the age-groups of children being adopted. In particular higher proportions of older children are adopted nowadays. The numbers of babies under one year who were adopted fell by 40 per cent between 1989 and 1992, whereas children aged one to four showed an increase of 21 per cent over the same period. A survey of agency adoptions in England and Wales in 1995 (i.e. excluding adoptions by close relatives) revealed that twice as many children aged five to nine were adopted as infants. One quarter of adoptions in London boroughs concerned children of minority ethnic backgrounds, though only four per cent in the shire counties (Dance, 1997). Satisfactory information is difficult to come by concerning intercountry adoption, which is often transracial too. However, it is clear that there has been a comparative upsurge from an insignificant number in the 1980s to probably about 200 per annum in the UK as a whole (BAAF, 1991; **Selman and White, 1994**; Dance, 1997).

The reasons for these changes are familiar: the greater availability of contraception and abortion facilities and the greater social acceptance of single parenthood led to fewer babies needing adoption. Potential adopters had to consider a wider range of children, including those who are no longer babies and those with disabilities or development difficulties. People interested only in adopting babies initially sought or were offered black children born in the UK. Transracial placement, once seen as a positive liberal response to a "social problem", gradually through the 1980s came to be regarded by adoption workers as unethical and contrary to the best interests of the children concerned. In addition, the merits of "closed" adoption, protecting the anonymity of the adopters and excluding birth relatives from the lives of their children post-adoption, have come to be challenged in favour of varying degres of openness, up to and including post-adoption contact between the child and his or her birth relatives. As a result of these developments, what might be termed "traditional" adopters, seeking healthy, white babies to bring up as their own without birth family contact, have sometimes turned to intercountry adoption. This was initially viewed as an humanitarian exercise in rescuing children from countries ravaged by war, but more recently has generated concern as a form of Western imperialism, with commercial interests taking priority over the rights and welfare of children or birth parents (Ngabonziza, 1991).

Section I
Principles and trends

1

Adoption is an enduring and flexible social institution, even though it only took on a legal form in 1926 in England and Wales (1930 in Scotland). 'The first recorded adoption in Western tradition is that of Moses, a transcultural and possibly transracial adoption in which an infant of a subjugated people was adopted by a woman of the ruling class – possibly a single parent' (Triseliotis *et al*, 1997, p 3). Once associated with ensuring male heirs, it came to be seen as an appropriate outcome for children in long-term foster homes. In the post-war period, the so-called "traditional" form of adoption predominated, with the infants of single mothers being placed with mainly middle-class couples **(Triseliotis, 1995)**.

As noted above, the patterns are now more diverse, even though smaller numbers of children are affected. Thus certain core elements of adoption persist, while other aspects evolve in response to changing circumstances and attitudes. The central ingredient remains the idea of permanent transfer of responsibility for a child from one family household to another, though in the case of step-parent adoptions even this applies only partially.

The first articles in this collection set the scene by offering a range of perspectives on contemporary adoption. **Hill (1991)** reviewed the functions which have historically been performed by adoption. His analysis of the nature of parenthood and parenting helps to illuminate the issues and dilemmas which are prominent in present-day adoption. He identified the major challenge for adoption in the 1990s as being to reconcile openness with providing children with a sense of lifelong belonging, i.e. permanence.

The ideas of permanence and permanency planning were developed through the 1970s and 80s, prompted in the UK by the publication of *Children Who Wait* (Rowe and Lambert, 1973). This revealed widespread occurrences of what was called "drift", i.e. children remaining in foster or residential care with no definite long-term plans, sometimes in inappropriate placements, yet with no apparent possibility of returning them to their families of origin. To counteract drift, it was argued that the aim of any placement, apart from assessment and short-term care, should be to provide a child with a "permanent" family. This meant either their own or an adoptive family, rather than residential or foster care, which were viewed as inherently unstable and unsatisfactory. Despite the priority given by writers on permanence to returning children home (e.g. Maluccio *et al*, 1986), in practice adoption services benefited more than preventive or rehabilitative services from the application of this philosophy. Legal changes brought in by the Children Act 1975 made it easier to arrange adoption without parental consent. Changes in local authority policies emphasised seeking adoptive homes for children who remained in care after two years and/or who had little prospect of a satisfactory return home (McKay, 1980; Hussell and Managhan, 1982). Recruitment strategies became more inclusive, while adoption allowances enabled foster carers and other prospective adopters on low incomes to proceed to adoption (Hill *et al*, 1989). "Freeing" for adoption was introduced in the mid-1980s. A child could now be freed for adoption through a court hearing which dealt with the issue of parental agreement, prior to the identification of suitable adopters or to a full adoption application (Lambert *et al*, 1990; Murch *et al*, 1993).

The pursuit of permanency planning policies varied considerably and was less strong in Northern Ireland (Kelly, 1989; Kelly and

Pinkerton, 1996). At its height, permanency was criticised for neglecting the rights and needs of birth parents (Harding, 1991) and disregarding the potential of permanent fostering (Thoburn, 1994; 1996). During the 1990s, adoption has come to be seen as incapable of providing a universal remedy, especially for older children and adolescents with emotional and behavioural difficulties. Contested adoptions run counter to principles of partnership embodied in the Children Act 1989 and which apply to divorce situations (Ryburn, 1994, 1997). It was also realised that birth parents often provide their children with their least inconsistent continuity and security while moving from placement to placement and social worker to social worker.

Reviewing the position, **Triseliotis (1991)** noted that the permanency movement had been successful in achieving stable homes for many children who would otherwise have lacked them. He also noted that the imposition of rigid time limits for restoration followed by legally enforced severance of contacts with birth families was 'one of the big blemishes'. **Smith (1995)** observed that adoption could provide lifelong belonging and commitment and need not rule out continued contact if that was in the child's interests. She observed that an American approach of Concurrent Planning was attractive to many agencies and practitioners. This involves recruiting carers who can work intensively to help a child return to his or her original family, but be prepared to keep the child permanently if restoration does not work out. It seems to require special qualities to strive genuinely for a child to return home (and so "lose" the child) at the same time as preparing for the possibility of keeping the child for good, but apparently some carers with careful preparation and support are able to do this (Katz, 1996).

A more far-reaching critique of permanency planning was

ovided by **Gilligan (1997)**. He acknowledged the achievements f permanence, but also identified a number of serious limitations. At times insufficient effort has been placed on restoring children home rather than moving them to a new family. Permanence is not achieved and probably not achievable for many looked after children (especially adolescents). Children's other needs may be neglected in the pursuit of psychological bonding as the overriding goal. Gilligan proposed that practice should aim to achieve three qualities for children which help them to be resilient and overcome adversity. These are a secure base (as permanency emphasised), good self-esteem and a sense of efficacy. Among the main implications are that more attention should be given to preserving continuity of positive relationships from the past, encouraging positive school experiences, encouraging peer friendships, promoting talents and interests, and helping the child develop specific coping skills. These are important tasks alongside seeking a secure alternative family home when that is possible and in the child's interest. They become even more vital when it is difficult or impossible either for a child to return home or to move to an adoptive or permanent fostering situation.

In 1995, **Triseliotis** provided an update on his thinking about the development of adoption. After reviewing the historical changes in the nature of adoption, he identified the professionalisation of adoption services as one of the key aspects of the last 30 years. He cited evidence that better outcomes are produced when knowledge and skills are applied in the recruitment and support of carers. This development has been accompanied by a focus on the child's needs and rights as the central consideration. For example, in the past babies had to be assessed if they were "fit for adoption", i.e. fitted the wishes of childless couples for a healthy baby. Nowadays, the issue is reframed so that appropriate adopters are sought for children who have health conditions or disabilities. The adopters chosen should fit the needs of the child.

Triseliotis observed that the increase in intercountry adoptions was likely to continue and these would require their own kind of preparation and support. Concern about intercountry adoption was one of the factors which prompted a desire for new adoption legislation in the early 1990s. On the one hand, some adopters complained of the obstructive approach they experienced from government officials and local authorities. On the other hand, professionals were concerned at the unregulated way in which intercountry adoption was taking place, with dangers and indeed actual instances of trafficking, improper consents and adopters poorly equipped to assist children from different parts of the world to adapt to life in Britain. **Ball (1996)** outlined the influences which slowly led up to an Adoption Bill in 1996, 20 years after the previous Adoption Act 1976. As it turned out, the Conservative Government did not proceed to legislate and at the time of writing it is unclear what the successor government plans. Part of the Bill was to apply to the whole of the United Kingdom, putting into effect the Hague Convention on intercountry adoption. The rest of the Bill applied to England and Wales. It strengthened consideration of the child's welfare, including it as part of the grounds for dispensing with parental consent. An important proposed innovation was the placement order to replace freeing for adoption as a means of enabling local authorities to place a child for adoption without parental consent, yet with safeguards for the parents to make an early legal challenge if they wished.

Although the law for England and Wales has not so far been changed, the Children (Scotland) Act 1995 brought in a number of revisions to the Adoption (Scotland) Act 1978. For example, the child's welfare has become the *paramount consideration* and refers to welfare *throughout life*; time limits were introduced (e.g. for reports, dates of hearings) to speed up procedures; and post-placement support duties were extended (Tisdall and Plumtree, 1997). Unlike the English and Welsh Adoption Bill, the 1995 Act introduced a duty for courts and adoption agencies to have regard to the child's religious persuasion, racial origin, culture and linguistic background (section 95).

Northern Ireland had no adoption legislation for 20 years after 1967 and so missed out on the kinds of changes introduced by the Children Act 1975 to promote permanency planning in the rest of the UK (Kelly and Coulter, 1997). For instance, freeing orders and adoption allowances were not introduced until 1989 and 1995 respectively, and neither provision has been much used. In Northern Ireland, Health Trusts rather than local authorities manage children's social work services and act as adoption agencies. Some are too small to offer comprehensive services.

1 Perceptions of permanence

John Triseliotis PhD, OBE

*John Triseliotis is Emeritus Professor at the University of Edinburgh
and Visiting Professor and Senior Research Fellow at the University of
Strathclyde. He has been carrying out research on separated children in
the fields of adoption, foster care and residential care for over 25 years.
He has co-authored or edited many books and articles including: "In
search of origins", "Hard to place", "Achieving adoption with love and
money", "Freeing children for adoption", "The practice of adoption and
fostering", "Parting with a child for adoption", and "Adoption with
contact". He has presented papers at many national and international
conferences and has lectured on child welfare in several countries.*

This paper was published in Adoption & Fostering 15:4, 1991.

It is tempting to start by saying that permanency through adoption for
children with special needs is on the defensive, and that adoption policy
and practice are at the crossroads because of the challenges they face.
The fact is that adoption, as an institution, has always been at the
crossroads, as it mirrors the society within which it is practised. Because
society is not static but changes all the time, so adoption changes and
adapts to new needs and challenges. For example, over the last 20 or so
years there have been radical changes in patterns of living, including
changes in personal, sexual, couple and family relationships. What is
understood by the concept of family has been re-defined to take account
of diverse life-styles, divorce, reconstitution and single parenthood.
These changes are here to stay and adoption has had to respond to them.

In considering the various ways in which families are constituted now,
and how atypical they are of our traditional image of the family, it is hard
not to claim that adoptive parenthood has been a pace-setter in this
direction. Psychological parenting is no longer confined largely to
adoption but is becoming far more common, along with step-parenting
and parenting through various forms of assisted reproduction.

Changes in personal and social relationships have always been the main dynamic underlining the evolution of the practice of adoption throughout history. Had I been writing on this topic five years ago, I might have been tempted to say that, for reasons that have not escaped you, adoption as an institution was moving towards its sunset. Permanence through adoption, for children with special needs, was then seen as the final remnant of what was once a big field of social work policy and practice. The end of this final form of adoption was expected to come with the provision of better preventive and supportive services to families to ensure permanence for children within their own families.

Two new issues have surfaced in the meantime, however, to give adoption a new dimension. Open adoption, which was previously characteristic of mainly non-European cultures, is gradually coming into prominence, along with intercountry adoption which Britain, compared to some other countries, resisted for a long time. Concepts of permanence cannot be examined in isolation from these other recent developments.

The concept of permanence

There is no agreed definition of the concept of permanence. Perceptions, therefore, are bound to vary. Different protagonists, depending on the ideologies and value positions they hold about the place of the family and the role of the state in relation to families and children, place different emphases on what is good for families and children. Polarised positions between the so-called "defenders of the family" and those who are perceived as "savers of children" can only delay the development of an agreed and coherent theoretical framework, based mainly on what empirically is known to be good for children. Insights gained from empirical studies can only illuminate part of the debate, because research is still lacking in many areas of practice. Some things we will also never know about because of the ethical objections to certain types of research involving human beings. Neither can the ethical dilemmas surrounding some of the issues be resolved totally by empiricism. For example, can permanence outside the family of origin be justified solely on the ground that it works? Or would, for example, the moral issues surrounding intercountry adoptions disappear, if research were to show that the children eventually do well or even very well?

It could be reasonably argued that in a world of instability with high divorce rates, marital reconstitution, step-parenting and a large number of single parent families, it is somewhat paradoxical to talk of permanence for children coming into public care. Thus the concept of permanence can only be examined in relative terms and in the context of the society within which it is being pursued. At the same time, when planning for children who have already experienced a chequered background, there is perhaps an extra responsibility to ensure, if not guarantee, an added form of stability in their lives.

My own studies have led me to define permanency in practical terms, these being to provide each child with a base in life or a family they can call their own, and more hopefully a family for life (Triseliotis, 1983; Triseliotis and Russell, 1984).

Studies have been showing that the difference between those who manage to cope in adult life and those who don't is closely related to the kind of support systems they continue to enjoy and whether or not they have a base in life they can call their own and turn to for practical and emotional support when needed. This applies even more so to individuals who have spent a large part of their childhood in public care. Our own studies have shown that those who had no birth families to return to, but were fortunate to secure relative permanence within foster or adoptive homes, fared infinitely better in adult life, compared to those who left the care system with no such base. This empirical reality is one of the concepts which underpins the policy to secure permanence for children with special needs.

Few would disagree that it is in every child's interests that a strenuous effort is made to achieve permanence first and foremost within the child's own family and country of origin, where biological and psychological parenting, including ethnic identification, can occur simultaneously. Where this is not possible, and in the light of what has been said earlier, permanence may have to be pursued outside the family of origin. It would be hard to argue that everything possible was done to achieve permanence within their own families for all the children with special needs who have been adopted over the last two decades. For many though, adoption has provided the base which was missing from their lives.

Whether permanence for special needs children is on the defensive or not it is difficult to say. It is proper, though, that after 20 or so years we take stock and look at both the successes and blemishes. In the following pages an attempt will be made to identify the various forces that gave the impetus to the adoption of children with special needs, examine the permanency movement's achievements and challenges, and briefly look at outcomes and the future.

The forces which gave the impetus to the adoption of children with special needs

A number of events seem to have coincided in the early 1970s to stimulate interest in permanence through adoption for children with special needs. First, the dwindling number of babies being available for adoption and, second, the realisation that there were large numbers of children in public care whose families were unable to have them back or who had no families to return to. Neither were there any realistic plans for the future of these children. Attention then was drawn to the needs of these children for continuity of care and for a family to call their own. It is doubtful, though, whether this new "move" would have taken place if it wasn't for the declining number of baby adoptions.

The third factor was an empirical one. Besides research, already referred to, concerning the plight in adult life of those who were formerly in public care, and who grew up in unstable arrangements, two other types of studies provided added impetus and optimism. First, a small but increasing number of studies were beginning to demonstrate the reversibility of early psychological trauma which came about through separations and deprivations. In other words, that children could overcome early adversities, provided suitable new conditions could be ensured (Kadushin, 1970; Clarke and Clarke, 1976; Triseliotis and Russell, 1984; Bohman and Sigvardsson, 1980). Second, that psychological parenting such as adoption and long-term fostering were a reality. Those who matter to children are generally the people who bring them up and not necessarily those who give birth to them (Triseliotis and Russell, 1984; Hill *et al*, 1989).

In this new type of adoption, the future psychological well-being of these children was dependent, not only on the accomplishment by adoptive parents of the traditional tasks associated with adoption, but adoptive parents were now expected to take on a treatment type role with many of the children.

If Britain responded to the decline in baby adoption by going all out for securing adoptive families for older children and children with disabilities that were previously thought unadoptable, a number of countries on the continent of Europe responded by turning mainly towards inter-country adoptions. It can be assumed that older children and those with disabilities or learning difficulties with no birth families to return to were either found long-term foster homes or kept in residential homes. This may be a somewhat simplified picture, but if the adoption statistics coming out of these countries are correct, then the adoption of own country children with special needs has hardly featured in recent years. One explanation why intercountry adoption did not develop in similar numbers in Britain, as on the continent, was possibly the stance taken by many black and white social work practitioners; the prohibition of non-agency adoptions and stricter immigration laws. A second explanation is the close links maintained by researchers, trainers and practitioners in Britain with the USA. It was the USA where the first ideas and service programmes for children with special needs were developed and these quickly crossed the Atlantic. Though the United States were pioneers in this field, eventually they followed a middle path to that of Britain and the continent of Europe by paying attention to both children with special needs and to intercountry adoptions.

Achievements and challenges
After more than a decade of pursuing a policy of permanency through adoption for children with special needs, there have been some astounding successes, but equally challenges and blemishes.

1 Achievements
• *Families for life*
The policies formulated and the practices developed seem to have had considerable success. If studies are right, within a period of three to five years following placement, something like eight out of every ten children with special needs seem to stabilise with their new families (Thoburn and Rowe, 1988; Borland *et al*, 1991). This may not be a long enough

period to judge outcomes. As we shall also see later these figures hide significant variations in outcome, depending on age at placement, and sometimes on the agency making the placement. On the earlier definition of permanency, these children were provided with a possible base in life. This has not been achieved easily and the cost to some families has been considerable. We are not talking about older children only, but children displaying serious emotional and behavioural problems, children who have been physically or sexually abused, children with learning and physical disabilities and children who are HIV positive. For a variety of reasons, today's "special needs" displayed by children who need new families appear more intense and intractable compared to those of ten or 15 years ago. The question arises as to whether we have reached the limits of what can reasonably be expected of permanent new families, without a much more comprehensive network of supportive treatment-oriented services being made available.

• *A body of new knowledge and expertise*
As a result of the challenge to place children with special needs with new families, child care practitioners have developed a large body of new knowledge and expertise covering the preparation, assessment and post-placement support of new families and of the children involved, using both individual and group methods. This body of knowledge and expertise is now being recognised more widely and is being transferred to other areas of child care work. The permanency movement has also demonstrated what can be achieved by agencies who develop coherent policies with accompanying services in this area.

• *Empowerment and partnership*
A less recognised achievement is the realisation that through organised, explicit and collaborative forms of preparation and assessment, adoption workers have provided 'the script for the expected behaviour for adoptive parenthood'. (See also Kirk, 1987.) The role of adoptive parents and the parenthood tasks to be carried out were not only better defined, but an explanation for the rationale behind them was also offered. This has included information and help to adoptive parents to understand and use child development theory, particularly as it emerged from the studies of

separated children. This was an empowering approach and far removed from the "all powerful" adoption social worker image. Adoptive parents were being prepared, trained and supported to become their own experts within realistic limits. As a result a climate of increased partnership began to develop between adoption workers and adoptive parents well before the word "partnership" became fashionable in social work. This type of relationship formed the background against which post-placement support was provided. I am aware that this shift in practice is not yet uniform across the country. Far from being complacent, we have to be reminded that some applicants still complain of long waits to obtain a response or to be prepared/assessed. Worse is the way that non-accepted applicants are left with little or no support following a long period of preparation/assessment.

- *Intensified rehabilitation efforts*

Because of the need to make the case before the courts to free some children for adoption, studies suggest that after about the mid-1980s the pursuit of permanence sharpened, and efforts for the rehabilitation of children with their own families intensified (Lambert *et al*, 1990).

Challenges

A number of recent challenges seem also to have put the pursuit of permanency outside the family of origin on the defensive. These challenges have to do with the legitimacy of adoption, the setting of time limits and the clean-break approach, and the role of the birth parents.

- *The legitimacy of adoption*

The first challenge concerns the legitimacy of adoption for children who enter public care without their parents having originally asked for adoption. As an example, approximately 40 per cent of children adopted each year in Scotland, England and Wales have been in public care. In England the percentage leaving care through adoption has been rising since the late 1970s. The critics of adoption argue that this is because not enough is being done to enable children to stay or return to their families of birth.

Some critics also contrast the attention being paid to children with special needs for new families, including the pre-placement and post-placement support offered, with the negligible help offered to children and their families before and during admission to care or following return home from public care. The payment of adoption allowances, to secure permanence for children with "special needs", is also quoted as an example which has exposed the weakness of general social provision for ordinary families and children. If similar allowances and attention were paid to birth families, it is argued, these might have helped to keep families and children together.

The legitimacy of adoption will continue to be challenged so long as much of child care need is generated as a result of extremes of poverty and homelessness in relation to the rest of the population. The lack of adequate provision and of supportive services undermines the coping resources of many parents. An acceptable policy of child care, and therefore of adoption, has to include adequate resources at the general, the preventive and tertiary levels to enable families to raise their own children, before permanency through adoption can be legitimised. While Teague's (1990) argument that adoption represents a deliberate child care policy for "ideological mastery" or "social control" is extreme, the critics of adoption have to be taken seriously. Ideological domination are the words used by opposing sides to accuse each other either of excesses in the separation of children from their families or in unfounded professional optimism about the chances of rehabilitation.

The close relationship that exists, though, between poverty and the relinquishment of a child for adoption, whether voluntarily or involuntarily, cannot be dismissed easily. It is mainly improved social conditions that have reduced own country adoption to almost nil in some northern European countries such as Scandinavia and Holland. It is, equally, the extremes of poverty in some Third World countries that force parents to part with or sell their children. If we are serious about children's best interests, then concepts of permanence have to start with permanency in family of origin and country of origin, moving away from a position 'of viewing all children admitted to care as potentially free for adoption'.

The provisions in the Children Act 1989 for support to families are to be welcomed, but the test will be its implementation and how the resourcing of preventive and rehabilitative services will be achieved. It

18

is also the view that, with "child protection" capturing the headlines and resources, little is left for mainstream child care work. Is it not a paradox that a few dramatic cases of child abuse capture the attention of both the profession and the media, but not the extreme conditions of poverty and homelessness affecting thousands of children?

We have to accept, however, that even in the best regulated societies, of which we are not one, there will always be situations where, irrespective of how much provision there is and how well services are delivered, some parents for personal or social reasons, or most likely for both, will be unable to continue or resume the care of their children. Worst still is the fact that where children are concerned, social workers have to act from how the situation stands now, instead of how it might have been if past mistakes had not been made. The dilemma is how to respond to an existing situation, knowing that to be able to grow up and face the demands of adult life, children require stability, security and continuity of care with a base in life to call their own. They should obviously have the right to attain these conditions within their own families, but in my view they also have a right to achieve permanence with new families, when everything else has failed. The example of the harsh circumstances of children who leave public care without a base in life has already been referred to and does not offer an attractive alternative.

Farmer and Parker (1991) found that one in five children in care were unlikely to return home and long-term arrangements seemed desirable. Furthermore, they found that for 38 per cent of the children return home broke down and the outlook for second and third attempts was not good.

Obviously we have to satisfy ourselves that the children and their families had the best possible help to resume the care of their children, and had adequate support following the children's return home. We have not yet used with birth families the experience gained from supporting new families to maintain placements. Dingwall *et al* (1983), though, observe that it is right and reassuring that social workers think the best of parents but wonder if sometimes they are over-optimistic about achieving rehabilitation.

It is a sad fact that we lack a shared philosophy of child care policy and practice which explicitly, rather than implicitly, also includes permanence through adoption. This can result, as McMilland and Wiener

(1988) argue, in 'resistance, often mute, to permanent care plans (outside the family of origin). At worst, this will show in deliberate sabotage of the plan . . .' As a result, in their view, plans to move children on to permanent homes are often not realised and they continue to drift through the care system and placement. Information is also emerging that with devolved and tight budgets in some social services departments, adoption allowances receive less sympathetic attention than before.

- *Time limits and the "clean break" approach*
Rigid time limits and the "clean break" policy, which went alongside permanency planning through adoption, and possibly still does, has been one of the big blemishes in the permanency movement's short history. While many children moved into new families without leaving behind important links, others had meaningful ties severed before joining their new families. The significance of the emotional links between especially an older child and a mother or a father or a grandparent were often underestimated and some children were cut off from emotional life-lines before they had established new ones. Some of the examples are too painful to relate here. Margaret Forster's recent book, *The Battle for Christabel*, should become compulsory reading for all adoption workers with regard to this topic.

I challenged this policy in 1985 and I would like to think that each child's meaningful ties to past figures are assessed and maintained in a form of open adoption. A range of studies suggest that contact does not threaten the stability of the placement, provided the new family have agreed to it. On the contrary, contact seems to help stabilise the arrangements. I am not saying that all contacts are worth preserving, but as Fratter (1989) has also shown, it is possible to provide legal and emotional security to children through adoption without cutting them off from earlier important links.

Why and how such a situation came about is difficult to explain. There are those who attribute it to the legacy of the poor law with a strong desire to "save children" from what are seen as neglectful parents. Like a hundred or more years ago, the importance and meaning of parents to their children have again been underestimated. Older children, particularly, quickly lose their sense of identity and self-concept when communication with their biological parents is suddenly altered or terminated (Gibson and Noble, 1991). Jenson and Whitaker (1978) add that the bond that unites parent and child does not totally dissolve when a child is placed with another family. This does not mean that children cannot develop psychological bonds with a new family, but they can do this more easily when their earlier attachments are recognised and, where necessary, maintained. Not surprisingly, arranging adoption with contact is a far more complex process compared to closed adoption.

Both the concept of adoption with contact and open adoption, used appropriately, should help to expand the boundaries of adoption. With few exceptions, such as where the law has to protect children, parting with a child through adoption should be a voluntary act and free of pressures. Tentative research findings suggest that some parents of both younger and older children within the public care system who are unable to care for their own children would not be unwilling to agree to adoption, provided the links were maintained. When it comes to baby adoption, openness could give rise to increased altruism. Altruism, as a motivating factor in adoption, already operates in some societies where adoption is seen as a donation without severing contact. However, altruism, openness and contact have also to be shown to be in a child's interests, irrespective of the adults' intentions and preferences.

A sense of altruism, though, can only develop if birth parents come to feel equal, have a choice, are in control and own the adoption decision. It could be rightly argued that there is no such thing as pure altruism without some self-interest. In this case the satisfaction for the birth parent comes not only from the knowledge that she/he can be of service to other human beings, but also from safeguarding the well-being of her child without the feeling of total loss if it includes contact or continued updating. No doubt there is still much more that needs to be learned about the long-term impact of open adoption. In the meantime, social workers are not only facing the emotional challenge of finding families for children with special needs, but also families that can accept contact and openness.

• *The role of birth parents*

One shift in attitude that seeking new families for children with special needs has brought about has been the recognition that such families offer a service. This has helped to lower the barriers between professionals and adoptive families and contribute to a climate of greater collaboration and partnership. Sadly, this has not been matched with a similar change in relationships between many birth parents and social workers. Increasingly we are faced with angry birth parents and stressed social workers experiencing a gap in communication and in constructive relationships.

During the early part of the permanency movement, conflict featured very little, if at all, because many of the children had been in public care for a long time and most parents had disappeared or lost interest in their children. As those children moved on, a new generation of parents and children emerged, but with different needs and expectations. More parents are readier now to challenge social work decisions, including the use of the courts. At the same time, social workers' awareness of the need to plan early to prevent drift in children's lives has increased the likelihood of conflict with parents, resulting sometimes in bad feeling, acrimony and stress. The handling of the increasingly conflict-ridden nature of adoption work seems to have contributed to some of the disillusionment towards permanency planning currently found among practitioners. Around 600 parental consents to adoption are dispensed annually by the courts in England and Wales as having been 'unreasonably withheld'. [Source: Report to parliament on the operation of the Children Act, 1975 (1979)].

Like other users of services, parents of children in public care are readier now than before to challenge social work decisions at every stage and especially when adoption is being considered, and this is likely to increase under the concept of "parental responsibility" provided for in the Children Act of 1989. Social workers are rightly encouraged to look upon parents as partners and to try to plan jointly with them, but partnership does not always stand the strain arising from different perceptions of what is good for a child and especially as the parents' power does not match that of the worker. As an example, conflict is inevitably generated when freeing procedures are used which give parents the right to defend

2

themselves before a court of law, and some have successfully done so. Yet social workers mirror in some ways the parents' agony and stress in their experience of protracted and stressful court procedures, something *the envia* for which they have little preparation or support. There are no clear criteria for decision-making when the children are not free for adoption. In addition, the adversarial aspects of many proceedings before the courts often exacerbate rather than reduce conflict.

Outcomes

Do the outcomes achieved so far justify the pursuit of permanency through adoption for children with special needs, or do the challenges referred to earlier call for a much more cautious approach? Similarly, are the breakdowns experienced unacceptably high or within acceptable limits? To answer some of these questions we have to turn to outcome studies. The studies themselves are far from unproblematic. Inconsistencies and contradictions abound, but some agreement is also beginning to emerge about specific issues and circumstances.

I am not alone in recognising the complexities and hazards of trying to assess and compare outcome studies involving children placed for adoption or foster care. This is not the place to discuss in detail the methodological complexities but some of these include: not comparing like with like; failure to establish children's baselines on entering the system; questions of definition and measurement about such concepts as "satisfaction", "well-being" and "self-esteem", and variations in the length of time between placement and the studies taking place. Where long-term criteria are used to assess outcome, the intervening variables can distort the picture. Finally, long-term or follow-up retrospective studies have not yet emerged.

A simple example of how outcomes for older children can be distorted is whether those children who are adopted by their long-term foster parents are included in the sample. Foster parents don't usually proceed to adoption before considerable stability in the placement has been achieved. An additional point to be borne in mind is that an increasing number of British studies now refer in their findings to both permanent family foster care and to adoption because of the many overlaps between these two types of substitute parenting. A further complication with

 .ption studies is that some have concentrated on disruption before and after the adoption order was granted, while others focus only on what happened following the granting of the adoption order.

In assessing satisfactory or unsatisfactory outcomes, studies have used the rather crude criterion of the placement continuing or breaking down following a certain period of time after the arrangement is made. Of course continuity of a placement is not always synonymous with success. Nor is a disruption or breakdown always disastrous for the child.

Highlighting the dangers of comparing outcome studies is not meant to paralyse thinking and action but it serves to add caution to the making of too definitive statements. We have to start somewhere though, if we are ever to be able to build more sophisticated and sensitive measures.

Children with special needs

A spate of studies which have been monitoring and evaluating perm-anency through adoption for children with "special needs" began to emerge in the 1980s, and are still doing so. These have been appearing, mainly in the USA and Britain, where such policies and practices have been pursued. While in the case of baby adoptions the characteristics of the adopters were found by earlier studies to be the most crucial factor, when it comes to children with special needs the picture is much more complex. In this instance both the characteristics of the child and of the adopting family seem crucial to outcome, including what Belsky (1981) calls 'the context within which parenting takes place'.

On average, something like eight out of every ten children seem to settle down with their new families reasonably well. Looking at the figures, though, in greater detail, they show that children placed when under about the age of ten have a consistently lower rate of breakdown than those who are placed when older. For the under ten-year-olds the rate may be as low as ten per cent, but it rises from between 15 and 50 per cent for those who are older, depending on which study is examined. The breakdown rate for the age group of ten and over is not monolithic but varies, usually rising with increased age and increased difficulties displayed by the child. A breakdown rate of between 25 and 40 per cent may, therefore, be accepted as usual. What happens to those who are adopted in adolescence presents a complex tableau of benefits and losses with breakdowns reaching sometimes 50 per cent and over. Older age is not infrequently accompanied by emotional and behaviour difficulties which many carers find difficult to handle. The child's ambivalence about commitment to the placement is often a further factor posing a threat to the placement.

Other pointers from the studies are that adoption with contact does not seem to threaten the stability of the placement, provided the adoptive family has agreed and has been prepared for this. Similarly, siblings placed together seem to experience fewer disruptions than when they are split, though other factors may be more important than the sheer fact of being a member of a sibling group, such as the quality of relationships between siblings. Children with learning difficulties and physical disabilities have been found to do very well by more than one study and they demonstrate consistently low breakdown rates. The main explanation for this is that such children are mostly adopted by people with previous experience of caring for children or adults with some disability.

Placing young children with families who have other children near the new child's age continues to carry a high risk for the placement. While childless couples were found in our recent study to be more successful in parenting young children, experienced parents were more successful in parenting older children who were disturbed (Borland *et al*, 1991).

Who can successfully parent a child and which children can be parented by new families is still far from clear, but a crucial variable contributing to disruptions, and mentioned by several studies, is the failure of the child to bond or attach itself. This is not always a one-way process, but can relate to characteristics in both the child and the carer. Without some form of attachment to provide a degree of mutuality and satisfaction in the relationship, the arrangement usually breaks down from between 12 and 18 months. In other words, when no rewards begin to emerge after a period of time, carers tend to give up. As in marital relationships, and in line with "exchange" theory, something is expected back at some point. Similarly, breakdown is more likely if carers find that the adjustment and well-being of other children in the family is threatened as a result of the new child's behaviour. Estimating, however, the possibilities of attachment when matching family and child is far from easy. It is an area where much more refinement in assessment processes is required. Though commitment and perseverance by the new parents is essential for successful outcome, a realistic view from the start of what the parents are taking on can also be decisive. Combining temporary optimism with realism from the outset is not always easy.

It remains difficult to predict which individual children will settle well with their new families, but certain features of the social work service increase the likelihood of stability for children of all ages. These are more accurate assessment; better planning and preparation; the provision of adoption allowances; and a wide range of post-placement support services with specialist staff being available for use and consultation by families as the need arises. Staff who are knowledgeable and experienced in the field of child care seem to be more successful in making more stable arrangements compared with others.

The adoption of adolescents

As already pointed out, permanency through adoption for adolescents carries many risks, with breakdown ranging between 30 and 50 per cent. A number of agencies, possibly discouraged by the high rate of break-downs among older children, including the high investment demanded in human and physical resources and the distress that usually follows from breakdowns, are either far more cautious and discriminating, or have given up altogether considering adolescents. Yet a blanket approach is not in the children's best interests. After all, even among the most difficult to place groups, at least half the children settle down in their new families.

How do practitioners distinguish between those who are going to succeed from the rest? Good assessment and good preparation of both children and families are again emerging as important variables that contribute towards placement stability. Above all, especially with adoles-cents, it is important to listen to them, obtain their views and establish their wishes and feelings. In the past, we have perhaps not always listened carefully and enough to what they had to say, or failed to involve them more fully in planning and decision-making. Some of them may not want adoption, but something different; others may want security through adoption but without severing links with their birth families; others still may want to commit themselves fully to an adoptive family.

26

It is too early to predict how the concept of "parental responsibility" built into the 1989 Children Act is going to affect adoption, but a possible unwelcome outcome would be to deprive, especially older children, of a badly needed secure base in life through adoption. Based on our studies here, adoption as an option should not be ruled out for older children and for those who wish to retain links with members of their birth families. Possibly the best chance for older children entering care, and who cannot return to their families, is fostering with a view to adoption, even if it takes some time. Otherwise such children will be condemned to a life of rootlessness. Adoption through foster care has achieved considerable success in the past, but the move by many agencies towards contractual, time-limited placements could jeopardise this route unless more flexible placement policies are developed.

It is the legality of adoption and the emotional security that goes with it that sets it apart in the minds of the children and their adoptive parents from other forms of substitute parenting. A second tier of adoption order will only be perceived as a second-class type of adoption. A second tier adoption may have worked, for example, in France, though I am not familiar with any French studies in this area, but the historical backgrounds and contexts between Britain and France are not the same. Other ways could be found to provide security for children who cannot return to their families and where adoption, as we understand it now, cannot be pursued.

The way forward
The permanency movement has demonstrated what can be achieved in the placement of children with special needs. A small group of practitioners and managers can take a lot of credit for these achievements. Many of the children who found new families were emotionally damaged and often displayed behavioural difficulties. There is a lot of evidence now which points to the capacity of many children to overcome deprivation and emotional damage. For some very damaged children we may be unable to undo all the earlier damage but we could provide a range of compensating experiences. Mistakes have also been made in the past – taking stock can only help to produce a more measured response.

It would be a retrograde step, though, to relax the efforts and the impetus developed in finding new families for children who have no-one to turn to. Social workers cannot be held responsible for the defects in social policy and for its failure to provide supportive and rehabilitative services to all families and children.

Caring for children with special needs has also proved stressful and painful. Besides offering care, many adoptive and foster parents are also expected to provide therapy to some very disturbed children without having been trained or equipped to do so. More attention must therefore be paid to how to furnish them with problem-solving skills and with a network of treatment services they can call upon without being labelled as dysfunctional. Permanence can be achieved through a number of routes and care arrangements. Joining a new family through adoption still remains the preferred option for some vulnerable children with no-one else to turn to. There are strong pressures here and in other countries to see the abolition of adoption, especially for older children, for the wrong reasons. This should be resisted. Adoption will phase itself out only when every child can live with his or her own family and in his or her own country, thus maintaining continuity and stability. This position has not yet been reached. Its discouragement could prove detrimental to many children who would be condemned to a life of rootlessness for ideological reasons.

Since this article was written permanence, through adoption, for children with no realistic prospects of returning to their families has been in some decline. There are many reasons for this making adoption for looked after children more complicated and more difficult to achieve than in the past. Long-term fostering has a definite place as a form of substitute care, but the recent trend of using the term "permanence" to describe it is misplaced because, unlike adoption, the term is inconsistent with the legal realities.

References

Belsky J, 'Early human experience: a family systems perspective', *Developmental Psychology*, 17, pp 3–23, 1981.

Bohman M and Sigvardsson S, 'Negative social heritage', *Adoption & Fostering*, 101:3, pp 25–31, 1980.

Borland M, O'Hara G and Triseliotis J, 'Placement outcomes for children with special needs', *Adoption & Fostering*, 15:2, 1991.

Clarke A M and Clarke A D B (eds), *Early Experience: Myth and evidence*, Open Books, 1976.

Dingwall R, Eekelar J and Murray T, *The Protection of Children*, Blackwell, 1983.

Farmer R and Parker R, *Trials and Tribulations*, HMSO, 1991.

Fratter J, *Family Placement and Access*, Barnardo's, 1989.

Gibson D and Noble D N, 'Creative permanency planning: residential services for families,' *Child Welfare*, 70:3, 1991.

Jenson J and Whitaker J, 'Parental involvement in children's residential treatment', *Children and Youth Services Review*, 9:2, 1978.

Kadushin A, *Adopting Older Children*, Columbia University Press, 1970, USA.

Kirk D, *Adoptive Kinship*, Butterworth, 1981, Canada.

Lambert L, Triseliotis J and Hill M, *Freeing Children for Adoption*, BAAF, 1990.

McMillan and Wiener R, 'Preparing the caretaker for placement', *Adoption & Fostering*, 12:1, pp 20–22, 1988.

Teague A, *Social Change, Social Work and the Adoption of Children*, Avebury/ Gower, 1990.

Thoburn J and Rowe J, 'A snapshot of permanent family placement,' *Adoption & Fostering*, 12:3, pp 29–34, 1988.

Thoburn J, *Success and Failure in Permanent Family Placement*, Gower, 1990.

Tizard B, *Adoption: A second chance*, Open Books, 1977.

Triseliotis J and Russell J, *Hard to Place*, Gower, 1984.

Triseliotis J, 'Identity and security in adoption and long-term fostering', *Adoption & Fostering*, 7:1, pp 22–31, 1983.

2 Concepts of parenthood and their application to adoption

Malcolm Hill

Malcolm Hill is a Professor of Social Work and Director of the Centre for the Child & Society at the University of Glasgow. He previously taught social work students at the University of Edinburgh, where he did postgraduate research into the care of pre-school children. He has an MA in geography, a Diploma in Applied Social Studies and a PhD in Social Science. He also has ten years experience as a child care officer, generic social worker and senior social worker. His publications include books on child care in early parenthood, adoption, children's services and family support.

This paper was published in Adoption & Fostering, 15:4, 1991.

Introduction

There have been many changes in the nature of both adoptive and non-adoptive parenthood in recent years, which means that it is timely to review commonly held assumptions. I would like to examine how our ideas about parenthood influence adoption policy and practice.

I shall deal with modern Western forms of adoption, since that is the form which I know best and which is more familiar to most readers, but I would like to acknowledge from the start that there are many other traditions of adoption. Moreover, after a long period during which the Western model has been widely imposed elsewhere, we have recently witnessed a reverse process whereby this dominant legal form is now being challenged by some of those different traditions. This is a trend which I consider to be a positive one. I shall refer largely to the modern Anglo-Saxon basis for adoption, again recognising that there are significant differences in continental Europe as regards the meaning and scope of adoption (Rieg, 1985; France, 1990).

Modern adoption has proved a remarkably resilient and popular institution since its inception in North America less than 150 years ago. It has adapted rapidly to social and policy changes so that it now encompasses a range of family circumstances. Its roots lie in legal mechanisms for the acquisition of heirs and transmission of property (Benet, 1976). Later, adoption became formalised in the modern laws of many countries to provide recognition for situations where children had already moved from their original families to stay with relatives, friends and neighbours. In North America, Australia, New Zealand and Southern Africa, adoption was also used to legalise the status of children "rescued" from urban squalor and placed with settler families (Bean and Melville, 1989; Cole and Donley, 1990). Subsequently, adoption became the favoured route for childless couples to create a family of their own by raising infants who were previously strangers to them. Mostly, of course, this involved the placement of babies born outside marriage. Increasingly, it also became a common means of confirming step-parent relationships.

Over the last 20 years, as the number of local babies available for adoption declined in all Western countries, we have seen the development of intercountry adoption and the adoption of older and special needs children, mostly from public care. This last type has also been associated with a growing willingness to arrange adoptions not only without parental consent, but even in the face of their active opposition. There has also been a shift from discouraging foster carers from considering adoption to active promotion of foster adoptions. Different countries have markedly different proportions of these various kinds of adoption (Hoksbergen, 1986).

We have reached the position where adoption has become very diverse and complex. Indeed, often it is more accurate and helpful to talk of adoptions in the plural, rather than adoption as a single phenomenon. Each type of adoption has a very different social and psychological nature, even though there is the same legislative basis. This point, that legal certainty and uniformity can accompany wide psycho-social variations, is one to which I will return.

Expectations about adoptive relationships need to be adapted to these variations, so that a single model of adoptive parenthood is inappropriate. Yet much adoption practice remains based on a particular view of adoption as a total transfer of parenthood. This in turn is related to conceptions of so-called normal parenthood. These include ideas that parents should carry out all major responsibilities for their children, that they should provide for all their material and emotional needs and that there should be only one parental figure or couple for a child. Hence Western adoption has been dominated by the idea of the complete break – that an adopted child completely and permanently severs ties with the original parents and becomes totally the child of new parents. In recent years, this position has become modified with the development of openness, but as yet the change has been marginal and by no means universal.

While this concept of adoption as the total transfer of parenthood is reflected in the legal situation in many countries, it seems to be an excessively narrow view of the psychological and sociological realities of both adoptive and non-adoptive parenthood. Therefore, I would like to outline an approach to parenthood which corresponds better with emerging trends in adoption and, I believe, will be more helpful in guiding adoption practice in the 1990s.

Five vital features of parenthood (both non-adoptive and adoptive) have particular significance for the themes that will be highlighted in the rest of the conference papers [International Conference on Adoption, 1990]. These are:

- Parenthood and parenting are highly variable and culture-specific.
- Parenting functions can be shared.
- Parental relationships must be viewed as part of a wider network of relationships.
- Parent-child relationships are developmental – they alter over time.
- Parents have needs as well as children.

It may be helpful in considering these five aspects to bear in mind a crude distinction between parenthood as a broad set of responsibilities and parenting as more specific day-to-day tasks and functions.

The variability of parenthood and parenting

If we examine families in general, it is evident that there is no uniformity in the way the tasks and roles of parenthood are carried out. The population movements and technological changes of recent times have meant that most societies have become culturally pluralistic and contain a diversity of family structures. Expectations vary greatly about such matters as the involvement of kin networks in child-rearing and decision-making, gender roles, parent-child communication and acceptable forms of discipline. Multiple households are common among some peoples, rare for others. In many countries there have been growing proportions of single parent households and stepfamilies following divorce (Sorrentino, 1990). Patterns of male and female employment and unemployment have altered substantially. Assisted forms of reproduction have enabled children to be born to previously infertile people with special implications for the nature of parent-child relationships.

In adoption two kinds of decision are made with respect to parenthood and parenting, which need to take account of this diversity and cultural relativity. Firstly, the birth parents are considered by themselves or others not to be suitable for raising their children. Secondly, prospective adopters – unlike the vast majority of new parents – have to be formally approved as eligible to be parents. Such decisions are influenced by assumptions about the quality of parenting and desired types of parent. For example, adoption legislation often excludes unmarried couples and may specify minimum or maximum age differences between child and adopter.

In relation to voluntary relinquishment of infants, the choices of pregnant single women have clearly been affected by the extent of stigma towards unmarried mothers and the amount of support they may receive, as well as by attitudes about the rights and wrongs of abortion and adoption. When children are compulsorily removed from parents and placed for adoption, value judgements are involved in assessments of the quality of parenting which override parental rights to determine where children live. While there are probably universal norms about children's physical safety, decisions about neglect and even harsh discipline are open to cultural misunderstandings and to differing responses (Cross, Bazron, Dennis and Isaacs, 1989; Woodhead, 1990).

In North America, Australasia, Britain and elsewhere prevailing attitudes about the parenting of black, native and aboriginal children have been challenged as culturally insensitive, racist and even potentially genocidal (McKenzie and Hudson, 1985; Ahmad, 1989; Edwards and

Egbert-Edwards, 1989). Disproportionate numbers of children have been removed from their families as a result of culturally inappropriate judgements. This has included "rescuing" children from the harsh effects of colonialism without tackling the basic social and economic conditions. As a result many children were then placed transracially in culturally alien settings. Only recently has this trend been partially reversed. A vital element in this shift in policy and practice has been to recognise the strengths in ethnic minority communities and to work with them to locate suitable substitute families when these are needed (Ahmed, Cheetham and Small, 1986; Kaniuk, 1991).

Turning now to judgements about adoptive parents, in the past adoption agencies have been accused of having a white, middle-class bias in their selection processes which have favoured material well-being and a conventional breadwinner-housewife division of roles (Pascall, 1984). Over the last 15–20 years some places have witnessed substantial changes in approach prompted by the desire to widen the pool of potential adopters for special needs children. This has required new, active approaches to recruitment and flexibility about who can be acceptable as adopters. Types of people who were previously discouraged or barred from becoming adoptive parents are now positively sought after. This includes the poor and unemployed, black people, working mothers, single parents, single people, divorced people, parents with several children of their own – indeed much of the adult population. Once considered not good enough to adopt in the competition for a diminishing supply of available infants, they may have special things to offer to older or disabled children. It remains the case, however, that the more people deviate from the so-called "normal" couple, the more restricted are the kinds of child available to them.

Parenting functions can be shared

A major element of the permanence philosophy of the 1970s and '80s was the view that children are only able to cope successfully with one set of parents, and that legal authority should be vested in the person or couple to whom the child has the primary attachment (Goldstein, Freud and Solnit, 1973; Hess, 1982; Maluccio, Fein and Olmstead, 1986; Black, 1990). The value of this perspective is that it emphasises the importance of children knowing clearly who carries the legal responsibilities of parenthood towards them. Whenever possible, those legal parents should be people the child loves and trusts. However, it does not follow that the day-to-day parenting tasks or even longer-term parental roles have to be restricted to one individual or couple. It is clearly beneficial for a child to have at least one parental figure, but cross-cultural evidence indicates that in most non-Western cultures several adults (usually relatives) have shared the tasks and loyalties of parenting (Smith, 1980). Mothers tend to be the main caregivers in most societies, but sharing care of children with others from infancy onwards is also nearly universal. What children need from adults is material security (food, shelter and safety) and qualities such as nurturance, continuity, stimulation and mutuality. These can be provided by a set of familiar people and need not be confined to one individual or couple (Maccoby and Martin, 1983; Hill, 1987).

When children live apart from one or both of their original parents, sharing parental functions can become more problematic, but it remains possible for a separated parent to meet some needs. It is possible to draw certain parallels between the double families produced by divorce and those produced by adoption, although there are also important differences. About one in five children in Britain will now experience divorce by the time they are 16 (Haskey, 1983) and the figure is higher in places like Sweden and California. The evidence about families divided by divorce is complex and ambiguous, but the indications are that children can accept two sets of parents fairly readily when the adults can co-operate reasonably well (McGurk and Glachan, 1987; Benjamin and Irving, 1989). In adoption, too, the relationships between key adults is likely to affect considerably children's willingness and ability to handle divided parenting. When a divorced parent ceases contact, the result may often be grief reactions for both the child and the adult, which has led experts to advocate policies and practice which preserve the relationship.

Similarly, many forms of non-Western adoption have included some continuing role for the original parents as a normal expectation (Triseliotis, 1970; O'Collins, 1984). The authority of parenthood is vested in adopters, but one or more of the tasks of parenting may still be carried out by a birth parent. In Western adoption the role of the birth parent will often be narrow, but that need not be the case, especially in adoptions by foster carers and of older children. At the very least, birth parents have a part to play (whether directly or symbolically) in an adopted person's evolving sense of identity. There can be difficult dilemmas in contested adoptions when there is little prospect of birth parents ever providing a satisfactory home (on account of alcohol or drug problems, for instance), but they may still be able to offer contact, love or concern (Lambert, Buist, Triseliotis and Hill, 1990). However, the guiding principle as regards any continuing parental role by birth parents should be the interest and wishes of the adopted person.

I would not wish us to return to the period of indeterminacy and drift of the 1960s and '70s, but it does seem to me that in planning adoptive placements, where of course it is expected that most of the primary parenting and all of the legal control will rest with the adopters, consideration should routinely be given to what role if any the birth parents may retain in meeting current or future needs of the child, rather than assuming that they are excluded for ever.

Parental relationships are part of a wider network
Children's upbringing normally occurs within a wide social network, yet thinking about adoption has often concentrated on the parent-child relationship exclusively. Adoption law is usually framed in terms of parental responsibilities and rights, hence the position of other relatives is often neglected. In Britain, the question of birth grandparents having legal access after adoption has been disputed. The situation of siblings adopted in separate homes has received little attention. These and other relatives are now being included in some post-adoption and adult counselling services, but need these relationships have been invariably terminated in the first place? In some countries a distinction is made between adoptions which confine the new legal relationships to parents and those which substitute wider kin relationships too (Van Loon, 1990).

In a wider sense, children can be seen as belonging not just to a family, but to a community or nation. Decisions about relinquishment and in particular involuntary removal of children for adoption can have implications for the larger social group, especially when that is itself small or threatened. For example, native peoples in Canada and New

Zealand have fought to gain control of child welfare services, since their own future had been placed at risk by the frequent removal of children to substitute care and adoptive homes in distant places (Alcoze and Mawhiney, 1988; Rockel and Ryburn, 1988). The black communities in North America and Britain have made similar arguments against transracial adoption. Some countries have stopped international adoptive placements because they do not want their children sent overseas (Pilotti, 1990), even though in individual cases the main short-term alternative to a family home abroad will be a large, local institution. It is vital to provide the material and social basis to ensure that there are enough family placements within the country of origin so that these policies may succeed.

Parent-child relationships alter over time

Too often, the various stages in an adopted person's life course have been viewed in isolation. Furthermore, insufficient account is taken of the ways in which people's needs and capacities change. Expectations about adoption have been primarily influenced by considerations current at the time of placement, yet it is also necessary to prepare for changes as the adopted person, adoptive parents and birth parents progress through life.

This is most evident in relation to the secrecy which has typically surrounded the placement of infants for adoption. This largely suited the needs of the adults concerned, but provided an unsatisfactory framework for many adopted persons as they grew up and found their desire to know more about their origins thwarted by the inaccessibility of vital information (Schechter and Bertocci, 1990). Of course, this pattern is now changing, but there is still a tendency to deal separately with just two periods in an adopted person's life – early childhood and early adulthood. Increasingly practice and legislation are being modified to provide for more involvement and even contact by birth parents at the point of placement, and for readier availability of personal details to adopted people at the age of majority, but without examining closely how these changes should be linked during the intervening period. Services are sometimes divided in relation to pre-adoption work and support for adult adoptees. The latter are sometimes called post-adoption services, but in practice focus on the time 17 years or more after adoption. Agencies dealing with special needs placements have come to realise that the demands of taking older and sometimes disturbed children from care warrant post-adoption support available as required or requested at any time (Argent, 1988).

For children with a more straightforward history, all that may be needed is more attention in preparation interviews and groups to the issue of how best to maintain dialogues with children as they grow up about their adoptive status. Single or occasional "telling" is inadequate. Indeed the word "telling" is misleading, since it implies one-way communication. What is needed are ongoing dialogues embedded in everyday conversations. Again, studies of divorce have shown how one-off or occasional explanations can leave children mystified and confused (Mitchell, 1985). It is clear from the work of Brodzinsky and his colleagues (1984) that adopters require considerable skills in adjusting their discussions of the meaning and implications of adoption as children's cognitive abilities develop. This process may well be easier when there is some occasional contact directly or indirectly with birth families.

Professionals, too, may get stuck in their perceptions. For example, some counsellors continue to treat adult adopted people as children. While it is necessary to include some safeguards when legislation about open records has been retrospective, as in England and elsewhere, it is vital to acknowledge both the rights and abilities of adults to make their own decision when properly informed. The evidence is that nearly all adoptees are very sensitive about the feelings and reactions of other parties in the minority of situations where they envisage some kind of reunion with birth relatives (Lambert, Hill and Triseliotis, 1990).

Changes over the life course affect birth parents too. They can mature and their social situations may change in ways which affect what they can give to a child. Some who have little to offer an infant may still have a role later on. While primary parental functions like caregiving and decision-making are carried out by the adopters, birth parents may be able to assist adopted persons directly or indirectly in understanding their personal history and working out their identity (Laird, 1981; Walby and Symons, 1990). For children who are adopted internationally, parents and other relatives may be able to convey part of their cultural inheritance.

Parents have needs too

We would probably all agree that children's needs should come first in shaping the nature of adoption. Nevertheless, compared with other cultures and historical epochs, present-day Western attitudes to parenthood are unusual in the nature of their "child-centredness" (Jahoda, 1982). Norms for women in particular encourage self-sacrifice. One result is that many parents, especially mothers, feel guilty about having their own needs met.

Such needs include emotional and practical ones. It is increasingly acknowledged that birth parents may want help in handling grief at the loss of their children (Winkler and Van Keppel, 1984; Bouchier, Lambert and Triseliotis, 1991). Their pain may be lessened if they can feel they still have something to give.

Parents who bring up children born to them take for granted their right to do so, but many adopters may have to acquire their sense of entitlement in order to feel fully a parent. Openness can only work if adoptive parents feel assured that the centrality of their role is not undermined. This requires sensitivity to adopters' feelings, especially those who have had to come to terms with infertility (Walby and Simons, 1990). While there is evidence that some adopters find birth family contact quite acceptable and even beneficial, undoubtedly for others it is threatening and discomforting (Fratter, Rowe, Sapsford and Thoburn, 1991). It is very important, therefore, to continue to safeguard the *legal position* of adoptive parenthood, even as its *social nature* becomes more varied and permeable. Both children and adults clearly see a crucial difference between fostering and adoption, with adoption conferring a greater sense of security, belonging, public recognition and shared identity (Triseliotis, 1983; Hill and Triseliotis, 1989). The United Kingdom has experimented with legal statuses which give most of the controls of adoption but stop short of full transfer of legal parenthood, but these alternatives (custodianship, custody and guardianship) have not proved popular except for some children living with grandparents, aunts and uncles (Bullard and Malos, 1990).

As regards practical aid, the reality is that all but the most isolated of parents have much help from their relatives and social networks. Furthermore, in spite of the challenges of the 1980s (Alber, 1988; Munday, 1989), the state nowadays usually provides support to all families and not just a safety net for a minority. Even in poor countries, or those with less developed welfare states, there is assistance with education on a universal basis. In most wealthier countries, there is some kind of family allowance. There are often additional forms of help for families with particular needs. Some countries now have schemes offering financial assistance to certain kinds of adopter, in recognition of their special costs or low income. Initially controversial , subsidy schemes have come to be seen as quite acceptable ways of facilitating adoptions by foster carers and of special needs children (Southon, 1986; Hill, Lambert and Triseliotis, 1989). In Sweden some monetary help is now given for inter-country adoptions. Other adopters may want non-cash help, such as aids for a disabled child, respite care, assistance with housing or mutual support (Macaskill, 1985; Argent, 1988; Hill, Hutton and Easton, 1988).

Conclusion

I have argued that adoptive parenthood, like non-adoptive parenthood, is able to embrace a variety of social forms within a unifying framework of clear legal authority and responsibility. We appear to be at a stage where Western adoption is undergoing a shift in paradigm. It is changing from one set of ideas based on secrecy and unitary identity to one embodying greater honesty and recognition of the continuing duality of adoptive parenthood and identity. That double nature occurs whenever genetic and social parenthood are partially or wholly separated, whether through adoption, divorce, assisted reproduction techniques or widowhood.

This provides a challenge for adoption in the 1990s. How can we best reconcile greater openness with children's and adopters' needs for security, belonging and positive social status, in other words – *permanence?* It is important not to swing from one extreme to another but to blend the best features of both permanence and openness in a range of ways suited to the individual circumstances of each child. There are particular difficulties in doing so when the birth parents and adoptive parents are separated by hundreds or thousands of miles, and a wide cultural gulf, as in intercountry adoption. These three issues – openness, permanence, intercountry adoption – are the main themes of the papers which follow [in the original collection, *Adoption & Fostering*, Special Issue, 1991].

References

Ahmad B, 'Child care and ethnic minorities', in Kahan B (ed), *Child Care Research, Policy and Practice*, Hodder & Stoughton, London, 1989.

Ahmed S, Cheetham J and Small J (eds), *Social Work with Black Children and their Families*, BAAF/Batsford, 1986.

Alber J, 'Is there a crisis of the welfare state? Cross-national evidence from Europe, North America and Japan', *European Sociological Review*, 4:3, pp 181–207, 1988.

Alcoze T and Mawhiney A-M, *Returning Home*, Laurentian University Press, 1988.

Argent H (ed), *Keeping the Doors Open*, BAAF, 1988.

Bean P and Melville J, *Lost Children of the Empire*, Unwin Hyman, 1989.

Benet M K, *The Politics of Adoption*, Free Press, 1976, USA.

Benjamin M and Irving H H, 'Shared parenting: critical review of the research literature', *Family and Conciliation Courts Review*, 27:2, pp 21–35, 1989.

Black D, 'What do children need from parents?', *Adoption & Fostering*, 14:1, pp 43–51, 1990.

Bouchier P, Lambert L and Triseliotis J, *Parting with a Child for Adoption*, BAAF, 1991.

Brodzinsky D, Singer L M and Braff A M, 'Children's understanding of adoption', *Child Development*, 55, pp 869–78, 1984.

Bullard E and Malos E, *Custodianship*, University of Bristol, 1990.

Cole E S and Donley K, 'History, values and placement policy issues in adoption', in Brodzinsky D M and Schechter M D (eds), *The Psychology of Adoption*, Oxford University Press, 1990.

Cross T L, Bazron B J, Dennis K W and Issacs M R, *Towards a Culturally Competent System of Care*, Georgetown University Child Development Centre, 1989, USA.

Edwards E D and Egbert-Edwards M, 'The American Indian Child Welfare Act: achievements and recommendations', in Hudson J and Galaway B (eds), *The State as Parent*, Kluwer, Dordrecht, 1989, The Netherlands.

France E, *International Perspectives, Background Paper Number 1, Inter-Departmental Review of Adoption Law*, Department of Health, London, 1990.

Fratter J, Rowe J, Sapsford D and Thoburn J, *Permanent Family Placement*, BAAF, 1991.

Goldstein J, Freud A and Solnit A J, *Beyond the Best Interest of the Child*, Free Press, 1973.

Haskey J, 'Children of divorcing couples', *Population Trends*, 31, pp 20–26, 1983.

Hess P, 'Parent-child attachment concept: crucial for permanency planning', *Social Casework*, pp 46–53, 1982, USA.

Hill M, *Sharing Child Care in Early Parenthood*, Routledge & Kegan Paul, 1987.

Hill M, Hutton S and Easton S, 'Adoptive parenting – plus and minus', *Adoption & Fostering*, 12:2, pp 17–23, 1988.

Hill M, Lambert L and Triseliotis J, 'The transition from long-term care to adoption', in Hudson J and Galaway B (eds), *The State as Parent*, Kluwer, Dordrecht, 1989, The Netherlands.

Hoksbergen R A C, *Adoption in Worldwide Perspective*, Swets and Zeitlinger, 1986, The Netherlands.

Jahoda G, *Psychology and Anthropology*, Academic Press, 1982.

Kaniuk J, 'Strategies in recruiting black adopters', *Adoption & Fostering*, 15:1, pp 38–42, 1991.

Laird J, 'An ecological approach to child welfare: issues of family identity and continuity', in Sinonoglu P A and Maluccio A (eds), *Parents of Children in Placement*, Child Welfare League of America, 1981, USA.

Lambert L, Buist M, Triseliotis J and Hill M, *Freeing Children for Adoption*, BAAF, 1990.

Lambert L, Hill M and Triseliotis J, *An Evaluation of an Adoption Counselling Service*, Report to Social Work Services Group, Edinburgh, 1990.

Macaskill C, 'Who should support after the adoption?', *Adoption & Fostering*, 9:2, pp 21–25, 1985.

Maccoby E and Martin J, 'Socialisation in the context of the family: parent-child interaction', in Hetherington M (ed), *Handbook of Child Psychology*, Wiley, 1983, USA.

McGurk H and Glachan M, 'Children's conception of the continuity of parenthood following divorce', *Journal of Child Psychology and Psychiatry*, 28:3, pp 427–35, 1987.

McKenzie B and Hudson P, 'Native children, child welfare and the colonization of native people', in Levitt K L and Wharf B (eds), *The challenge of child Welfare*, University of British Columbia Press, 1985, Canada.

Maluccio A, Fein E and Olmstead K A, *Permanency Planning for Children*, Tavistock, 1986.

Mitchell A, *Children in the Middle*, Tavistock, 1985.

Munday B (ed), *The Crisis in Welfare*, Harvester Wheatsheaf, 1989.

O'Collins M, 'The influence of western adoption laws on customary adoption in the third world', in Bean P (ed), *Adoption: Essays in social policy, law and sociology*, Tavistock, 1984.

Pascall G, 'Adoption: perspectives in social policy', in Bean P (ed), *Adoption: Essays in social policy, law and sociology*, Tavistock, 1984.

Pilotti F, *Intercountry Adoption: Trends, issues and policy implications for the 90s*, Social Affairs Unit, Montevideo, 1990, Uruguay.

Rieg A, 'Adoption – introduction comparative', *Revue Internationale de Droit*, 3, pp 511–24, 1985.

Rockel J and Ryburn M, *Adoption Today: Change and choice in New Zealand*, Heinemann, 1988, New Zealand.

Schechter M D and Bertocci D, 'The meaning of the search' in Brodzinsky D M and Schechter M D (eds), *The Psychology of Adoption*, Oxford University Press, 1990.

Smith P K, 'Shared care of young children: alternative models to monotropism', *Merill-Palmer Quarterly*, 26:4, pp 371–87, 1980.

Sorrentino C, 'The changing family in international perspective', *Monthly Labour Review*, March, pp 41–58, 1990.

Southon V, *Children in Care: Paying their new families*, Department of Health and Social Security, London, 1986.

Triseliotis J, *Evaluation of Adoption Policy and Practice*, Department of Social Administration, University of Edinburgh, 1970.

Triseliotis J, 'Identity and security in adoption and long-term foster care', *Adoption & Fostering*, 7:1, pp 22–31, 1983.

Van Loon J H A, *Report on Intercountry Adoption*, Permanent Bureau of the Conference, The Hague, 1990.

Walby C and Symons B, *Who am I?*, BAAF, 1990.

Winkler R and van Keppel M, *Relinquishing Mothers in Adoption*, Institute for Family Studies, 1984, Australia.

Woodhead M, 'Psychology and the cultural construction of children's needs', in James A and Prout A (ed), *Constructing and Reconstructing Childhood*, Falmer Press, 1990.

3 Permanence revisited – some practice dilemmas

Sheila Smith

Sheila Smith (now Sheila Byrne) is a Child Placement Consultant at BAAF's Southern Regional Centre. She has written several papers for various journals and is the author of "Learning from Disruption: Making better placements".

This paper was published in Adoption & Fostering, 19:3, 1995.

The history and development of what is commonly known as permanence planning has been well documented and needs no repetition (Triseliotis, 1991 and others). Its central principles – that continuity of care and mutual lifelong commitments are vital foundations in a child's development – are commonly accepted. Similarly, no-one would dispute that for the great majority of children permanence is best achieved within their family of origin. The principles behind the Children Act 1989 rightly refocused social work practice by highlighting the partnership, honesty and clarity that should underpin good preventive work. While the changing legislative framework has created opportunities for some innovative and creative practice with families, it has also stimulated fresh debate concerning the continuum of permanence. Simultaneously, the complexities of adoption and fostering in the mid 1990s are by necessity forcing us to review our response to the needs of all involved.

Over this past year, staff at British Agencies for Adoption and Fostering (BAAF) have been pooling their knowledge and experience of consultancy and training requests concerning permanence together with practice dilemmas raised by member agencies through our regional centres and groups. Consequently we have been working on a strategy which aims to address some of the most common concerns around effective planning for children and which it is hoped may stimulate debate and thinking about important issues.

The first task was to review BAAF's policy statement concerning permanence, bearing in mind the immense changes which have taken place since its inception in the 1980s. We have restated our fundamental premise that permanence is essential for healthy emotional growth. It provides children with a foundation from which to develop their identity, values and relationships throughout childhood and into adulthood. For most children the best place for this to be achieved is within their family network and every effort should be made to sustain this situation. If separation cannot be avoided, the child should be restored to their family as quickly as possible. When this is not in the child's best interest, an alternative family should be found which can provide continuous care and commitment to the child into adulthood. Such a family should be able to maintain the child's ethnic, religious and cultural heritage, acknowledge and respect their family of origin and maintain ongoing links and relationships which are responsive to changing needs.

As our awareness of the complexities of individual needs has increased, the policy statement acknowledges that for those children who cannot return home, permanence can be satisfactorily achieved in a variety of ways. However, it was felt important to reiterate that adoption does have an important role to play in securing a legally permanent and stable future for some children – albeit a small minority. Adoption continues to offer an experience of belonging and mutual lifelong commitment which is intrinsically different from other forms of permanence, and recognised as such by the child, by birth and adoptive families and, indeed, by society at large. The welcome move towards openness within adoption practice has meant that adoption can now combine needs for permanence with those of contact, while recognising that there is much to learn in this area. The challenge of working more openly and purposefully with birth families and their children cannot and should not be ignored, but neither should the potential benefits of adoption for some children who cannot return home.

Requests for BAAF training on permanence issues have risen considerably and seem to reflect the struggle that many child care professionals face in their day-to-day work of planning for children. Experience has also shown that for many more recently recruited social workers, awareness of the contextual framework of permanence as well as the significance of changes in adoption practice was absent. In an attempt to give practitioners a broader perspective on which to base their decision-making for children, a new Practice Note on permanence will be published later this year. It will outline the historical development of permanence, and will comment on the various routes by which it might be achieved for individual children along with pointers for good practice.

The starting point for planning in child care must be a genuine commitment to maintaining children within their family of origin. When separation threatens it signals a critical phase for both child and family and the nature, purpose and clarity of social work involvement can have a profound impact on the long-term outcome. Planning for children is by necessity a multi-factorial process, and the complexities of individual circumstances can sometimes be overwhelming. It is necessary – indeed essential – to operate within a shared and explicit framework which is respectful of the wishes and feelings of those involved, delineates goals, mutual expectations and supports, and is child focused within appropriate timescales. These characteristics are all reflected in the Children Act, yet still some children are remaining too long in very damaging and dysfunctional family settings, and others drift in foster care with no clear objectives.

The myth that the Children Act makes planning for children more difficult is still alive and well and is sometimes used to justify indecision, misguided optimism (which often lacks any basis of evidence) and poor practice. In fact, the Act gives agencies the opportunity to plan well for children and places upon them a clear responsibility to make decisions that are in the best interests of the child (see also DoH, 1994). For the great majority this will mean working purposefully towards reunification with their parent(s) or within their family network; for the remainder it will involve a thorough consideration of how permanency might best be secured and how parental responsibility is to be exercised reliably and unambiguously.

These ends cannot be achieved if professional thinking is polarised or entrenched. It is as dangerous to believe that every separated child should be adopted as it is naïve to believe that every parent/family can work constructively towards meeting the needs of their child. While underlining the comments of Ryburn (1992; 1993) concerning the essential importance of improving our work with birth families, court action is sometimes the only way an agency can protect and plan effectively. It is unfortunate not only that our current legal system reflects such an adversarial tone, but that social workers making recommendations of such immense importance about the future of children are not required to have developed a recognised level of skill and experience.

In order to address permanency planning issues and to encourage debate around policy and practice, BAAF invited Linda Katz to present several seminars in England and Scotland this autumn. Katz's work in the USA on concurrent planning attempts to combine a philosophy which values family-centred practice and the essential importance to the child of a permanent placement, together with a structured approach to case management which emphasises honesty, goal setting and timescales. Thus, concurrent planning actively and specifically supports reunification, while at the same time developing an alternative plan in case it is necessary. It will be interesting to contrast Katz's thinking and experience with the sequential planning which characterises most child care practice in the UK. It is hoped that the subsequent exchange of views will be lively and challenging, and will contribute towards reflective evaluation of current service provision.

Attachment

While our understanding and awareness of attachment has grown over the years there undoubtedly remains much more to learn about this crucial area. Within the child placement field the contribution of Vera Fahlberg (1981; 1994) has been considerable, yet perhaps because of its inherent complexity there remains a worryingly simplistic view of attachment which sometimes can be at the root of planning dilemmas. Patterns of attachments, both primary and secondary, are vital to make sense of as they can frequently tell us so much about a child's behaviours, responses and needs. Decision-making which does not take account of the entirety of a child's history and experience can lead to inappropriate planning and unrealistic expectations.

When a child is apparently settled in a short-term foster placement the nature and quality of the existing relationship must be critically assessed before it is used as pivotal evidence, either for maintaining the placement, or for portraying the emotional progress of the child and his or her capacity to make positive use of family life. At times either may prove appropriate conclusions, yet experience shows how deceptive temporary arrangements can be and that they have a propensity to mask deeper problems. The implications of a child's attachment history and patterns of behaviour have been highlighted in disruption work (Smith, 1994) and are critical in seeking and sustaining effective placements. The relevance of transgenerational attachment patterns (Main, 1984) cannot be ignored, as it may inform positive family intervention, increase the potential for successful reunification and could provide important information for alternative carers.

When we really appreciate the purpose and function of attachment and recognise the fundamental part it plays in healthy emotional, cognitive and social development, observation and evidence of both past and present attachments will then be scrutinised more critically. The multi-dimensional experience of attachment common within black communities challenges our Eurocentric perception in planning for black children while expedient measures which place such children trans-racially can lead to a multitude of difficult decisions. Acknowledging that an additional dynamic is at work when black children build attach-ments is the first step towards more purposeful planning with longer-term objectives. Attachment is a continuum but if, especially for younger children, it is seen as an essential part of building identity, self-worth, social connectedness and the capacity to cope with stress and frustration as well as other vital life skills, we cannot overestimate the implications of this for black children who develop their primary attachments to white carers, however positive these may be.

Recently there has been much publicity concerning Reactive Attach-ment Disorder and a great deal of informative material emanating from the USA. There are undoubtedly a small number of children/young people with particularly severe attachment problems which cause both them and their carers immense pain and stress and make family life almost intolerable. The determination and commitment of carers in such situations are to be respected and supported, and they need access to as much information and help as we can provide. Yet there is a danger of inappropriate labelling that requires a degree of caution. Every separated child who cannot return to their family network will have attachment and loss issues to deal with, including the infant (Verrier, 1994). Attachment and separation are at the core of family placement work and experts in Reactive Attachment Disorder would agree that, while their confrontational style of therapy has often been effective, they are working with a very small group of young people with particularly destructive and dangerous symptoms. What can be learned from their experience is the crucial importance of a deeper and more informed awareness of the individual child, as well as the value of tools, strategies and support services to equip carers to meet the difficult demands of substitute parenting.

Fortunately, very few children are completely unattached but the majority who cannot return home frequently present a dysfunctional attachment history which has considerable implications for preparation of the child, family finding and parenting. At a recent BAAF seminar, 'Making Placements Work', held in June 1995, David Howe gave a fascinating and all too brief glimpse of his recent research on long-term perspectives in adoption and the developmental histories of the children involved. The significance of the data was such that Howe was diverted from his study and prompted to write, in addition, a book about attachment theory (1995). His research reports, due early next year, which consider the different attachment patterns of approximately 250 adopted children, together with their adoptive parents' views on outcomes, will be essential reading.

Contact
The emphasis within the Children Act on the value of contact has led generally to more appropriate, child-centred practice which respects the child's needs for continuity of attachments and experience. Many BAAF training requests have resulted from the efforts and concerns of agencies to plan effectively for children, while acknowledging the necessity of maintaining important links. Yet for those children requiring permanent placements, contact needs can sometimes appear so dominating that other considerations – including at times a clear long-term plan – can be jeopardised (see also DoH, 1994). In helping agencies we have started from the belief that children need a sense of both permanence and identity, and ideally one should complement the other. Separated child-

ren depend on the adults in their lives to hold these two aspects together for them with all the inherent tensions, and this has considerable implications for recruitment and preparation as well as ongoing support services for birth relatives and carers.

The potential contribution of birth families in gathering information, giving permission and maintaining continuity is rarely valued appropriately within social work practice. There is a need for more understanding of the long-term implications of regular, direct contact within adoption while there is growing evidence that it can be positive for all concerned (Fratter, 1989; 1994). It is encouraging to note the increasingly positive attitudes of prospective adopters towards contact arrangements, but experience within a busy urban adoption panel reflects a wide range of complex histories and relationships, and the ongoing reality of sustaining initial agreements, especially to face-to-face contact, has not proved easy for some. Contact is never static and will have to adapt and respond to changing needs and circumstances. Difficulties arise for a variety of reasons but it seems there is a need to be clearer, not only about the purpose and nature of contact but also to recognise the crucial importance of the attitudes, commitment and flexibility of the adults involved. The implications for the values and expertise of social workers in child placement are also immense.

In contrast to adoption, contact has been assumed to play a more central role in foster care (although see Bilson and Barker, 1995) and the different parental status of foster carers can lead to less tensions. But adoption will be the best route to permanence for some children and in certain situations, whether adoption or fostering, difficult decisions will need to be made that preserve and enhance the child's identity as much as possible, while recognising that face-to-face contact may not facilitate a sense of safety and belonging. The distinction between contact with primary and secondary attachment figures brings its own challenges and at times the complexity of contact arrangements for children from large scattered families can seem daunting. BAAF will be working on a forthcoming Practice Note to help professionals assess individual children's needs in a more structured way.

Identifying and supporting resources

However well planned, permanence cannot be achieved without an appropriate range of family resources. Yet many agencies are currently experiencing a severe crisis in recruitment, particularly of foster carers but also of adopters for children with severe emotional difficulties. Speculation on why this is so might well include economic, social and financial factors but it is also true that social work agencies are asking more of alternative carers than ever before. Living with the nation's most hurt children is taxing in every sense and carers have a right to expect skilled preparation and ongoing training and support in order to meet the demands expected of them. The move towards competency-based training in foster care is to be welcomed but it is important that it is underpinned by a genuine sense of reciprocity and partnership. Competency in a range of areas can and should be appropriately expected of foster carers, but they too have an equal right to expect from social workers and their agencies a similarly competent and facilitating service which supports and develops their capacity to care effectively for troubled youngsters. Competency-based training may also have lessons for adoption preparation, which remains fragmented and *ad hoc* in this country. BAAF's Scottish Centre is currently exploring potential funding in order to work on developing materials for preparing prospective adopters.

In a climate of scarce resources one of the real dangers is the potential for assessment to diminish in importance. It can seem something of a luxury to spend time on building up an accurate picture of a child's needs if at the end of the day there is little or no placement choice. Yet without the thorough assessment which is an integral part of family placement work, and especially of linking, all involved can be set up to fail. While recognising the realities of the world in which we live and work, careful assessment can at least help to identify and prioritise need and alert us to the areas and degree of risk that any placement will involve. It is only then that the planning of contingency or compensatory action can be constructively discussed in order to best support each placement.

Determining the route to permanence for individual children involves a range of considerations, not least the wishes and feelings of the child/ young person. Depending on age and development their views, while essential to obtain and respect, need to be seen in context. There is a need to understand where children are coming from and what informs and potentially distorts their perceptions. Fear, confusion, internalised racism, divided loyalty are just some of the aspects which can impact on a young person's perception of the present and future. Holding the pain, building inner strength and creating an environment of trust and hope, while attempting to identify the best chance of permanence, is rarely easy. An increasing number of young people in the 11–12 plus age range appear to be causing particular concern within the public care system. Many of them have experienced a succession of short-term placements and as a result become more and more hurt and angry. This older age group present particular dilemmas as so many of them have little to draw on in terms of positive and continuous healthy relationships while their need for the intimacy, trust and controls of the younger years are clearly manifest. Often their needs are so disguised by angry, hurt behaviours that achieving permanence within a family is viewed as being unrealistic.

Hard decisions have to be made about how best to support these youngsters into independence and yet provide them with some of the basic tools necessary for emotional growth – and for many time is short. The urgency often implies a task-centred approach which identifies a small number of potentially achievable goals along with specific parenting skills. Adoption is no panacea and often seems inappropriate to consider for such youngsters who, while desperately seeking the commitment and belonging that adoption can offer, are simply unable to respond in the way many adopters would hope for. There is a delicate path to tread between arbitrarily seeing adoption as an unacceptable option for the older age range, and perhaps developing a more skilled and focused approach to recruitment and preparation which recognises the different challenges and rewards of caring for youngsters approaching adolescence.

However, there is little hope of increasing family resources in this or indeed other demanding areas of need unless the support networks so urgently needed by adopters and their children are better established and more readily available. Admirable efforts are being made throughout the country but post-placement support is still extremely variable in quality and accessibility, and carers and workers continue to express their frustration at being expected to care for such needy children in the absence of a clearly defined and well co-ordinated support network. BAAF has been working on a new policy statement to be considered by the Management Committee this autumn which reiterates its conviction that post-adoption support must be an integral part of any adoption service. On a broader front the BAAF AGM/Seminar in November 1995 will focus on the need for ongoing support services for all permanent placements, and how this might best be achieved.

Conclusion

This article has reflected on just a few concerns arising from personal experience of current practice in achieving permanence for children who need long-term care. Such children may be small in number but the time and effort required to work constructively with all parties in order to identify and sustain appropriate placements is remarkable. The imminent organisational changes faced by so many agencies means that, yet again, there is a danger that vital time, energy and finance will be absorbed by structural demands. Children's needs must not get lost. Their childhoods will not come again and they have a right to expect those with responsibility to act in a considered and decisive way in order to secure their future. It is to be hoped that BAAF's efforts to promote the welfare of separated children and to encourage agencies to review their practice and response will contribute to a continuing debate about how best we can all help vulnerable children and the families who care for them.

References

Bilson A and Barker R, 'Parental contact with children fostered and in residential care after the Children Act 1989', *British Journal of Social Work*, 25, 1995.

Department of Health, *Planning Long-term Placement Study*, 1994.

Fahlberg V, *Attachment and Separation*, BAAF, 1981.

Fahlberg V, *A Child's Journey Through Placement*, BAAF, 1994.

Fratter J, 'Contact with birth parents', *Adoption & Fostering*, 13:4, 1989.

Fratter J, *Perspectives on Adoption with Contact: Implications for policy and practice*, PhD Thesis, August 1994 and then published as *Adoption with Contact: Implications for Policy and Practice*, BAAF, 1996.

Howe D, *Attachment Theory for Social Work Practice*, Macmillan, 1995.

Main M, 'Predicting rejection of her infant from mother's representation of her own experience: implications for the abused-abusing intergenerational cycle', *Child Abuse and Neglect*, 8:2, 1984.

Ryburn M, 'Contested Adoption', *Adoption & Fostering*, 16:4, 1992.

Ryburn M, 'Adversarial decision-making', *Adoption & Fostering*, 17:3, 1993.

Smith S, *Learning from Disruption: Making better placements*, BAAF, 1994.

Triseliotis J, 'Perceptions of permanence', *Adoption & Fostering*, 15:4, 1991.

Verrier N, *The Primal Wound*, Gateway, 1993, USA.

4   Adoption – evolution or revolution?

John Triseliotis

John Triseliotis is Emeritus Professor at the University of Edinburgh and Visiting Professor and Senior Research Fellow at the University of Edinburgh. He has been carrying out research on separated children in the fields of adoption, foster care and residential care for over 25 years. He has co-authored or edited many books and articles including: "In search of origins", "Hard to place", "Achieving adoption with love and money", "Freeing children for adoption", "The practice of adoption and fostering", "Parting with a child for adoption", and "Adoption with contact". He has presented papers at many national and international conferences and has lectured on child welfare in several countries.

This paper was published in Adoption & Fostering, 19:2, 1995.

Documentary evidence suggests that some form of informal or *de facto* adoption was practised in Britain during the pre-Reformation period, but it was neither widespread nor connected with the fate of non-marital children or the needs of childless couples. Adoption as a response to the needs of non-marital children did not emerge until after World War One and equally the use of adoption as a means to resolve problems of childlessness and infertility was mainly a feature of the post-1945 period.

Occasional references to adoption are not missing from English literature. For example, there is reference to it in Shakespeare's *Richard I* and *Henry VI*. George Eliot (1861), in her novel *Silas Marner*, which depicts village life during the late 18th and early 19th centuries, remarks that 'adoption was more remote from the ideas and habits of that time'. Nancy, one of the characters in *Silas Marner*, expresses fears that an adopted child may not turn out well and is quoted as saying to her husband:

> *Don't you remember what that lady we met at the Royston Baths told us about the child her sister adopted? That was the only adopting I*

ever heard of: and the child was transported when it was twenty-three.
(p 159)

The adoption, though, of Margaret Gigs by Sir Thomas More, hardly childless, was a fact. Another example is quoted by Gerin (1967) in her biography of Charlotte Brontë. She writes that the Hudsons, with whom Miss Brontë stayed, had been married in 1830 but were childless. At the time of Miss Brontë's visit they had staying with them a seven-year-old niece of Mrs Hudson 'whom they later adopted'. In the absence of any adoption laws, it doesn't say how this was formalised.

The Oxford Dictionary traces adoption and its cognates back to the 14th century but the Foundling Hospital, which was set up in London in 1739 with the object of accepting mainly non-marital children, has no record of any of these children being adopted before 1802 and after that only infrequently is an adoption recorded. A letter written by a Lady Montagu from Constantinople in 1718 tends to suggest that there was ignorance in Britain of the practice of adoption. In a letter to a friend describing its practice there among Greeks, Armenians and Turks she writes:

The adopters are mainly childless couples who chose a child of either sex among the meanest people, and with the consent of the parents before the cadi that the child they received will be their heir . . . a child thus adopted cannot be disinherited. (p 170)

Lady Montagu goes on to urge the introduction of the system in Britain.

As I said earlier, the number of *de facto* adoptions was on the increase after the middle of the last century and was an offshoot of the fostering system which had just been introduced. Few deliberate adoption arrangements, though, are recorded. Long-term fostering then was similar to adoption, including being closed, in the same way that much of adoption today is similar to permanent fostering and is largely open!

Those wishing to understand the development or "evolution" of adoption policy and practice in Britain need, in my view, to study how the following four main factors have influenced, held back or promoted it over the years:

• Economic and class factors;

- Attitudes towards inheritance;
- Attitudes to heredity; and
- Attitudes to non-marital children.

Economic and class factors

The connection between adoption, poverty and destitution can be illustrated in a number of ways. To take one such example, that of infanticide and the exposure or sale of babies and children that had been going on for as long as European history is recorded, it was largely a form of family limitation because many families could not economically afford them. In the process, some children like Oedipus and Moses were rescued and benefited from the "kindness of strangers" who reared them as their own.

Right through to the Middle Ages, infanticide and the increase in the number of exposed, abandoned or sold children or the oblation of children to monasteries, usually coincided with periods of famine and its decrease with periods of improved economic conditions (Boswell, 1988). Similar forms of infanticide, with "adoption" becoming a byword for "baby farming" and exposure, did not come to a halt in Britain until the early start of this century, which again coincided with some relative economic prosperity. Those who have studied the recent Romanian situation would confirm that many of the children found in nurseries or *leaganes* there were placed by parents because it was the only place the children could obtain the basic necessities of life. As with the sale of children from Third World countries, so in Romania there are many examples of parents selling their children to Westerners because they cannot afford to rear them (Triseliotis, 1994).

An examination of adoption statistics in a number of Northern European countries from the end of the Second World War onwards shows also how the reduction in the number of babies made available for adoption over the years went hand-in-hand with improvements in the standard of living of each country and of improved welfare provision to single parent families. There may have been other factors, such as the lowering of the stigma attached to out-of-wedlock births, but the economic factors appear to have been the most decisive. As an example, in recent years only one or two Swedish born children have been adopted each year and only about four or five Dutch children. Britain has always followed the Scandinavian statistical pattern, albeit decades later. However, possible changes at some future date in the economic climate and the pursuit of punishing social policies towards single parents could again alter the picture.

Even Third World countries that have experienced economic growth and improved social welfare provision, such as Korea, have seen a drastic reduction in the number of children taken out of the country for adoption. Irrespective of the arguments for and against intercountry adoption, nobody denies that apart from wars and large-scale catastrophes, most intercountry adoption is of children from very poor countries being adopted in wealthier ones. Some of the economic arguments advanced now against intercountry adoption are broadly the same as those traditionally advanced to criticise own country adoption and they cannot be dismissed easily (Teague, 1989).

It is of course unlikely that a time will ever come when the parting with children for adoption will be free of any internal or external constraints and become a pure form of altruism from those who have children to those who are childless. Even the extensive form of surrogacy practised by the Romans was not entirely altruistic. It is possible that greater openness and contact in adoption may eventually come to generate feelings of altruism resulting in more cases of shared parenting.

Economic factors also played a part, in my view, in the process whereby modern adoption laws which departed from Roman Law first appeared in Massachusetts in 1851 and in Western Australia and in part in New Zealand at the start of this century. It was not accidental that it was another 75 years or so before adoption legislation was introduced in Britain. Push-and-pull factors operated in the countries I mentioned, and particularly in the United States, to account for the introduction of modern adoption laws. I said before that modern adoption is an offshoot of the fostering system and this is also true of the North American experience. The push factor in the USA was the need to empty children's institutions to make space for newcomers and the pull factor was the needs of a homestead economy for cheap labour. These factors resulted in the emptying of institutions by fostering the children with farming families. No doubt, as is always the case, some of the children – nobody knows how many – found good homes and considerate new families, but there was also harsh exploitation. The early Massachusetts' adoption law was reactive to this situation and had as its main purpose the offer of some protection to the children.

Britain was not a homestead economy but a highly industrialised one. The nearest equivalent to the USA – that is the emptying of institutions which Dr Barnardo and others were keen to achieve – was the shipping of children to the new Commonwealth countries whose homestead economies, like that of the USA, required cheap labour (Parker, 1991).

Economic factors have not altogether disappeared from being at the root of some parents parting with their children for adoption in Britain. No doubt there are other complex personal and social factors and characteristics operating. However, until we demonstrate that our preventive and rehabilitative services offer comprehensive and uniform cover, the legitimacy of adoption will always be challenged for being biased against the poorer sections of the community. One of the positive contributions resulting from the recent efforts to place older children for adoption was that it made agencies more sensitive to the need for preventive and rehabilitative services, mainly because they had to convince the courts of the need to free the children for adoption. We have to recognise though that, even in the most ideally organised society, there will always be some children who will need the protection, security and social base offered by a new family.

Poverty was not the only class factor that played a part in shaping adoption policy and practice over the years. I said earlier that adoption as a response to the needs of the childless was mainly a post-1945 phenomenon. Not only that, but during the next 20 or so years, childless, mostly middle-class, couples were prized by adoption agencies. It was then very hard for poorer families to adopt because they were viewed as marginal unless, as we have found, they were prepared to adopt children who were viewed as equally marginal (1970). Today it is mainly couples with a different family structure and from a different social background that are prized because of the need to place children with special needs. One of the many positive contributions of adoption allowances, introduced in 1983, was that it made it easier for poorer families to adopt with an allowance attached. However, younger and healthier children still go to predominantly middle-class families.

Attitudes to inheritance

One other crucial factor that delayed the introduction of adoption legislation in Britain was attitudes to inheritance. The British were not alone in disliking the idea of property passing from consanguineal to adoptive kinship relationships, that is away from the blood line. This explains, for example, the continued pull in many countries of adoption by relatives. It is well known that adoption from ancient times onwards has been practised mainly between relatives and only when that source was unavailable did families then turn to outsiders.

The decisive move towards large-scale adoption by non-relatives, as well as foster care, is both recent and mostly a characteristic of Western Europe, North America and the New Commonwealth. There may be different reasons for this, but it appears that families which have diffuse boundaries between themselves and the community, as opposed to rigid ones, are readier to accept outsiders. The stronger the family unit and the loyalty to the wider family group, the less space is made for outsiders. (I was told that in Romania it was seen as a big stigma for one's child to be fostered by a non-related family. In contrast, no stigma apparently is attached to the child being brought up in an institution.) Improved economic circumstances, social mobility and better social welfare provision seem to encourage families to be more outward looking and more inclusive of "outsiders".

Feelings about inheritance in Britain appear to have been particularly strong among the landed aristocracy and, though in a minority, they yielded legislative and economic power which they used to block moves to introduce adoption laws that would allow adopted children to inherit from their adoptive parents. The arguments about inheritance were very influential both in delaying adoption legislation in Britain and also in shaping the 1926 English Adoption Law and its Scottish equivalent later. Lady Montagu, quoted earlier, deprecated in her letter the reluctance in Britain to adopt because of the reluctance to pass property on to an outsider:

Methinks 'tis much more reasonable to make happy and rich an infant whom I educate after my own manner brought up upon my knees, and who has learned to look upon me with a filial respect than to give an estate to a creature without other merit or relation to me than by a few letters. Yet this is an absurdity we see frequently practised. (p 170)

Faulds (1975), in her article on adoption in the Highlands and Islands of Scotland, gives graphic accounts of the strong feelings attached to the ownership or occupation of land and the reluctance to see any pass out of the hands of the family and adds:

The feelings of the people for their meagre birthright demonstrates a great preoccupation with kinship and its relationship to land tenure. It is generally regarded as unacceptable that a stranger or someone not related takes over a croft which has been in the family's possession for many generations.

Interestingly enough, it is claimed that early US adoption legislation had the support of many "adoptive" parents who wanted to make the children's position legal in order to enable them to inherit from their adoptive parents. What seems to have won the day for adoption legislation in Britain was the agreement to leave out matters of inheritance. As a result, the first Adoption Act of 1926 excluded the adopted child from inheriting from his or her adopters. The child could, however, inherit from the birth parents. The passing of the legislation was also helped by concern about the increasing numbers of *de facto* adoptions in England and the number being contested in courts by parents at the time.

The biggest contribution of modern adoption laws, in my view, has been the conferment of legality and respectability to adoption especially in the post-World War One period when adoption in Britain had a very poor image. As we have found from a couple of our recent studies, legality has a strong emotional significance for children growing up as adopted, including those transferring from long-term fostering to adoption. As for the conferment of respectability, again we know that even until the 1960s adopted children and adopted people were looked upon as second-class citizens and they felt like that (Triseliotis, 1973; Hill *et al*, 1989). The diversity of family life styles, and the assertion of rights by minority groups that have become key features of the last two decades, have made people more accepting towards those who do not fit traditional familial images. Adopted people, as noted from a recent study, no longer feel either second class or ashamed for being adopted (Craig, 1991).

An amendment to the Adoption Act in 1949 allowed eventually adopted children in England to inherit property, but not a title, from their adoptive parents. The change in the law with regard to inheritance did not occur in Scotland until 1964. It was also because of concerns around inheritance that the Scottish law made it possible for adopted children to obtain a copy of their original birth certificate on attaining the age of 17. The significance of such information to the formation of the adopted person's identity was not to be recognised until much later (Triseliotis, 1973).

Fears about heredity and bad blood

Another important factor that held back adoption legislation in Britain was the strong stigma attached to out-of-wedlock births and especially the strongly held belief that immorality, criminality and badness were either hereditary and/or transmissible from parents to children.

Because of these twin factors, non-marital children were not accepted by a number of philanthropic and child care organisations for placements in institutions or for "adoption" out of fear that any association with the unmarried mother and her child would lead to the cessation of charitable contributions. Until after World War One, and apart from Josephine Butler, no organisation was prepared to stand up publicly in support of single unwed parents and their children. Some softening of attitudes began to emerge after about 1918 when it was pointed out that some of the children were the offspring of the "heroes" who fell in the First World War.

It was also mainly because of fears about heredity and bad blood that adoption, until about the late 1940s, was practised mainly among the working classes who were not supposed to be too much bothered by such fears. Apparently the Romans, unlike the ancient Greeks or Egyptians, did not attach much importance to the blood relationship or to heredity (Dupont, 1989). Yet the blood relationship has been supreme in Western culture for 2000 years and the few dents have only appeared in the second half of this century.

Adoption practice was reversed after the end of the Second World War when heredity seemed to be out among the middle classes and nurture rather than nature was seen to be paramount in determining how children eventually turn out. It may not be accidental also that this coincided with the greater optimism, even if misplaced, ushered in at the end of the Second World War. It was from then onwards that a strong relationship was established between childlessness and non-marital births.

However, this apparent optimism concerning the benefits conferred on children by a benevolent environment was carried in the knowledge that adoption agencies would ensure that all babies placed would be well screened beforehand, to eliminate those suspected of "bad blood" or physical or mental conditions. The trend of eliminating children with a poor medical or social history from being placed for adoption has its apparent origins in the Horsbrugh Committee report of 1937. The Committee was set up in the 1930s to examine the practices of adoption agencies and it showered praise on those agencies that took great care to avoid placing children for such reasons as bad health, mental defect in the mother, or dubious parentage (Horsbrugh, 1937).

By the 1950s, the Horsbrugh Committee's recommendations were reinforced by Bowlby's studies on "maternal deprivation". He claimed, among other things, that children who had experienced separations and early deprivations were irreparably damaged and therefore unable to benefit from adoption if placed, especially when older than about two years (Bowlby, 1951).

The studies on deprivation, and especially about the irreversibility of early psychological adversities, were to be challenged in later years, but by then adoption and general child care practice had incorporated these warnings. Influenced by these writings and by the Horsbrugh report, adoption workers were now looking for the "perfect" baby to be placed with the "perfect" family and adopters were socialised into these expect-ations. Kornitzer (1968) gives many examples of the kind of children would-be adopters were asking for. For example, "an upper-class family" asked for "an aristocratic child"; another "not one from the gutter"; and the child of a tailoress was rejected as the background "didn't fit" with the adopters' idea. In fact Kornitzer claims that some societies would not accept "low-class" adopters or children, confirmed also by Triseliotis (1970) and Triseliotis and Russell (1984).

In the pursuit of the "perfect" baby, medical advisers to adoption agencies declared thousands of children as unadoptable, either because of physical or other handicaps and not infrequently because of the birth mother's "dubious" way of life (Triseliotis and Russell, 1984). Though doctors were only advising the agencies, as Margaret Kornitzer points out (1968), it would be most unusual for adoption agencies to go against the views of the medical profession.

With the above in mind, it is puzzling that in the recent Consultative Document issued by the Department of Health, *Adoption: The Future* (1993), medical advisers are given what appear to be extensive powers to advise adoption agencies, not only on medical matters, which is understandable, but also on issues of child neglect and abuse, which largely involve social factors. My reading of the document is that the extensive powers conferred on medical advisers could undermine the morale and enthusiasm of adoption workers who are expected to play second fiddle to the medical profession. Yet the recruitment of new families, their preparation and assessment, and that of the children, will still have to rely largely on the enthusiasm and commitment of the adoption workers.

Attitudes to non-marital births

Reference has already been made to how non-marital children were linked to fears about heredity, bad blood and the transmission of immorality until about 1945. This is not the place to discuss society's treatment of the unmarried mother, or of non-marital children. However, as our theme is "evolution or revolution", I could not resist the temptation to draw at least one parallel with the past. I was reading recently Lawrence Stone's (1992) fascinating book, *Uncertain Unions – Marriage in England between 1600 and 1753*, and came across the following passage which reminded me of some of the approaches of the Child Support Agency:

Since illegitimate children were becoming an increasing burden on the community by the eighteenth century, every effort was made by the parish to identify the father by prior interrogation of the mother either by a JP before the birth or during her labour by the midwife on threat of withholding assistance. Once paternity was ascertained, a filiation order was issued by a JP against the father, who was required to give bonds and provide sureties to pay an annual sum sufficient to cover the cost to the parish of maintaining the child for the first seven years of life. (p 14)

Recent American literature on adoption suggests that although the numbers of non-marital babies and of very young children released for adoption may have decreased dramatically, there is evidence that some of the children are now coming into care when older, many of them requiring new permanent families (Centre for the Future of Children, 1993). In Britain the picture may not be exactly the same. The number of all children coming into care has fallen significantly over the last ten years, and though the percentage of those who exit from care through adoption has slightly risen, in terms of numbers they have decreased. Much, in my view, will depend on whether preventive work with families and children is increased or takes a back seat.

The future
Turning to the future, I have no prophetic powers, and I am no Cassandra. To predict future developments in adoption requires the ability to foresee social change and changes in social policy, which adoption mostly reflects. Barring social upheavals here and elsewhere, adoption is likely to become rarer and more difficult. The main reasons are shifts in the legislation, particularly the Children Act 1989 and, I would like to think, increased confidence on the part of single parents to bring up young children on their own.

Leaving aside the empirical and practical arguments about the rights and wrongs of intercountry adoption, its future regulation in Britain is likely to lead to some increase in numbers. This will happen in spite of the fact that there is evidence suggesting that other European countries are turning away from it because of the commercialism surrounding it. In the interests of children, an increase in intercountry adoption will require adoption workers to develop new skills for preparing and supporting families adopting intercountry to cope with the additional tasks involved. Agencies will also have to be prepared to offer some familiar, but also some new, forms of support to children adopted inter-country. Similarly, the increased use of open adoption and of adoption with contact will require new mediation skills on the part of adoption workers and skills on how to negotiate and defuse conflict or its potential.

The lessons emerging from studies covering the post-placement stage of children with special needs highlight how much more remains to be learned, particularly on how to match older children and new families. The studies so far have been too general to be of much help, either to policy makers or to practitioners. No doubt a lot has been achieved, but equally a lot still remains to be learned to avoid exposing some children and families to impossible situations. It is also unfair to ask families to undertake onerous responsibilities in the light of the present variability between the amount of preparation and post-placement support agencies offer to new families and children before and after placement. Apart from the apparent reluctance of adoptive families to return for help, possibly out of fear of being seen as dysfunctional, the availability of support is still patchy, unco-ordinated and far from uniform.

Finally, one of the many ways in which adoption has changed over the last 30 or so years has been the increased professionalism with which it has been practised. I know that it is not popular to champion "profession-alism" at a time when "common sense" is meant to rule. However, I have no hang-ups about the use of the word. What it conveys to me is purpose-fulness in the application of knowledge and skills rather than relying solely on intuition and experience, which sometimes can lead to the repetition of mistakes. Research evidence suggests that better outcomes, in both fostering and adoption, are associated with the application of such knowledge and skills (Berridge and Cleaver, 1987; Borland et al, 1991).

Much of the professionalism achieved in adoption work in Britain could be attributed to the close collaboration developed over the years between adoption and social work, which has proved beneficial to both. The possible association of adoption with another profession, such as psychology, may have brought about similar benefits, but we do not know. It is my view, based on observations from a number of other European countries, that where the profession of social work is weak or almost non-existent, the interests of children seem to feature less also in adoption arrangements. (I recognise that it is not enough to have a pro-fession with a commitment to children's best interests. You also need to have the right legislation plus a network of social work services to implement the law.)

There are also a number of concerns about the future. These arise mainly from some shifts in practice that are taking place now within social work departments. While I welcome the move towards more defined specialisms within social services, such as children and families which I urged some 20 years ago (Triseliotis, 1973a), nevertheless child care work, including adoption, is facing a number of threats. First, increasing demands are being made on social workers' time without a corresponding increase in resources, shifting them into a largely reactive response connected with child protection rather than child care. Second, community care work, with its emphasis on the customer/purchaser relationship, on budgeting, accountancy and on form-filling, seems to be becoming the benchmark for the rest of social work, even though such a wholly instrumentalist approach does not appear to meet the needs of families and children. In addition, the competencies-driven functional analysis of social work spearheaded by the Central Council for Education and Training in Social Work is leading to the fragmentation of tasks, losing sight of the person. This mechanistic approach may suit a factory assembly line, but it does not suit the needs of many users of social services. Attention to process, and relationships between social workers and service users, are still central in family and child care work, as we have found from our recent research on teenagers and their families (Triseliotis *et al*, 1995). Third, the recent re-organisation of many social services departments to take account of recent community care legislation has resulted in the disbandment, in some authorities, of specialist fostering and adoption units. In the past such units were pioneering, along with the others, the development and application of new knowledge and skills in this field of work. As a result, valuable expertise built over many years could be lost and total reliance will now be on the voluntary sector to continue this tradition.

References

Berridge D and Cleaver H, *Foster Home Breakdown*, Blackwell, 1987.

Borland M, O'Hara G and Triseliotis J, *The Outcome of Permanent Family*

Placements in Two Scottish Local Authorities, Scottish Office, 1991.

Boswell J, *The Kindness of Strangers*, Penguin, 1988.

Bowlby J, *Maternal Care and Mental Health*, World Health Organisation, 1951.

Centre for the Future of Children, 'Overview and major recommendations', *Adoption*, 13:1, pp 14–16, 1993.

Craig M, *Not a Big Deal*, Scottish Adoption Society, unpublished report.

Department of Health, *Adoption: The future*, HMSO, 1993.

Dupont F, *Daily Life in Ancient Rome*, Blackwell, 1989.

Eliot G, *Silas Marner*, The Thames Publishing Co, 1861.

Faulds M, 'Adoption in the Highlands and Islands', *Child Adoption*, 79:1, pp 41–44, 1975.

Gerin W, *Charlotte Brontë*, Clarendon Press, 1967.

Hill M, Lambert L and Triseliotis J, *Achieving Adoption with Love and Money*, National Children's Bureau, 1989.

Horsbrugh Committee, *Report of the Departmental Committee on Adoption Societies and Agencies*, HMSO, 1937.

Kornitzer M, *Adoption and Family Life*, Patman, 1968.

MacIntyre A, *After Virtue: A study in moral theory*, Duckworth, 1981.

Montagu W M, *Letters from Lady Montagu, 1709–1762*, Everyman's Library, Vol 1, 1925.

Parker R, *Away from Home*, Barnardo's, 1991.

Stone L, *Uncertain Unions – Marriage in England 1600–1753*, Oxford University Press, 1992.

Teague A, *Social Change, Social Work and the Adoption of Children*, Avebury, 1989.

Triseliotis J, *Evaluation of Adoption Policy and Practice*, Department of Social Administration, University of Edinburgh, 1970.

Triseliotis J, *In Search of Origins*, Routledge & Kegan Paul, 1973.

Triseliotis J, 'Issues in child care practice', *Child Adoption*, 73:3, pp 15–21, 1973.

Triseliotis J and Russell J, *Hard to Place*, Heinemann/Gower, 1984.

Triseliotis J, 'Setting up foster care programmes in Romania', *Community Alternatives*, 6:1, pp 49–74, 1994.

Triseliotis J, Borland M, Hill M and Lambert, L, *Social Work Services to Teenagers*, HMSO, 1995.

This article is an abridged version of a speech delivered at BAAF's 1994 Annual General Meeting.

5 Adoption: A service for children?

Caroline Ball

Caroline Ball is Senior Lecturer in the Schools of Law and Social Work at the University of East Anglia, Norwich

This paper was published in Adoption & Fostering, 20:2, 1996.

Major reform of adoption law takes place, on average, every quarter century, with some amendment in between. Each reform in its turn reflects, in broad terms, contemporary public and professional concerns regarding the process and consequences of the adoption of children. With the publication of a Draft Adoption Bill for consultation, we are now near to another statutory landmark, which in its turn represents an attempt to reframe adoption legislation better to meet the increasingly diverse and complex needs of children in need of a permanent placement outside their birth family.

The historical context
In the 1920s when the introduction of legal adoption was being debated in the aftermath of the social upheaval of the 1914–18 war, the focus was on the need for formal legal mechanisms by which illegitimate babies and, less commonly, orphaned children could be adopted by childless couples and brought up in families rather than in the Poor Law and other impersonal institutions which formed the main public provision for abandoned and destitute children (Parker, 1990). There were also many children already informally "adopted" by relatives or strangers who needed security within the new family and the avoidance of what was the then crushing stigma of illegitimacy. After several failed attempts, the Adoption Act 1926 introduced legal adoption in England and Wales; a similar statute was enacted for Scotland in 1930.

Once adoption was legalised, the process of refining the statutory framework to meet the needs of the adoptive population began. The first major reforms reflected a dual determination to:

- regulate the adoption process to eliminate financial abuses and inappropriate placements; and
- equate the position of adopted children for purposes of succession more nearly to that of birth children within a family.

Greater regulation of the process was initially addressed in separate adoption legislation. The unexpected popularity of adoption, as evidenced by the rapid rise in the numbers of orders made, from just under 3,000 in 1927 to over 5,000 in 1936, was accompanied by abuses which resulted in the recognition of a need for stricter regulation, particularly in regard to the suitability of adopters (DoH, 1937). The responsibilities of local authorities for registering adoption societies and supervising children placed for adoption, which began with the Adoption of Children (Regulation) Act 1939, was increased in all subsequent adoption legislation, culminating in all local authorities becoming adoption agencies in 1988. The gradual extension of rights of succession to adopted people ran parallel. Beginning with the Adoption of Children Act 1949, amendments over the years have had the effect of totally equating the adopted child's rights of inheritance with those of birth children (apart from succession to titles of honour).

By the early 1970s the profound changes in social attitudes, particularly in regard to illegitimacy, and in child care policy and practice that had taken place since the war, were reflected in both the legalising of abortion and in changing patterns of adoption. The Departmental Committee on the Adoption of Children, chaired by Sir William Houghton, took evidence at a time when the numbers of children adopted annually had just passed its peak of nearly 27,000 in 1969. The Committee addressed many contemporary concerns and in particular the increased diversity of children for whom adoption was a possibility (DoH, 1972). Provisions reflecting many of the Houghton Committee's radical recommendations were enacted in Part 1 of the Children Act 1975 and subsequently consolidated into the Adoption Act 1976. These included the outlawing of third-party placements and measures discouraging step-parent adoption. The Act also introduced the procedure of freeing for adoption, an innovative mechanism by which courts were empowered to deal with issues of parental consent before, and separately from, the adoption application.

Part 1 of the Children Act 1975 was implemented incrementally and it was only in 1988 that the Adoption Act 1976 finally came into force. By that time it was apparent that the statutory framework was not sufficiently flexible to meet the increasingly varied needs of children for whom their birth families could not provide a permanent home. The main concerns clustered around a number of key issues:

- The *needs of children* requiring permanent placement into adulthood outside their birth families were often fundamentally different to those of the illegitimate babies on whom, despite all the intervening changes, legislation still appeared predicated.
- Research findings, the perceptions of legal and social work professionals, and the bitter experience of families showed that the procedure for *freeing for adoption* was deeply flawed. Damaging delays disadvantaged parents wishing to contest plans for their children's adoption, and after freeing some children were left in a legal limbo for long periods.
- There were increasing numbers of children for whom there was need for some kind of post-adoption contact, and differing perceptions surrounding the term "open" adoption.
- After an initial drop following implementation of section 10(3) of the Children Act 1975, *step-parent adoptions* had risen significantly, at a time when it was recognised that second and subsequent marriages were particularly vulnerable to breakdown.
- Additionally, and most importantly, what amounted to a *traffic in babies* from Eastern Europe and Third World countries to the United States and Western Europe was already being addressed through preparation of the Hague Convention on the Protection of Children and Co-operation in Respect of Intercountry Adoption, which would have to be incorporated into domestic law before the United Kingdom would be able to ratify the treaty.

All these factors contributed to recognition of the need for a radical review of adoption law, similar to that which informed the underpinning principles and provisions of the Children Act 1989.

The process of reform

The current reform process started in the productive climate of the Children Act reforms, and with the model of that Act in place. In July 1989 an inter-departmental working group supported by officials from the Department of Health and the Law Commission was set up. It produced consultation papers looking at all aspects of adoption, including a review of research, and commissioned background papers on international perspectives, intercountry adoption and research relating to adoption. This group reported to Ministers in the Review of Adoption Law (the review), published as a consultation document in October 1992. The wide-ranging Review addressed all aspects of the adoption process and suggested many reforms. These included: the replacement of freeing orders with orders made prior to a child being placed for adoption; an order giving parental responsibility to step-parents without severing the child from half of his or her birth family; the requirement that children aged 12 or over should give their own consent to adoption; the introduction of a new order giving the child and the people with whom the child would live greater security and continuity than that provided under a residence order, without legal severance from the birth family; and the incorporation within domestic law of provisions necessary to enable ratification of the Hague Convention on Intercountry Adoption.

In November 1993 the Government responded to the review recommendations with proposals for adoption law reform, set out in the White Paper *Adoption: The future*. Following somewhat critical response to the sketchy content of many of the proposals, further consultation papers on the key issues of placement orders and adoption panels were circulated and responded to in 1994.

In an unusual and most welcome final step in the consultation process, in March of this year the Government published *Adoption: A service for children*, containing a Draft Adoption Bill, together with an invitation to comment on the provisions, prior to the possible inclusion of the (hopefully amended) Bill in the next legislative programme.

The Bill

Contrary to the initial somewhat hysterical press reaction when it was published, the Bill has received a cautious welcome in many quarters.

There are, however, critical areas in which well-researched, well-argued recommendations or emphases in the Review, many of which were echoed in the White Paper, appear to have been altered. Whether this represents an intended shift of policy or misunderstandings in the drafting process is not entirely clear. Many organisations and individuals including BAAF will respond in detail on all the matters on which comment on the Bill is invited. Here there is only space to put forward a personal, selective, lawyer's view on some of the provisions which do not appear adequately to address the concerns of those with an expert understanding of the diverse range of needs of children for whom adoption may be being considered. These concerns relate to:

- aspects of the welfare principles (clause 1);
- the criteria for dispensing with parental consent (clause 46);
- aspects of placement orders (Chapter 3);
- orders for step-parents (clause 85); and
- residence orders used as an alternative to adoption (clause 86).

The welfare principles

The provision of an introductory chapter is very welcome. This sets out, as in section 1 of the Children Act, the principles relating to the welfare of the child, applicable in all decision-making, not only by courts but also by adoption agencies. Unfortunately, a number of principles well addressed in the review, and mostly also in the White Paper, are either omitted or appear in a significantly altered form in the Bill. For instance, throughout the review and consultation process it was recognised that as '(u)niquely among interventions available to protect children's upbringing, adoption involves an irreversible legal separation of the child from his birth parents and the transfer of parental responsibility to other people', there should be 'a clear and positive duty on the court to address itself to the needs of the child and to the scale of potential advantage to the child of having a new family; and to satisfy itself that *the likely benefit of adoption is so significantly better when compared with other options as to justify an order*' (DoH, 1993; emphasis inserted). Unfortunately clause 1(5) of the Bill merely echoes section 1(5) of the Children Act. It concludes '. . . the court must not make any order under this Act unless it considers that making the order would be better for the child than not doing so'. This form of words may have the merit of consistency, but it fails to acknowledge the essential difference between the two Acts – clearly endorsed in the White Paper – that while other orders are time limited or revocable, adoption 'involves an irreversible legal separation'.

The omission of specific reference to the need to consider issues regarding the child's race and culture in the checklist in section 1(4) doubtless and sadly reflects the extremity of the current backlash against anything perceived as adherence to political correctness. Such a require- ment can easily be differentiated; far from being a gesture towards political correctness it would represent an acknowledgment that a proper regard for issues of ethnicity and culture are central to, though not necessarily determinate of, informed and sensitive decision-making in regard to children's futures.

Dispensing with parental consent

In the Bill, for the first time, statutory provisions relating to a court over- riding a parent's consent to his or her child's adoption are directly linked rather than explicitly separated from consideration of the child's welfare (clause 1(6)). The proposed criteria for dispensing with consent are that 'the parent or guardian cannot be found or is incapable of giving consent, or the court is satisfied that the welfare of the child requires the consent to be dispensed with' (clause 46). There is no doubt that the currently most commonly used test that the parent is "unreasonably withholding" consent has proved difficult to interpret in terms other than the child's welfare, and that the proposals to make this explicit were widely welcomed. The welcome was, however, for the review and White Paper test that 'adoption is likely to offer a *significantly better advantage to the child* than any other option' (emphasis inserted). Once again the omission of the "significance factor" in the Bill lay the changes wide open to criticism.

Placement orders

The placement order provisions set out in Chapter 3 are, as Nigel Lowe points out in a detailed and helpful analysis, the third set of proposals regarding the placement of children for adoption (Lowe, 1996). Under clause 23 local authorities who wish to place children for adoption, or change the status of foster carers and others to that of prospective adopters, are required either to obtain parental consent or a court order authorising placement. The principle underpinning placement orders, that they will enable parents to challenge the local authority's plans for their children's adoption at an early stage, is widely welcomed and not at issue. There are, however, some indications that the provisions are still in need of further consideration and possible amendment, particularly in regard to the legal status of the child and the prospective adopters when a placement order is in force, and the possible elision of care and placement order proceedings when the local authority's initial care plan is for adoption.

Step-parent adoptions
The amendment of section 4 of the Children Act 1989 to allow step-parents to acquire parental responsibility for their step-children, either by agreement or court order, provides a viable alternative to adoption for step-parents. For the acquisition of parental responsibility to replace adoption as the order of preference for step-parents, there may need to be an additional statutory direction to the effect that step-parent adoptions will only be made in exceptional circumstances. Given the terms of clause 1(5), such a direction might be seen as duplicitous, so alternatively the presumption will need to be made explicit in guidance. The extent to which birth fathers may welcome the adoption of their children as a means of ending liability under the Child Support Act is an issue which should attract separate attention.

Residence orders as an alternative to adoption
Throughout the reform process it has been recognised that there is a need for an alternative order giving the permanent carer of a child for whom rehabilitation is not possible, but who still has meaningful contact with their birth family, greater security and assured continuity in their relationship with the child than that currently provided by a residence order. At present guardianship, which most closely equates to the status envisaged, can only take effect after the death of parents. The concept of a status similar to that of guardian but to take effect with the consent of

living parents (an *inter-vivos* guardian) was explored in the review and endorsed in the White Paper.

Implementing the proposal raised seemingly intractable legal problems, particularly as regards issues of inheritance and liability for child support. The Bill provides instead for amendments to section 12 of the Children Act set out in clause 86, under which, with the consent of all persons with parental responsibility, a residence order may be made to last until the child is 18. In such cases applications to vary or discharge the order would only be able to be made with leave. This order would provide more security during the child's minority but no continuity. For instance in the event of the death of the person or persons with such an order a child could be left without anyone capable of exercising parental responsibility. It is suggested that the necessary continuity could be achieved by allowing holders of such residence orders to nominate persons to continue to hold the order in the event of their death.

Intercountry adoption

Parts 3 and 4 of the Bill extend to the whole of the United Kingdom. Clause 88 makes provision for the making of regulations to give effect to the 1993 Hague Convention on intercountry adoption. The way in which the regulations will interrelate with the provisions of the Bill are detailed in the consultative document, paragraphs 5.1 to 5.10. A draft of those for England and Wales is included. The procedure appears relatively straightforward as regards member states, but despite the outlawing of the bringing of children into the UK in contravention of the provisions of clause 91 on legal procedures for intercountry adoption, huge problems remain and are likely to remain unresolved in relation to the adoption of children from non-member states. Advice is sought in regard to the recognition under UK law of what is known as "simple adoption", a form of adoption not recognised in UK law, which avoids complete legal severance from the birth family and which is the only form of adoption in many donor countries.

Conclusion

The opportunity to reform adoption law comes at best no more than once in a generation. As the making of an adoption order is, and is intended to remain, an irrevocable step, outstanding issues must be satisfactorily resolved in this final stage of the consultation process. If there are issues that cannot be determined in a way that ensures passage of legislation in the next parliamentary session, it will be a pity since reform is badly needed. Even so it would be much less damaging in the long term for the children involved to delay in order to achieve a satisfactory conclusion which addresses the concerns raised in this article.

References

The following Department of Health publications are all published in London by HMSO: *Adoption: The future*, Cmnd 2288, 1993; *Draft Adoption Bill*, 1996; *Report of the Departmental Committee on the Adoption of Children*, Cmnd 5107, 1972; *Report of the Departmental Committee on Adoption Societies and Agencies*, Cmnd 5499, 1937.

Lowe N, 'Placement of children for adoption under the proposed Adoption Bill', *Childright*, 126, pp 14–18, 1996.

Parker R, *Away from Home: A history of child care*, Barnardo's, 1990.

6 Beyond permanence? The importance of resilience in child placement practice and planning

Robbie Gilligan

Robbie Gilligan is Senior Lecturer in Social Work and academic Co-director of the Children's Centre at the University of Dublin, Trinity College

This paper was published in Adoption & Fostering, 21:1, 1997.

The concept of permanence has cast a very long shadow over practice and debate in the child care field in the past few decades. Permanence has been represented in different ways but essentially seems concerned with stable, enduring and guaranteed placement as an alternative and antidote to ruptures in earlier care and primary relationships. The ideology of permanence has tended to concentrate on the child's need for one or more lasting attachments. In this regard, many have come to see permanence as based on a permanent placement for the child outside his or her own family. While not always achieved in practice, permanence has certainly become an influential standard by which the quality of care provision may be assessed. The concept of permanence has undoubtedly contributed a great deal to the child welfare field (Pecora, Whittaker and Maluccio, 1992). The purpose of this article, however, is to argue that there are problems with an excessive reliance on *permanence* as a guiding framework in alternative care, especially for older children. Instead it will be suggested that the concept of *resilience* now has greater potential as a more far reaching and inclusive concept for child placement policy and practice, partly because it can incorporate but extend beyond the scope of permanence. Resilience fits very well within the new outcomes paradigm which has growing influence in the child placement field. Resilience refers to qualities which cushion a vulnerable child from the worst effects of adversity in whatever form it takes and which may help a child or young person to cope, survive and even thrive in the face of great hurt and disadvantage. The concept of resilience has become extremely important in the wider child development literature and this article makes the case for its prominence in the child placement field more specifically.

The article initially argues that there are limitations inherent in the permanence paradigm. A too exclusive preoccupation with permanence may risk a policy or practice which fails to connect with important realities in child care services. The article then goes on to examine the concept of resilience and its potentially greater relevance for policy and practice in child placement. Resilience, it is suggested, can make a valuable contribution to a wider framework for assessing and responding to child care need. Finally some messages for practice are distilled from the research evidence on resilience.

The purpose of the article is not to dismiss permanence. It argues, instead, that a resilience-based perspective, while retaining certain strengths of the permanence framework, offers additional insights and principles which can accommodate more of the complexity of child care problems and needs. The article seeks to contribute to what Fein and Maluccio (1992) term 'the necessary move away from the search for simple answers to complex questions'. In the end, of course, it is not slogans or concepts which will transform the fortunes of individual children in care but sensitive and detailed assessment and planning on a case by case basis (Parker *et al*, 1991).

Limitations of permanence

The first difficulty raised by some commentators is that the ideology of permanence may operate in practice against the child's (re-)integration in the birth family The concept of permanence has at times been used as justification for a "clean-break" strategy where a child is in care because of family difficulties. In fairness, however, this has sometimes been a problem associated more with interpretations of the concept of permanence than with the concept itself. Indeed, in what is essentially an important refinement of the concept, proponents of the family continuity paradigm have asserted that the birth family and its social ecology is the context of choice for permanence or at least is an active resource for the child in placement (McFadden and Downs, 1995).

The second difficulty I would suggest is that permanence is so frequently unattained (or unattainable?) in practice. This brings into question its relevance or utility as a governing paradigm of child care practice and policy. We must distinguish between intentions and outcomes. Just because we wish or plan for a placement to be permanent and enduring does not guarantee its ultimate longevity or indeed continuing appropriateness. In one British study of 16- to 19-year-olds in the care system, fewer than ten per cent had had a single placement in their care career; the average number of placements was 4.4 per young person (Biehal *et al*, 1992). While this may seem to underline the case for permanence, it also raises important questions. If permanence often proves elusive, if it proves more aspirational than actual, how helpful can it be as a central guiding principle? The aphorism that the 'best is the enemy of the good' may be relevant here. By setting sights too high or by putting all the eggs in one basket, the danger may be that alternative (and feasible) intermediate and good objectives are obscured. So attention to important issues such as schooling experiences, health, links with extended family, hobbies and friendships may be sacrificed on the altar of permanence. The evidence of the rates of disruption and the fact that high proportions of young people leaving care drift home and/or into homelessness seem to challenge the wisdom of putting all the eggs into the permanence basket (Bullock *et al*, 1993; Courtney and Barth, 1996). A prudent policy should be based on ends which are desirable and attainable. While often desirable, permanence narrowly conceived may not be sustained in many individual cases.

The problem of diminished or insufficient relevance is partly accounted for by the third possible difficulty which can be identified with permanence. As a guideline for practice it seems unable, by itself, to accommodate the complexity of the issues involved. This complexity derives from three sources: the myriad of histories, problems and demands presented by individual children needing care; the range of categories of care which are required in response to this panoply of need; and our increasingly sophisticated understanding, courtesy of research, of the multiple influences on social development in the child and adolescent. A focus on permanence alone risks a too narrow response to a child's complex needs. It may obscure important factors in a child's social development beyond what may be said to be the key preoccupation of permanence: a new (or renewed) primary attachment relationship.

Prioritising permanence seems to assume the superior developmental and rehabilitative value of primary attachment relationships for a child who has suffered loss and separation. Attention to these relationships in isolation may lead to neglect of other resources and relationships in a child's life which may have an important role to play as supplements, or indeed substitutes, should the attempted (re-)establishment of primary attachment relationships fail. The research evidence suggests that relations with caring adults other than parents may be an important source of support, and indeed attachment. Even a young child is likely to have a hierarchy of attachments (Holmes, 1993). This can embrace in varying orders of importance parents, grandparents, siblings, godparents, and possibly pets or transitional objects (Kosonen, 1996b).

The developmental context which influences and interacts with a child's development is very complex (Belsky, 1981; Bronfenbrenner, 1986). A strategy to help children recover from and adapt to loss, harm and separation must itself reflect that complexity and avoid being too simple or uni-dimensional. Even in the most harmonious, child-centred and well-resourced of family circumstances, the child's development is nurtured not only by attachments to parent(s) but almost inevitably by relationships with siblings, grandparents and other relatives, as well as teachers and friends. Social and cultural competence – for children in or out of care – derives ultimately from a child's sense of belonging to a social network reflecting familial, school, neighbourhood, ethnic and cultural elements.

The fourth problem that may be associated with a preoccupation with permanence as a guiding principle is the neglect or at least the downplaying of the child as actor or subject in terms of his or her own experience or development. The child is not a passive receptacle of experience or caring. Even from a very young age children are active partners in influencing experiences and adult responsiveness to them (Belsky, 1981; Bronfenbrenner, 1986; Schaffer, 1996). Children themselves help to shape their own development, relationships and immediate psychosocial environment. A child with a pleasing and pro-active disposition is likely to have a positive effect on his or her own development. This is not of course to suggest that the child is responsible for her or his fate. Ultimately the child's pathway of development seems to reflect the evolving balance between competing protective and risk factors in the child's social ecology (Rutter, 1989; Bowlby, 1988). The upward curve of development in physical or psychosocial terms will be depressed or enhanced depending on whether risk factors outweigh protective factors or vice versa. The challenge for those who seek to influence the child's well-being is to try to cultivate, carefully, as many protective factors as possible and to minimise risk factors so that resilience may manifest itself.

The fifth and final problem – and perhaps the most telling for the purpose of the argument here – is that permanence essentially entails a focus on means rather than ends. Permanence constitutes a quality of the arrangements sought for a child's placement rather than a developmental outcome desired for the child from that care experience or episode. For effective child care planning at the individual or aggregate level we need to be clear about the difference between ends and means, i.e. between the final qualities, resources or circumstances with which we may wish to endow a child and the arrangements we put in place to try to secure the chosen ends.

Instead of aspiring merely to the quality of *permanence* in the child's care arrangements, I contend that it may be more helpful to strive to foster *resilience*, both in children and in their supportive social relationships. Resilience – the capacity to transcend adversity – may be seen as the essential quality which care planning and provision should seek to stimulate as a key outcome of the care offered. This emphasis on resilience is based on an impressive body of evidence now emerging largely from beyond child care literature in the fields of child and social development. This evidence points up factors which may explain why some children manage to develop well in the face of great odds. Understanding the reasons for this apparent paradox may help us to understand better how to draw more children into a virtuous rather than vicious cycle of development in the face of adversity – whether that adversity takes the form of long-term placement in care, chronic abuse, educational failure or whatever. If we can understand why some children have good outcomes following exposure to the care system, then we may have important clues about how to transfer those gains to wider numbers of children who might otherwise succumb to its widely acknowledged deleterious effects.

Resilience and its relevance to child development and child placement

A resilient child is one who bounces back having endured adversity or who continues to function reasonably well despite continued exposure to risk. 'Resilience is *normal* development under difficult circumstances', [original emphasis] (Fonagy *et al*, 1994). Rutter identifies three characteristics of the person imbued with resilience, rather than the sense of powerlessness and helplessness which may so often accompany chronic stress and adversity. The person who is resilient has (i) a sense of self-esteem and self-confidence; (ii) a sense of self-efficacy (a belief in their capacity to make a difference); and (iii) a repertoire of social problem-solving approaches (Rutter, 1985). In considering the nature of resilience it may also be helpful to bear three further points in mind. Firstly, resilience may have a social or constitutional origin. It is that portion of resilience, due to social experience, which is the subject of this article since it is that which is susceptible to influence. Secondly, Luthar (1993) argues that it is more helpful to think of resilience in different domains of functioning, rather than as a universal quality of the individual. So a person, for instance, may be resilient in terms of social competence but not in terms of academic performance. Thirdly, there is Bloom's (1996) contention that this (social) resilience resides more in the contexts, systems or relationships to which a person belongs than in the *individual* as such.

The findings of research on what may foster resilience in individual children can be usefully grouped into three different categories, as summarised in Table 1. They convey the multi-faceted nature of influences on resilience.

The items listed in Table 1 are factors which have been found to be associated with resilience in children and young people. Within the space constraints of this article it is not possible to discuss each item in turn. In addition, of course, only some of these factors are amenable to direct

Table 1

Why do resilient youngsters differ from their more vulnerable peers?

General attributes	Immediate circumstances	Psychological functioning
Higher social class	Competent parenting	High IQ and good problem-solving ability
Female gender (before puberty)	Relationship with at least one primary caregiver	Superior coping styles
Male gender (after puberty)	Good (and enduring) friendship	Autonomy or internal locus of control
Absence of organic deficits	Chores and responsibility at home	Higher sense of self-worth
Easy temperament	Supportive educational experience	Inter-personal awareness and empathy
Younger age at the time of trauma	Involvement with organised religious activity or faith	Good social skills
Absence of early separations or losses		Willingness and capacity to plan
		Sense of humour

Source: Derived from Fonagy *et al*, p.232, 1994; Werner, pp 108–10, 1990; Luthar, p 450, 1993.

influence by child welfare practitioners and policy-makers. For instance, some sources of resilience derive from a child's constitutional make-up rather than social experience. Also, where a characteristic might in principle be amenable to influence, the state of knowledge or practice may not yet extend to knowing what should be done and knowing how to do it. How, for instance, are we to encourage a sense of humour in a vulnerable child? What research evidence, if any, exists on this point? Has it been or can it be translated into simple and practical guidance for the busy frontline practitioner? While many questions remain to be answered, some insights of value to practitioners are emerging.

The three "building blocks of resilience"

In this section I propose three "building blocks of resilence" which I have distilled from the literature as core influences on a child's level of resilience. These are the child's sense of a secure base, the child's self-esteem and the child's sense of self-efficacy.

A secure base

As the child grows up, secure attachments supply him or her with a reliable secure base which encourages and renders safe exploration of the wider world (Bowlby, 1988). A young person's sense of secure base is cultivated by a sense of belonging within supportive social networks, by attachment relationships to reliable and responsible people, and by routines and structures in their lives.

Most adolescents not in care normally expect to have a secure family base with one or both parents, their siblings and other family members (Byng Hall, 1995). These youngsters, especially as they get older, may spend much time away from their secure base but they will return to it whenever needed, right into early to mid-adulthood, especially at times of illness, emotional distress or penury! Young people growing up will also probably enjoy being part of a social network of friends, colleagues and acquaintances. Adolescence does not usually involve some crude exchange of parents for peers as the key influence of support. As Hill (1993) puts it, 'as they get older, adolescents seem to extend their social networks rather than exchange them'.

Most children in care are heavily preoccupied with their family of origin (Whitaker, 1984), even where that might not live up to the standard of a secure base. An Irish proverb seems apposite: 'You can take the man out of the place, but you cannot take the place out of the man.' Or for our purposes here: 'You can take the child out of the family, but you cannot take the family out of the child.' In the case of youngsters in care, they seem both to care about their parents and hope to remain in their parents' thoughts. For young people in care it is important to feel cared about even if not cared for. A sense of mattering to one's parents (and presumably their substitutes) has been found to be crucial to the well-being of adolescents generally (Rosenberg and McCullough, 1981). It also, more generally, seems important that young people – in care or not – feel that there are supportive people in their lives. In an American study of child psychiatric in-patients, researchers found that children who reported fewer supportive persons in their lives appeared to be at risk of higher levels of behaviour problems and of hopelessness (Kashani et al, 1994).

For a young person without any such viable secure base in their immediate or extended family of origin, a network of social support based on work, social, recreational and professional helping relationships is probably the best practical alternative when faced with leaving care. The bigger this social network is, research would suggest, the more it can reduce loneliness and improve physical and emotional health (Sharkey, 1989). It is important to stress, however, that it is not the size of the network per se, but the person's perception (accurate or not) that they have a network containing people who are supportive which is crucial (Thompson, 1995). Just as a network of supportive base camps may be crucial to the physical survival of mountaineers operating in severe conditions, a personalised network of secure base camps may be essential to social and psychological survival for the young person coping with the adversities of life out of care. These "base camps", it is suggested, are the equivalent for the adolescent and young adult of the secure base which attachment figures offer the toddler. A major task of care takers and care providers in adolescence is to help a young person to develop the relationships necessary to sustain these base camps. The latter may be made up by, for example, a former foster carer, a distant but sympathetic relative, a friend at work or on a training course, a former neighbour, or the parent of a sports team-mate. Identifying and cultivating potential base camps takes care and time. This highlights the importance of a constant focus on 'preparing for adulthood (leaving care) in the entire placement' (Stein, 1990). The words of leading attachment theorist Peter Marris (1991) may be consoling in the face of these daunting challenges:

> The qualities of good social relationships and good experiences of attachment are essentially the same: predictability, responsiveness, intelligibility, supportiveness, reciprocity of commitment.

Self-esteem

Self-esteem is based on the person's sense of their own worthiness and competence. While comprising many aspects, it generally involves some comparison by the individual between how they would like to be and how they think they actually measure up (Schaffer, 1996). According to Rutter (1990), the two types of experience which seem most important in influencing self-esteem are (a) secure and harmonious love relationships, and (b) success in accomplishing tasks that are identified by individuals as central to their interests. Even one positive relationship in adulthood may do much to counter the harm of other failed relationships. Similarly, success in an endeavour which the person values may do much to combat a sense of failure in other spheres of one's life. Success here is not necessarily based on competition but more on the person's own ambitions and standards. It seems important to be alert to the cushioning potential for vulnerable young people's development of even one real taste of success in relationships or fields of endeavour.

A sense of self-efficacy

Parenting style can also influence whether a child develops a sense of internal control or competence in relation to attaining desired outcomes. Parenting may help children to believe they can make a difference in their situation or, on the contrary, to gradually believe that they are "helpless" children to whom life happens. Factors which promote self-directedness or self-efficacy include the parent's belief in the child's own sense of control, responsiveness (since responsive parents show the child that his/her behaviour has an effect), consistency, warmth, praise, support and encouragement to the child to engage in his or her environment (Sandler et al, 1989). It may be helpful for professionals to know that self-efficacy can be fostered by (a) a successful performance of relevant tasks (practice), (b) observing the successful performance of the tasks by someone else, (c) verbal persuasion, and (d) helping the young person to attune to their physiological state and its impact on their sense of self-efficacy. For example, while anxiety, tiredness and hunger can affect self-efficacy adversely, deep breaths, rest and food may help to restore it (Bloom, 1996b, citing Bandura, 1986). There are clearly many opportunities where child welfare professionals can consciously help young people in care to develop a sense of self-efficacy, not least by involving them in the planning process in relation to their own care (and to care services more generally) and by helping them rehearse and develop coping skills and strategies for later life. A sense of direction is very important to young people in troubled circumstances (Dowling, 1993). Effective and detailed care planning can help foster this important sense of what the future may hold and how to reach it (Parker *et al*, 1991).

Key messages for practice
- *Encourage purposeful contact with family members and other key adults from the child's past* Try to have conveyed through this contact a crucial message to the child of being cared *about*, even if not being cared *for* in a day-to-day sense. Try to keep threads of contact alive for children to past contexts. Recognise that positive ties with siblings (Dunn *et al*, 1994; Kosonen, 1996a; Kosonen, 1996b; Hegar, 1988), grandparents (Jenkins and Smith, 1990), or even well-functioning neighbourhoods (Brooks *et al*, 1993; Reiss, 1995) may be very positive for a child or young person in care. Use contact to help the child to see positive aspects of their social heritage, which may in turn help them build a more positive view of their own social identity. Use contact also as a means of rebuilding relationships which may lead to the child's return home (Warsh *et al*, 1994).
- *Encourage positive school experience* Recognise the contribution that positive school experiences can make to general development (Sylva, 1994). Appreciate also how success at school in the academic, sporting or social sphere may assist recovery from adversity (Romans *et al*, 1995). Convey high but reasonable expectations to the child about their educational progress. Ambition by carers in this regard can be helpful (Borge, 1996), a measured degree of which seems desirable for youngsters in care judging by the generally dismal evidence about their educational progress (Aldgate, 1990; Jackson, 1994). Active steps to facilitate the educational progress of youngsters in care or to coach carers in specific tutorial techniques are also important (Walker, 1994; Menmuir, 1994). Prioritise educational issues in care planning (Stein, 1994).

- *Encourage friendships with peers* Growing up, the capacity to build and sustain friendships with own age peers seems a useful barometer of emotional health (Savin-Williams and Berndt, 1990; Schaffer, 1996). It also contributes potential members of current and future social networks, and thereby vital sources of potential and precious social support. It is important that facilitating continuities in friendship receives adequate attention in care arrangements.
- *Actively foster interest, involvement and talents in sport, music, hobbies or cultural pursuits* Encourage accomplishment (but without great pressure) in fields of endeavour which appeal to the young person. Involvement in cultural and leisure activities serves many valuable preventive functions (Borge, 1996; Quinn, 1995).
- *Help the child to rehearse, observe and discuss problem-solving and coping skills and strategies* Involve children in discussions about their needs and about their future. Help them to contribute to care plans and reviews. Give clear information to the young person. Ensure he or she knows about (i) reasons for entering and remaining in care, (ii) rights while in care, and (iii) future plans and how he or she can influence these. Try to regard young people as resources in the process of seeking solutions in their lives or milieux. Encourage them to make choices and declare preferences in everyday living. Coach young people in how to resolve conflict with peers without recourse to bullying or violence. These various opportunities and experiences can teach them that their opinions are of value and help them learn some of the skills of influence, negotiation and problem-solving.
- *Promote pro-social qualities in the young person* Arrogance and selfishness may be associated with resilience as much as altruism or compassion. The natural pro-social tendencies of the child may have to be nurtured or reawakened. Certain behaviours by parents or carers are more closely associated with pro-social behaviour. They should provide clear rules and principles; give messages about expected behaviour with emotional conviction; frequently tell the child they are "good", "generous", etc (and they will be more likely to live up to the attribution); model, as an adult, the standards desired of the child; and be warm and responsive towards the child (Schaffer, 1996). On a more specific point relevant to everyday care, there is evidence that young

people who do housework of benefit to others in the home on a routine or self-regulated basis are 'more likely to show spontaneous concern for the welfare of others' (Gruesc *et al*, 1996). This gain seems not to apply to self-care tasks but only to those of benefit to others.

Conclusion

This paper suggests that the heavy emphasis on permanence in much of the child placement literature may do less than full justice to what is now known of influences on how children respond in the face of adversity. An excessive focus on permanence in a substitute placement at the expense of other factors may not only fail to reflect the complex web of influences on children's progress. It may also make even more difficult the task of restoring and promoting normal development in the face of disruption and instability in a child's primary relationships in their family or household of origin. This is because a "tunnel vision" focus on permanence may divert attention from other important protective factors in the child's life.

In considering resilience due to social experience, I have argued that it may have much value in child placement practice as part of a more extensive and inclusive organising frame based on developmental outcomes. Such *resilience* can subsume but move beyond what *permanence* can offer in the child placement field. The goal of intervention should be to foster positive developmental outcomes in a given child, that is ways in which the child and their resources are transformed positively by virtue of the care experience. One such key developmental outcome it is argued should be resilience, to which experience of permanence can certainly contribute (and vice versa). The strength of detailed resilience-led care planning, however, is that all may not be lost for the child if permanence is not attained or sustained, so long as the child has acquired relationships, experiences and qualities which in themselves foster and sustain resilience in the face of adversity. If the promise of permanence disintegrates without the cushion of resilience, so too may the child's prospects in many other ways. This is not to argue for consigning permanence to the dustbin, but to keep in perspective its significance as a means rather than as an end. In the final analysis, as has been observed earlier, "slogans" such as permanence or indeed resilience are no substitute for detailed and sensitive assessment and planning.

References

Aldgate J, 'Foster children at school: success or failure?', *Adoption & Fostering* 14:4, pp 38–49, 1990.

Bandura A, *Social Foundations of Thought and Action*, 1986, USA.

Belle D (ed), *Children's Social Networks and Social Supports*, John Wiley, 1989, New York.

Belsky J, 'Early human experience: a family perspective', *Developmental Psychology*, 17, pp 3–23, 1981.

Biehal N, Clayden J, Stein M and Wade J, *Prepared for Living? A survey of young people leaving the care of three local authorities*, National Children's Bureau, 1992.

Bloom M, 'Primary prevention and resilience: changing paradigms and changing lives', in Hampton P, Jenkins J and Gullotta T, *Preventing Violence in America*, Sage, 1996a, USA.

Bloom M, *Primary Prevention Practices*, Sage, 1996b, USA.

Borge A, 'Developmental pathways of behaviour problems in the young child: factors associated with continuity and change', *Scandinavian Journal of Psychology*, 37, pp 195–204, 1996.

Bowlby J, 'Developmental psychiatry comes of age', *American Journal of Psychiatry*, 145:1, pp 1–10, 1988, USA.

Bronfenbrenner U, 'Ecology of the family as a context for human development: research perspectives', *Developmental Psychology*, 22:6, pp 723–42, 1986.

Brooks-Gunn J, Duncan G J, Klebanov P and Sealand N, 'Do neighbourhoods influence child and adolescent development?', *American Journal of Sociology* 99, pp 353–95, 1993, USA.

Bullock R, Little M and Millham S, *Going Home: The return of children separated from their families*, Dartmouth, 1993.

Byng-Hall J, 'Creating a secure family base: some implications of attachment theory for family therapy', *Family Process*, 34, pp 45–58, 1995.

Courtney M and Barth R, 'Pathways of older adolescents out of foster care: implications for independent living services', *Social Work*, 41:1, pp 75–83, 1996.

Dowling E, 'Are family therapists listening to the young? A psychological perspective', *Journal of Family Therapy*, 15, pp 403–11, 1993.

Dunn J, Slomskowski C and Beardsall L, 'Sibling relationships from the preschool period through middle childhood and early adolescence', *Developmental Psychology*, 30:3, pp 315–24, 1994.

Fein E and Maluccio A, 'Permanency planning: another remedy in jeopardy?', *Social Service*, pp 335–48, September 1992.

Fonagy P, Steele M, Steele H, Higgit A and Target M, 'The theory and practice of resilience', *Journal of Child Psychology and Psychiatry*, 35:2, pp 231–57, 1994.

Grusec J, Goodnew J and Cohen L, 'Household work and the development of concern for others', *Developmental Psychology*, 32:6, pp 999–1007, 1996.

Hegar R, 'Sibling relationships and separations: implications for child placement', *Social Service Review*, pp 446–67, September 1988.

Hill P, 'Recent advances in selected aspects of adolescent development', *Journal of Child Psychology and Psychiatry*, 34:1, pp 69–99, 1993.

Holmes J, *John Bowlby and Attachment Theory*, Routledge, 1993.

Jackson S, 'Educating children in residential and foster care', *Oxford Review of Education*, 20:3, pp 267–79, 1994.

Jenkins J and Smith M, 'Factors protecting children in disharmonious homes: maternal reports', *Journal of the American Academy of Child and Adolescent Psychiatry*, 29:1, pp 60–9, 1990.

Kashani J, Canfield C, Borduin C, Soltys S and Reid J, 'Perceived family and social support: impact on children', *Journal of the American Academy of Child and Adolescent Psychiatry*, 33:6, pp 819–23, 1994.

Kosonen M, 'Maintaining sibling relationships – neglected dimension in child care practice', *British Journal of Social Work*, 26:6, pp 809–22, 1996a.

Kosonen M, 'Siblings as providers of support and care during middle childhood: children's perceptions', *Children and Society*, 10:4, pp 267–79, 1996b.

Luthar S, 'Annotation: methodological and conceptual issues in research on childhood resilience', *Journal of Child Psychology and Psychiatry*, 34:4, pp 441–54, 1993.

Marris P, 'The social construction of uncertainty,' in Parkes C M, Stevenson-Hinde J and Marris P (eds), *Attachment Across the Lifecycle*, Routledge, 1991.

McFadden E and Downs S, 'Family continuity: the new paradigm in permanence planning', *Community Alternatives: International Journal of Family Care*, 7:1, pp 39–60, 1995.

Menmuir R, 'Involving residential social workers and foster carers in reading with young people in their care: the PRAISE reading project', *Oxford Review of Education*, 20:3, pp 329–38, 1994.

Parker R, Ward H, Jackson S, Aldgate J and Wedge P, *Looking After Children, Assessing Outcomes in Child Care: The report of an independent working party established by the Department of Health*, HMSO, 1991.

Pecora P, Whittaker J and Maluccio A, *The Child Welfare Challenge: Policy, practice, and research*, Aldine de Gruyter, 1992, USA.

Quinn J, 'Positive effects of participation in youth organisations', in Rutter M (ed), *Psychosocial Disturbances in Young People: Challenges for prevention*, Cambridge University Press, 1995.

Reiss A, 'Community influences on adolescent behaviour', in Rutter M (ed), as below.

Romans S, Martin J, Anderson J, O'Shea M and Mullen P, 'Factors that mediate between child sexual abuse and adult psychological outcome', *Psychological Medicine*, 25, pp 127–42.

Rosenberg M and McCullough B, 'Mattering: inferred significance and mental health among adolescents', *Research in Community and Mental Health*, 2, pp 163–82, 1981.

Rutter M, 'Resilience in the face of adversity: protective factors and resistance to psychiatric disorder', *British Journal of Psychiatry* 147, pp 598–611, 1985.

Rutter M, 'Pathways from childhood to adult life', *Journal of Child Psychology and Psychiatry*, 30, pp 23–51, 1989.

Rutter M (ed), *Psychosocial Disturbances in Young People – Challenges for prevention*, Cambridge University Press, 1995.

Sandler I, Miller P, Short J and Wolchik S, 'Social support as a protective factor for children in stress', in Belle D (ed), as above, pp 277–307.

Savin-Williams R and Berndt T, 'Friendship and peers relations', in Feldman S and Elliott G (eds), *At the Threshold – The developing adolescent*, Harvard University Press, 1990, USA.

Schaffer H R, *Social Development*, Blackwell, 1996.

Sharkey P, 'Social networks and social service workers', *British Journal of Social Work*, 19, pp 387–405, 1989.

Stein M, *Living Out of Care*, Barnado's, 1990.

Stein M, 'Leaving care, education and career trajectories', *Oxford Review of Education*, 20:3, pp 349–60, 1994.

Sylva K, 'School influences on children's development', *Journal of Child Psychology and Psychiatry*, 35:1, pp 135–72, 1994.

Thompson R, *Preventing Child Maltreatment through Social Support*, Sage, 1995, USA.

Walker T, 'Educating children in the public care: a strategic approach', *Oxford Review of Education*, 20:3, pp 339–47, 1994.

Warsh R, Maluccio A and Pine B, *Teaching Family Reunification*, Child Welfare League of America, 1994, USA.

Werner E, 'Protective factors and individual resilience', pp 97–116, in Meisels S and Shonkoff J (eds), *Handbook of Early Childhood Intervention*, Cambridge University Press, 1990.

Werner E and Smith R, *Overcoming the Odds – High risk children from birth to adulthood*, Cornell University Press, 1992, USA.

Whitaker D S, Cook J, Dunne C and Roccliffe N, *The Experience of Residential Care from the Perspectives of Children, Parents and Care Givers: SSRC Contract No. RB 33/12/7 Final Report*, University of York, 1984.

Section II
Understanding processes and outcomes

Research evidence about the successful outcomes of adoption was an important influence on the permanence movement. It was clear that many placements worked well even when children were placed well beyond infancy (Tizard, 1977; Kadushin, 1988). As the boundaries of age and challenging behaviour were pushed back, it became vital to assess how the placements of older children worked out.

One of the agencies which pioneered intensive recruitment and support of adopters was Lothian Region. **O'Hara and Hoggan (1988)** described the development of the policy in Lothian and provided statistics on outcomes. They used the conventional criterion of whether or not the placement persisted. By itself, this measure has its limitations since placements may continue despite unhappiness or lack of progress, while a child may have made significant gains in a placement which ends. Nevertheless, breakdown rates are a valuable if flawed indicator of success, given that adoption is meant to last for life. The authors reviewed over 300 placements of children aged two or more for adoption or occasionally permanent fostering. About one in ten had broken down, which is a much lower rate than typically occurs in either foster care or residential care (Triseliotis, 1989; Rowe *et al*, 1989; Berridge, 1994).

Older children had a significantly greater risk of breakdown – one in five for those over ten. Even so a considerable majority of placements for teenagers did endure. The connection between age at placement and likelihood of disruption has been confirmed in a range of studies, including those in North America (Barth and Berry, 1987; Thoburn and Rowe, 1988; Borland, 1991).

On this and other evidence, it appears that most adoptive placements of school-aged children do achieve stability, especially those which begin before adolescence. It has become increasingly clear, though, that some of the adoptions which last are tense and demanding, mainly on account of the long-term effects of the children's previous histories of abuse, neglect and/or discontinuities of care (Hill, Hutton and Easton, 1988; Archer, 1996). **Hobday and Lee (1994)** described some of the difficulties faced by children adopted from care. These include grief reactions to past losses, ambivalence and splitting of love and hate, and stress symptoms like flashbacks and nightmares. Children who have been sexually abused may not distinguish affectionate from sexual contacts or may be very fearful of being touched or undressing. Hobday and Lee noted how adopters need to understand the roots of such behaviour, to plan coping strategies and to make use of both informal support and specialist services.

Over the years, the journal has included a number of articles from Britain and overseas which describe some of the techniques and strategies which may be used to help children and/or adoptive families adjust and minimise some of the negative effects of difficult early life experiences (Hutton, 1988; Kaniuk, 1992; Harper, 1994, 1996; Harvey, 1996).

In two seminal articles, **Howe (1995, 1996)** identified long-term patterns which linked children's attachment histories to outcomes in young adulthood. In this case, the measures of outcome included educational achievements and the quality of the adoptive relationship as reported by adopters. Howe provided a picture which supports both caution and optimism with regard to the adoptions of older children. The baby adoptions were nearly all very successful. Young adults adopted as babies had nearly all developed consistently secure and warm relationships and had done well at school.

In contrast about half of the "late-start" adoptions had led to mainly negative relationships at age 16 and a similar proportion of the children had no academic qualifications. Many of these children had angry-ambivalent, detached or indiscriminate attachment patterns related to inconsistencies of parenting and/or a lack of affection in their early years. More encouraging was the finding that some of the relationships which were poor at 16 had improved substantially by the age of 23. Howe presented some vivid quotations which revealed the heartache, the persistence and the ultimate rewards of this group of adopters. They also point to the vital importance of support – a matter to which we return later.

The first of Howe's two papers prompted a letter to the journal from Sally Baffour, a member of BAAF's Black Perspectives Advisory Committee. She registered disappointment that the article had not adequately addressed the question of transracial adoption and asked for answers to a set of questions about patterns in transracial placements. In a detailed reply, Howe observed that his data were based entirely on adopters' perspectives, but from what they said 'it was not possible to detect any significant differences in children's psychosocial development between same-race and transracial placements, holding the quality of pre-placement experience constant' (Vol. 20, Issue I, Page 6).

The section of this book on Ethnic and Cultural Issues will explore further the tension between positive research findings such as these and practitioners' encounters with individuals distressed by what Baffour termed the 'culturally lacking ethnic input' in their upbringing (Vol. 20, Issue I, Page 5).

7 Permanent substitute family care in Lothian – placement outcome

Gerry O'Hara and Pauline Hoggan

Gerry O'Hara is Scottish Director of Social Work, NCH Action for Children, and Pauline Hoggan is Head of Children's Services and Criminal Justice Services in Argyll and Bute

This paper was published in Adoption & Fostering, 12:3, 1988.

Jane Rowe (1987) has pointed out how complex assessing placement outcomes and interpreting breakdown rates can be. She also reminds us that generally foster care is under-researched, although the Berridge and Cleaver (1987) study is a major contribution in this area. Placement outcome in special needs adoption and permanent fostering is also under-researched but will be considerably helped by Jane Rowe's recent study in six local authorities and by June Thoburn's (1986) evaluation of The Child Wants A Home adoption agency. There are also useful contributions from different agencies such as Parents for Children (Reich and Lewis, 1986), Barnardo's (Kerrane *et al*, 1980), Triseliotis and Russell's study of adoption and residential care outcome (1984) and the Adoption Resource Exchange placement study (Wolkind and Kozaruk, 1986).

However, most of the outcome studies into permanent placements are American and a good deal of evaluation in the UK needs to be done if we are to continue with confidence what has amounted to a permanent family placement revolution since the 1970s. The purpose of this article is to begin to assess the outcome of placements, intended to be permanent, made in Lothian Region (excluding under twos) by means of adoption or fostering, during the period September 1982 to September 1987. Lothian Region has a well-publicised permanency planning policy (McKay, 1980) which, whenever possible, involves maintaining children in their own homes, or at least returning them to their families, should they be received into care, as quickly as possible. If the return home cannot be achieved adoption is the preferred option, unless:

1 Parents are committed to and involved with the child, and the child would benefit from the relationship continuing.

2 The child is aged approximately ten or older and does not wish to have a relationship with his or her parents legally severed.

3 The foster parents are not willing to adopt, but the child would suffer if removed from their custody and placed for adoption.

In other words, children with meaningful links to their parents need to be returned home, or have a relationship which acknowledges these attachments, and only relatively young children with no meaningful contact or attachment to their family of origin are placed for adoption. This in fact amounts to a very small proportion of the total number of children who are received into care (i.e., less than four per cent) but tends to involve children who may well be described as among the most disturbed in the community. A recent survey in Lothian of 15 children placed by one adoption panel indicates that all but one had been subjected to some form of physical or sexual abuse.

Permanency planning

Maluccio *et al* (1986) described permanency planning as:

> *the systematic process of carrying out, within a brief time-limited period, a set of goal directed activities designed to help children live in families or, for continuity of relationships, with nurturing parents or caretakers and the opportunity to establish life-time relationships.*

Permanency planning, as the Short Committee (1984) noted, has become almost 'synonymous with adoption'. Margaret McKay (1980), who introduced permanency planning in the UK, saw it as an approach to the delivery of services to children in placement or at risk of being taken into care. The three strands of prevention, restoration and permanent alternative care make up the constituent parts of permanency planning but arguably too much emphasis has been placed on the third strand. In this context given that less than four per cent of the total number of children who are received into care in any one year remain permanently in care, it would seem that the identification in Lothian of permanency planning with adoption is one dimensional. Much of the debate about permanency planning happened in the late 1970s when there were large numbers of children who had grown old in the care system and who had no meaningful attachments with their families. In fact, as Triseliotis (1986) points out, the children identified by Rowe and Lambert in their 1973 study have grown up and left the care system and the scene is now much changed. Children placed permanently now are much more likely to have:

- Spent less time in care than in the past.
- Experienced repeated failed rehabilitation efforts.
- Been known to have been abused, either physically or sexually.
- Had very stormy and turbulent backgrounds with many different adults.
- Brothers or sisters who will need to be placed with them.
- Be in the main under ten years of age.
- Been actively worked with in relation to their family history, feelings and attitudes.

Additionally there are a small number of severely or profoundly mentally handicapped children who require permanent care, which may or may not also involve contact with their family of origin.

There are a number of agencies in the United States who have set up permanency projects which work with children in their own homes; away from their own homes with a view to restoration, and in permanent alternative substitute families. The evidence suggests that children can do very well indeed in permanent new families. (See Barth and Berry, 1987.)

Any outcome study of permanent placements should consider the possible alternative outcomes if different plans had been followed.

The service in Lothian

A specialist team was set up in September 1982 to recruit, prepare, assess and support families adopting or fostering children who were older and had special needs. In foster placements the intention was to achieve permanent placements.

Preparation in groups for both applicants and children to be placed has been available throughout the period of the evaluation, as has organised post-placement support and approved adoption allowances. The involvement of consumers in all aspects of the service is a fundamental and guiding principle. Many of these programmes have been described in various publications, (O'Hara, 1986, 1988; Hoggan, 1988 and Hutton, 1988). The placements are made and sustained by a combination of specialist workers from the central homefinding team and area team social workers. The authors since 1985 have been overall unit manager and team leader respectively and during the period 1982–1985 were team leader and team member respectively. Six of the original seven member team therefore still manage, organise and deliver the service.

The evaluation
We decided to identify every breakdown from the placements made during the period September 1982 to September 1987. Breakdowns were defined as any placement which ceased before the child reached the age of 16 years, regardless of the circumstances, other than in four cases where children returned to their birth family on a planned basis, after short stays in new families.

We have highlighted those placements made:
* Directly for adoption;
* Placed on a fostering basis with the intention of permanency; and
* Adopted after a period of fostering

We have excluded placements of babies or children under two which are made on behalf of the region by the Scottish Adoption Association. Every placement was formally made by one of Lothian's five adoption panels.

Comments
These statistics do not reflect the capacity of commitment, endurance, courage and imagination which families need to parent children who have suffered in early childhood. Two further studies in Lothian by Yates (1985) and Hill et al (1988) outline the need for support outside existing family and friendship networks which should be practical and financial, emotional and at times highly specialist. The Hill study suggests that some families have had to make enormous adjustments in their

STATISTICS

No. of children placed for adoption or fostering intended to be permanent in the period September 1982–1987		335
No. of placements disrupted/broke down		39
Percentage breakdown rate		11.3%
Disruption rate of children who were ten and over at the time of placement		21.7%
Disruption rate of children who were nine and under at the time of placement		4.6%

Adoption or fostering

Total no. placed		335
Placed for adoption	290 (86%)	
Placed for permanent fostering	45 (14%)	335

New adoptive placements or claims by existing carers

No. placed for adoption		290
No. claimed for adoption by existing carers	28 (9.6%)	
No. of new placements	262 (90.4%)	290

Approved adoption allowances

No. placed for adoption		290
No. of approved adoptional allowances paid		85 (29%)

Children with disabilities

No. of children with severe/profound mental disability		39
No. of breakdowns (ie two aged ten+: 1 aged – nine)		3 (7.7%)

Outcome of failed placements

Total no. broken down/disrupted		39
No. placed in teenage fostering scheme	18	
No. replaced in permanent placements	11	
No. in temporary foster care	6	
No. in residential care	3	
No. in supported accommodation	1	39

expectations and have been disappointed by the experience, and although Yates found that families could see the positive changes in children the cost was higher than they had expected. They worried a great deal about the future. Thoburn *et al* (1986) identified similar themes. Children were doing remarkably well relative to their past experiences, but at a high cost to families and consequently demanding of support services.

Our own experience echoes these research findings and we see the following components as essential for a permanent substitute family placement service in a large local authority:

- An approach which promotes clarity about the legal, policy, procedural, practice and knowledge frameworks in relation to planning for children in care.
- Specialist workers leading the service, but in partnership with area team non-specialist placement workers.
- Professional leadership from specialist managers.
- Constant evaluation of policy outcome and appraisal of practice "sacred cows".
- Consumer feedback and participation in all aspects of the service, including preparation and assessment work, adoption panel decision-making and post-adoption and post-placement support services.
- Realistic preparation programmes which are clear about the educative/preparation/ training components, but do not deny the responsibility of the agency to assess and evaluate capacities in partnership with applicants.
- Parent-focused support services.
- Approved adoption allowances for all families who take children with special needs.
- Informed help from specialist social workers, teachers and educational psychologists who have an understanding of special needs adoption and fostering and from health personnel with a similar understanding.
- An open door approach to support so that families can choose for themselves when they need it and an open door system when families request direct work to be done with the child in placement.
- A service to families after disruption.

These elements are not ranked according to any priority.

These initial findings from the Lothian experience require much more scrutiny. At the very least they need to be considered alongside the findings of Yates (1985) and Hill *et al* (1985), but we hope they will prove useful to other agencies who are looking critically at their permanency planning policies. There are plans to look specifically at the 39 placements which have failed, but the real test in relation to outcome will be to monitor these children's progress over the next ten years or more.

References

Barth R P and Berry M, *Outcomes of Child Welfare Services Under Permanency Planning*, University of Chicago, 1987, USA.

Berridge and Cleaver, *Fostering Breakdown*, Basil Blackwell, 1987.

Hill M, Hutton S and Easton S, 'Adoptive parenting – plus and minus', *Adoption & Fostering*, 12:2, 1988.

Hoggan P, 'Preparing children for family placement through the use of small groups', in Triseliotis J (ed), *Groupwork in Adoption and Fostering*, Batsford/BAAF, 1988.

Hutton S, 'An adopters' support group' in Triseliotis J (ed), as overleaf.

Kerrane A, Hunter A and Lane M, *Adopting Older and Handicapped Children: A consumers' view of the preparation, assessment, placement and post placement support services*, Barnardo's Social Work Paper 14, 1980.

McKay M, 'Planning for permanence', Adoption & Fostering, 4:1, 1980.

Maluccio A, Fein E and Olmstead K, *Permanency Planning for Children*, Tavistock, 1986.

O'Hara G, 'Post-placement support services in Lothian', *Adoption & Fostering*, 10:4, 1986.

O'Hara G, 'Preparing families in groups', Triseliotis J (ed), as overleaf.

Reich D and Lewis J, 'Placements by Parents for Children', in *Finding families for 'Hard to Place Children'*, Wedge P and Thoburn J (eds), BAAF, 1986.

Rowe J and Lambert L, *Children Who Wait*, ABAFA (now BAAF), 1973.

Rowe J, 'Fostering outcomes: incorporating breakdown rates', *Adoption & Fostering*, 11:1, 1987.

Short Committee, *Social Services Committee Report on Children in Care*, HMSO, 1984.

Thoburn J, Murdoch A and O'Brien A, *Permanency in Child Care*, Basil Blackwell, 1986.

Triseliotis J (ed), *Groupwork in Adoption and Fostering*, BAAF/Batsford, 1988.

Triseliotis J and Russell J, *Hard to Place: The outcome of adoption and residential care*, Heinemann, 1984.

Triseliotis J, 'Older children in care', Wedge P and Thoburn J (eds), *Finding Families for "Hard to Place Children"*, BAAF, 1986.

Wedge P and Thoburn G (eds), *Finding Families for "Hard to Place" Children*, BAAF, 1986.

Wolkind S and Kozaruk A, ' "Hard to place?" children with medical and developmental problems', in Wedge P and Thoburn J (eds), as above.

Yates P, 'Post placement support', MSc Research, University of Edinburgh, unpublished, 1985.

8 Adoption and attachment

David Howe

David Howe is Professor of Child and Family Social Work at the School of Social Work, University of East Anglia, Norwich.

This paper was published in Adoption & Fostering, 19:4, 1995.

Over the last ten or twenty years, there have been several major shifts in child care philosophy and practice which have changed the character of adoption. In turn, these changes have profoundly affected what is expected of adopters. Four of the more important shifts are:

- Adoption is designed to meet the needs of children and not those of parents.
- The adoption of older children, most of whom will have experienced some adversity in their upbringing prior to placement, is now commonplace. Adverse pre-placement experiences often leave these children disturbed and the demands they make of adoptive parents can be considerable, both in the short and the long term.
- The growing opposition to transracial placements has meant that some parents who have adopted transracially feel either guilty or angry or both.
- The demand that adoptions, particularly of older children, should be more "open" has meant that many adopters now have to cope with the continued involvement, in some form, of their child's birth mother or other birth relatives. In Western cultures at least, giving another set of parents some emotional rights in the upbringing of one's children can be a psychologically difficult thing to do.

Bearing in mind these shifts, it seems that the role of the modern adopter has become more important, more demanding and more difficult. The emotional balancing act that many adopters now have to perform requires parenting of a high order and people of rare motivation. In view of this it seemed to me that it would be valuable to study parents of adopted children. Such parents would have a great deal of first-hand experience of raising adopted children and they would possess much wisdom and insight into their children, their behaviour and development. In spite of the radical and basic changes in the character of adoption, the role of the adopter as parent has been strangely neglected. It was with these thoughts in mind that I sought the views and experiences of parents whose adopted children had reached late adolescence and early adulthood. I wanted to hear what adopters had to say about their children once they had reached maturity. I was interested to learn 'how things had turned out'.

I interviewed the parents of over a hundred families. I used a "snow-balling" technique to get in touch with potential respondents. With the help of three post-adoption agencies and some advertising, I made contact with a small number of adoptive parents who were willing to be interviewed. This initial core group then recommended other adoptive parents known to them and who were also willing to take part in the research. These in turn suggested other adopters and so on. Between them, the parents had adopted around 300 children including baby, toddler and older children adoptions. There were white children, black children and children of mixed racial parentage.

The full analysis of this research will be presented in a series of forthcoming papers. The purpose of the present article is to outline *six patterns of adoption* derived from the interviews. Each pattern is defined mainly by the children's (i) relationship history, (ii) behaviour, (iii) development, and (iv) emotional attitude towards the adoption as described by their parents.

In broad terms, there was a rough correlation between the quality of the children's pre-placement experience and the character of their post-placement development. The children with the more disturbed relationship histories prior to being placed tended to exhibit more anxious and insecure relationships, particularly with their adoptive parents. The quality of parental responses and the children's natural temperamental differences were the other major factors influencing the developmental pathways taken by particular children. However, the intention here is to concentrate on one particular strand in the developmental equation: the impact of pre-placement social environments on post-placement social developments.

Table 1

Attachment type	Behaviour pattern	Defensive strategy
Secure	*1. Secure/stable*	Selective approach
Insecure	*2. Anxious/compliant*	Approach and comply
	3. Short-term testing	Approach and test
	4. Angry	Approach and resist (ambivalence)
	5. Detached	Avoid/withdraw
Non-attached	*6. Casual*	Indiscriminate approach

The construction of the six categories has, in part, been informed by many of the ideas generated within attachment theory. (See, for example, Ainsworth *et al*, 1978; Main, 1994. For an outline of attachment theory for social workers, see Howe, 1995.) One of the key notions in attachment theory is that children who find themselves in close social relationships which are unreliable and unpredictable have to develop defensive strategies in order to cope with the psychological stress and anxiety that such relationships engender. Thus, if a child finds himself or herself in an unpredictable and inconsistent relationship, the defensive strategies adopted to handle the anxiety are *adaptive* in terms of the characteristics of that relationship. Ostensibly "maladaptive" behaviours therefore make sense when seen in the context of adverse social and emotional environments (see Howe, 1995). However, when the child approaches and handles subsequent relationships, particularly those charged with a high and meaningful emotional content (say with a new caregiver), they will be heavily influenced by the quality of past relationships and the defensive manoeuvres they triggered.

So, bearing in mind some of the principles of attachment theory and taking a developmental perspective, six patterns of adoption were identified (see Table 1).

The six labels given to the behaviour patterns emerged out of the interviews with adopters. Anxiety normally triggers attachment behaviour in which children "approach" their attachment figure seeking proximity, comfort, interest and affection. Over time, one or two people are "selectively" preferred as possibly providing a warm, secure base. When a child's attachment figure fails to supply comfort and affection, the emotional pain and anxiety this causes results in the child developing alternative defensive strategies. Rather than approach the unresponsive attachment figure, the child tries to cope by withdrawing from and "avoiding" the potentially rejecting relationship. The child attempts to become "emotionally self-reliant" (Bowlby, 1979).

1. Secure and stable patterns
Behaviours and relationships
In these secure patterns, we see relatively straightforward and trouble-free childhoods. Although there were the usual ups and downs, on the whole these children presented their parents with few problems and much pleasure. Self-esteem and confidence were reported as sound. These were trusting children who experienced no serious problems at school and did not steal or get into trouble with the police. They coped well with the normal changes and transitions of childhood and adolescence. Most left school with at least one or two qualifications and many went on to higher education. Once in employment, jobs ranged from hairdresser to barrister, car mechanic to research scientist. Leaving home occurred smoothly, either to attend college, live independently or get married. These seemed to be socially competent children. All the parents viewed the adoption as an unqualified success.

Pre-adoptive backgrounds
Most of the children in this group were placed as young babies, usually less than four months old. Indeed, most baby adoptions followed this pattern. Other than the one or two moves between birth mother, foster parents and adopters, the children experienced no major upsets. However, there were a small number of children who were adopted at an older age. The majority of these older placed children had enjoyed relatively stable and secure relationships with their caretakers before being adopted or removed into care, though a small number had experienced adversity.

2. Anxious and compliant patterns

Behaviours and relationships

These children could never take caring relationships totally for granted, particularly the love and interest of their adoptive parents. There was a barely conscious worry that rejection and emotional hurt might happen again if caretakers were bothered or upset. Feelings of mild insecurity were most pronounced in the early years. However, as time went by, feelings of security and confidence rose. Nevertheless, little threads of anxiety remained and could be traced through into adulthood. These children were more vulnerable to the upsets of everyday life. A change of school, move of house, parental exasperation, mother going into hospital, or the ending of an intimate relationship could easily trigger old feelings of fear, anxiety and insecurity. These were "home-centred" children.

At home, at school and with friends, these children were well-meaning and generally *anxious to please*. There was a need to "fit in" and be compliant. They were often over sensitive in relationships and were quick to fear disinterest or rejection. To this extent, they were emotionally a little immature. In attempts to gain attention or affection they could be silly and "show off". Boys in particular were easily led by friends. If they got into trouble, it was more through being thoughtless and "daft" than being devious or dishonest. Some parents described their children as "scatty". Anxiety could provoke tearful, irritable, moody or fretful behaviour.

Fear of failure coupled with the underlying anxiety meant that many of these children underperformed at school. They were happier in less testing environments. These anxieties often transferred to choice of work and career. As with other insecure patterns, there seemed to be a preference by many of these children to work with food, children, vulnerable adults or animals – jobs which involved an element of nurture and care. Many parents also noted that their anxious children were the last to leave home. While younger brothers and sisters went to college, got married or left to work in another city, the more anxious children remained at home, delaying separation and independence.

All adopters agreed that these were loving children and, although parents acknowledged that their sons or daughters could be exasperating, these children were liked and very much loved. Adopters viewed these adoptions in a very positive light and described their children with great fondness.

Pre-adoptive backgrounds
Children in this group might have been placed at any time *after* the age of five or six months. Typical were: (i) babies adopted after several months of being physically well-looked after in a nursery or by more than one set of foster parents; (ii) toddlers who had suffered some abuse or neglect often *after* a reasonably secure and safe start, though there were a few exceptions; and (iii) older children who had experienced some early love and attention which was subsequently lost or became increasingly unreliable. For example, Henry had been looked after quite successfully by his mother for the first 12 months. However, she began to suffer depression and her mental health deteriorated. After six months of worsening care, Henry was briefly fostered before being placed for adoption at the age of 20 months. In another case, Kirsty enjoyed a happy first few years of life being cared for by her single mother. When her mother married and had children by that marriage, Kirsty was harshly rejected by her step-father. After a period in care, she was adopted.

3. Short-term testing patterns
Behaviours and relationships
Once installed with their adopters, the children in this category behaved as if they did not trust the new demonstrations of love and interest. It seemed that the commitment of these parents had to be severely tested. The children were not convinced that this latest relationship was going to be any more reliable than previous ones. Accordingly, the children's behaviour showed much toddler-like defiance, contrariness and provocation. Such testing behaviour might go on for a few weeks or even a year or two. But if the adopters finally passed the tests and their care and commitment seemed reliable and permanent, the children suddenly seemed to relax and accept that they did belong and that they were wanted.

Donna was adopted when she was eight years old. She was the eldest of four children. According to her adoptive mother, she arrived "tired".

Donna's birth mother had worked long hours and left her daughter to look after the younger children for considerable stretches of time. The little girl was under increasing stress. After one or two spells in care all four children were adopted. 'Donna desperately wanted a family,' said her adoptive mother. There was a "honeymoon" period of six months before "all hell let loose".

She really, really, really tried to get us to give her up. She tested and tested us. She was never any trouble outside home, but at home she was very difficult. She argued over everything . . . If she was asked to wash the dishes, she'd deliberately do them in cold water. My husband felt like giving up. And yet she told the social worker that she loved us, especially her Dad . . . Over the years her anger seemed to evaporate.

But even after the children settled and became more trusting, like their anxious and compliant counterparts, elements of mild insecurity remained. They manifested most of the long-term behaviours, outcomes and personality traits of the anxious-compliant group. The combination of caring but vulnerable natures was often appealing to parents and teachers. In spite of the initial difficulties and testing behaviours, parents viewed both the adoption and their children in a very favourable light.

Pre-adoptive backgrounds
For these children, the first year or two of life was experienced as reasonably secure. However, this period of stability would be followed by disruption and disturbance. Parenting would become less consistent and there might be several changes of caretaker as the child moved in and out of local authority care before finally being placed for adoption. Love, initially reliable and consistent, began to be experienced as more erratic and disorganised.

4. Angry and ambivalent patterns
Behaviours and relationships
The children in this category were described as "angry" by their parents. The anger would persist throughout childhood and reach a peak during adolescence. In some cases the hostility and aggression would last into

early adulthood before finally exhausting itself.

Those adopted as babies seemed to get off to a "bad start". The reasons for the bad start varied. Some adoptive mothers felt that from the day they arrived their babies were irritable, fractious and difficult to comfort. The word that was most often used to describe their children as babies was "demanding".

Luke was a difficult baby. He was highly demanding. He woke up every night until he was three . . . He could never amuse himself. He demanded your whole attention the whole of the time . . . I couldn't bond with him. I felt guilty the whole time because I felt I should be loving him.

Other adopters felt that motherhood had come at the wrong time – two adoptive mothers said they felt very depressed; two had suffered the trauma of "losing" babies when birth mothers changed their minds about the adoption. 'I hadn't got over the loss of Simon going back to his mother when poor little Jessica arrived,' said one adoptive mother. 'I just wasn't ready for her.'

Whereas feelings of anxiety and insecurity caused the "anxious" children to become worried, agitated and *compliant*, the same feelings resulted in *anger, hostility and turmoil* in this group, whether adopted as babies or older. The anger was directed at those closest to them. They seemed to fight and *resist* becoming close and intimate with their parents. Birth mothers, too, were the target of much of the children's anger and resentment (at having been "rejected"), although in a few cases she was idealised and contrasted with the alleged "uselessness" of the adopters.

In spite of their apparent hostility towards their parents, these "angry" children were nevertheless "preoccupied" with the quality of their relationships with those closest to them. Parents described the seemingly odd behaviour when their children would follow them around, not letting go, saying 'I hate you' and 'You don't love me'. They seemed unable to leave the relationship that they claimed was so hateful to them. There was confusion and ambivalence about becoming too emotionally involved, even though being loved and wanted were what they appeared to crave. Although it was very difficult for many parents on the receiving end of these hostilities to understand, emotionally they were the most important people in their children's lives. Some children said that they felt that they didn't "belong" or "fit" in their families. In many cases, the angry child would be inordinately jealous of a brother or sister. A lot of children used food as a weapon, either refusing it, destroying it or eating too much of it.

During adolescence, all of these children lied excessively. The majority stole from home, particularly money from mothers and fathers. Deceit and deviousness became routine. And all the time there was anger and even violence towards parents. Some children began to commit offences outside the home. They adopted an attitude which seemed to say, 'No-one cares for me, so I don't care what happens'. Schoolwork became incidental. All the children performed badly at school. Concentration was always described as very poor. A few played truant or were expelled. They were not popular children with peers. Friendships were shallow or short-lived. They did not cope well with change. Nearly all of these children had been seen by a psychologist or psychiatrist at some stage during adolescence. Parents suffered great stresses and strains, and not a few either felt like giving up or did give up. In the latter cases, children left home aged 16 or 17 to live on their own or entered residential care. Few found permanent work or went on to higher education immediately after leaving school.

In post-adoption work, this group of children is probably the most prominent in terms of referrals and requests for help. The children are often diagnosed as suffering a "reactive attachment disorder" (e.g. Cline, 1992), although it seems more helpful to see them in terms of the more established and diagnostically useful category of "anxious resistant attachments" in which there is a deep *ambivalence* about committing oneself to emotional intimacy and a turbulent *preoccupation* with attachment figures (Ainsworth, 1978; Bowlby, 1988; also see Howe, 1995).

Anita was adopted just before her second birthday. She had been neglected, though not abused, by her mother. From the day she arrived, her adopters said she was 'difficult, demanding and awkward'. Although there were no major upsets in the early years, Anita found it hard to keep friends and there were worries that she bullied some of the younger children at school. Adolescence marked the beginning of a serious worsening in her behaviour She began to steal money from her mother's purse but always denied it if challenged. She refused to eat with the rest of the family. Her mother would find food and old cans of drink stuffed at the back of drawers and under the bed. By the time she was 14, Anita began stopping out late at night. She was disruptive at school and was suspended on a number of occasions.

Rows at home seemed never ending. Her mother describes one occasion when she came home one evening to find Anita drunk. Anita attacked her mother with a poker, then broke down in tears, crying, 'Why did that bitch [meaning her birth mother] have me adopted? What was wrong with me? You don't love me. This family is total rubbish and I wish you were all dead.' Leaving school with no qualifications, Anita moved into a squat. There was the suspicion that she was taking drugs and shoplifting. A year later she was pregnant, but at 14 weeks she suffered a miscarriage. She came home. The rows and arguments continued for a year. Her mother then decided to help her daughter find her birth mother.

Their meeting was strange and something of a non-event. They keep in sporadic contact now but nothing more. But it seemed to help Anita sort out her feelings. I can't say she's been the easiest person to live with since, but life is much better. She keeps buying me flowers which I can't quite adjust to! She seems to have no memory of the hell she put us through. She's started catering college and we're feeling more optimistic now than we've ever felt.

Parents who were able to "stick with" their angry children reported that the aggression and hostility all but disappeared by late adolescence or the early twenties. The grown-up children remained somewhat immature as well as insecure but most of the anger seemed to have evaporated. In this period of reconciliation, many of the children became particularly generous. They increased the amount of contact they had with their parents to frequencies that seemed high for children of their adult age. It was as if they had finally accepted the unconditional love of their parents. Meeting the birth mother sometimes helped resolve the ambivalence. The anger generated by the original "rejection" was diffused.

Some adopters were unable to "stay with" their children's violence and hostility and they viewed the adoption more negatively as well as with sadness and regret. For those who were still in touch with their children, there was a growing feeling of optimism, although they did not deny that the turbulent times had been highly stressful.

Pre-adoptive backgrounds

This category of children split into two major sub-groups: those adopted as babies under six months of age and those adopted as older children aged six months and older. The older placed babies and children had suffered several changes of caretaker, neglect or abuse during their first few months and years of life. From the start, their lives had been characterised by grossly inconsistent parenting. Their parents were not hostile or rejecting but rather unpredictable and unreliable, insensitive and lacking in accurate empathy. The children were uncertain whether their caretakers would be available when they were needed. Feelings of safety, being loved, understood and accepted were regularly compromised and undermined. The intensification of attachment behaviour was therefore mingled with anger and resentment at the uncertainty that seemed inherent in the relationships. After a period in residential or foster care, the children were placed for adoption.

5. Detached and avoidant patterns

Behaviours and relationships

Few of these children were able to become fully involved in the emotional life of their new families. They appeared to remain on the edge, looking in on family relationships. Parents felt that these children were somewhat wary or detached. Most of them received some kind of psychological or psychiatric help. It was difficult to get close to them and as they progressed through adolescence they drifted further away, eventually choosing to live on their own either at boarding school, in a bedsit or a hostel. Some parents described their teenage children as "wanderers". They would disappear from home and go missing for days, weeks or months before re-appearing again. A few children disappeared out of their parents' lives completely and had not been seen or heard for many years. Others who had left home and had not made contact for some time, nevertheless did seem to need to "touch base" periodically. 'He seemed to want to get close,' said one mother, 'but I don't think he really knew how.'

Whereas "angry children" were attention-seeking, needing family life to revolve around them, "detached children" coped with rows and disagreements by "switching off" or *walking away*. The children were evasive. They "held on" to their feelings. Lying and stealing were common. They had few friends; indeed most parents described them as "loners". School performance was always poor and disappointing. Once they left home, many children found themselves in trouble with the police. Although a few children were beginning to lead more settled lives as young adults, their behaviour continued to be immature and to suggest that they still felt insecure and uncertain in close relationships. However, in a number of cases, children in their mid-twenties began to make clumsy but noteworthy attempts to get closer and become more involved with their parents.

After a troubled and disturbed adolescence, Garth left home and became unemployed. Some time later he went to college to study and practise catering. 'He did extremely well,' said his father, 'but we didn't know he did extremely well until a long time after because he never told us anything.' Aged 24, Garth had a girlfriend.

She is a most splendid girl who has helped him enormously; helped him work things out . . . He seems to be beginning to "own us" and our family . . . We're just beginning to get birthday cards and Christmas presents. He even brought his girlfriend to meet us. We keep chalking up firsts even though he's 24!

Pre-adoptive backgrounds

These children were all adopted as either toddlers or older children. Prior to adoption they had experienced *rejection* or *indifference* as well as neglect or abuse. Multiple moves and changes of caregiver were also a common experience. Love and affection seemed largely absent from these young lives. The only way they had learned to cope with the anxiety and pain of such rejection and neglect was to become "compulsively self-reliant" and try to avoid emotional involvement and commitment.

6. Casual and indiscriminate
Behaviours and relationships

These children were casual, superficial and indiscriminate in their emotional dealings with other people, who were often treated as a means to an end. Anyone, it seemed, would do. The children found it difficult to control their impulses and feelings of aggression. If an immediate need was not met, they tended to lose their temper. Uncontrolled violence became a serious worry.

After a history of neglect, malnutrition and several short stays in foster care, Neil and Polly were placed in a children's home. Four years later, aged seven and five respectively, they were adopted. As children they were "hyperactive". Their parents never found them easy children. They were disruptive at school and had no close friends. Their behaviour was generally "attention-seeking". Quarrels and fights between them were common. 'I found it difficult to get their feelings about things, even now when they're in their twenties,' said their mother. 'I think I managed them rather than mothered them!' In his teens, Neil's behaviour became so aggressive and destructive that neither home nor school could cope. He was sent to boarding school. 'He couldn't seem to control himself . . . He would kick and swear and get into a total frenzy.' However, he seemed to settle at his boarding school. His mother thought he preferred the structure and routine of the institutional setting.

The children in this group had problems at school, academically, socially and behaviourally. Once they left school they were either unemployed or in casual, part-time labour. It was a struggle for these children to take advantage of their parents' love, though most did show a very slow but increasing susceptibility to the care and concern shown by their families. For example, at times of upset there was a greater preparedness to seek the support of parents and a reduced inclination to react aggressively and impulsively.

Pre-adoptive backgrounds

Essentially, children in this group failed to develop selective attachments and relationships of any kind during their early years. They received highly inconsistent and unpredictable parenting. All the children experienced long periods in residential care, often starting in babyhood. All the children were adopted at a relatively late age, the youngest being five.

Conclusion

Analysing adopters' views of their children's development within an attachment framework allows us to recognise six patterns of adoption. The taxonomy is merely a device to help both parents and professionals make sense of the range of behaviours described by adopters. In general, and not surprisingly, children with more disturbed backgrounds developed more demanding and difficult behaviours (also see Thoburn, 1991). However, the classification offered here is an attempt to refine the broad picture and paint in some of the more subtle details. Indeed *some resilient children, in spite of adverse beginnings, emerged relatively unscathed emotionally.* It must also be observed that although we have described some very disturbed behaviour patterns, only a few of the adoptions broke down irretrievably (usually those involving the most difficult "angry" or "detached" children). The more parents could "make sense" of their child, the more they seemed able to "stay with" them. Although asking a great deal of many parents, particularly those with angry and avoidant children, patience and persistence often seemed to pay off. In most of the difficult cases, relationships showed distinct improvements by the time the children were in their early to mid-twenties.

Very few of the parents who found themselves involved with the mental health services (educational psychologists, child psychiatrists, psychotherapists) said they found their help useful or effective, though there were notable exceptions. In many cases, criticisms of these professionals ran particularly high. It seemed that they showed little understanding of either adoption, the child's psychology or the parents' distress. However, specialist post-adoption support which is more sophisticated and sensitive is growing. Advances in our understanding of children's psychosocial development *and* the psychology of adoption are helping us to make better sense of adopted children's needs, behaviours and relationship styles. Frameworks such as the one developed in the present paper suggest ways in which both parents and professionals can find their bearings in the increasingly complex world of adoption and post-placement practice.

Acknowledgement

I am extremely grateful for the time and help given by the many adoptive parents who allowed me to interview them. Their reflections were thoughtful, encouraging and insightful.

This article is based on the lecture, Patterns of Adoption, *given at a BAAF seminar (London, 15 June 1995).*

References

Ainsworth M D S, Blehar M, Waters E and Wall S, *Patterns of Attachment: A psychosocial study of the strange situation*, Erlbaum Associates, 1978, USA.

Bowlby J, *The Making and Breaking of Affectional Bonds*, Tavistock, 1979.

Bowlby J, *A Secure Base: Clinical implications of attachment theory*, Routledge, 1988.

Cline F, *Hope for High Risk and Rage Filled Children*, Evergreen Co: EC Publications, 1992, USA.

Howe D, *Attachment Theory for Social Work Practice*, Macmillan, 1995.

Main M, 'A move to the level of representation in the study of attachment organisation: implications for psychoanalysis'. Annual research lecture to the British Psychoanalytical Society, London, 6 July 1994.

Thoburn J, 'Survey Findings and Conclusions' in Fratter J, Rowe J, Sapsford D and Thoburn J, *Permanent Family Placement: A decade of experience*, BAAF, 1991.

9 Adopters' relationships with their adopted children from adolescence to early adulthood

David Howe

David Howe is Professor of Child and Family Social Work at the School of Social Work, University of East Anglia, Norwich.

This paper was published in Adoption & Fostering, 20:3, 1996.

Some of the most complex and difficult cases in post-adoption work are with parents and their adopted teenage children. During adolescence, the behaviour of a small but significant number of adopted children – a few placed as babies, more joining their new families as older children – becomes increasingly disturbed and problematic. Such behaviour puts huge strains on the relationship between parents and their children. The problems often outpace the skills and understanding of many child care professionals. One way and another, these children and their behaviour sound like bad news as they cast a gloomy shadow over the long-term outcome of agencies' more ambitious placement policies and practices.

However, although there is no denying that some adopted children do have serious behaviour problems in their teenage years, an even longer-term perspective, carrying the view into early adulthood, sees the beginnings of a more promising outlook for both these parents and their children. The developmental pathway for the emotional growth of some behaviourally disturbed adopted children seems to be particularly long and hard. In terms of feeling secure, confident and relaxed in their relationships with those emotionally most important to them, these children appear to need several extra years in which to mature and overcome their feelings of anxiety, doubt and anger. This study looks at the evolution of the relationship between parents and their adopted children from adolescence to early adulthood.

Background

Although in comparative terms the adoption of older children is a relatively successful practice, we know that there is an increased risk of these children showing a variety of problem behaviours (Hodges and Tizard, 1990; Borland, O'Hara and Triseliotis, 1991; Thoburn, 1991; Fergusson *et al*, 1995; Rushton, Treseder and Quinton, 1995). However, it has been suggested that problem behaviour is not directly associated with older age at placement but rather with the degree of adversity experienced by children prior to placement. More specifically, children who experience neglect, abuse, rejection and inconsistent care from a very young age prior to being placed for adoption appear most at risk of experiencing problem behaviours after placement. The problem behaviours become most pronounced during adolescence. Of course, by no means all older placed children whose pre-placement care was poor experience problem behaviours. And it is equally the case that a small percentage of children adopted as babies become extremely difficult and problematic in their teenage years.

We need to recognise, therefore, that some adopted children, whether adopted as babies or older, present their parents with behavioural difficulties during adolescence. The problems are much more severe than the normal upsets that some parents suffer with their teenage children. These disturbed children may steal from their mothers, be expelled from school, show anger and even violence towards their parents. They appear confused by and preoccupied with all relationships which have a strong and meaningful emotional content (see Howe, 1996). A proportion of these adoptions do break down but the majority of parents continue to look after their children, even while they are being difficult.

The study

The aims of the study reported in this paper were twofold: (1) to consider adopted children's early adult life achievements in the light of their pre-placement backgrounds; and (2) to examine the range of views of parents whose adopted children are now grown up.

The broader study, of which the findings presented in this paper are a part, sought the views and experiences of parents whose adopted children had reached late adolescence and early adulthood. I wanted to hear what adopters had to say about their children once they had reached maturity. The adopters were invited to talk about their current relationships with their children and the relationships they had with them during adolescence. Particular attention was paid to the experiences of parents who found their children difficult as teenagers.

I interviewed the parents of 120 families (91 joint interviews with both parents, 28 interviews with the adoptive mother only and one interview with the adoptive father only). I used a "snowballing" technique to get in touch with potential respondents (see *Adoption & Fostering* 19:4, 1995). With the help of three post-adoption agencies and some advertising I made contact with a small number of adoptive parents who were willing to be interviewed. This initial core group then recommended other adoptive parents known to them and who were also willing to take part in the research. In turn, they suggested other adopters and so on. Between them the parents had adopted around 300 children including baby, toddler and older children adoptions.

Two hundred and eleven of the adopted children were aged 18 years or older at the time of interview. However, for the purposes of this study I shall be considering only those 100 adopted children who were at least 23 years old at the time I spoke with their parents. (The convenient figure of 100 just happened to be the number who had reached the right age.) By the time the children reached 23 most had either left home or finished college. It was an age that seemed to mark the beginnings of independent adulthood. This sample of parents offered the prospect of a reasonably long-term view, sufficient to pick up any movements in the quality of parent-child relationships between mid-adolescence (16 years) and early adulthood.

Forty-nine of the young adopted adults were men and 51 were women. Their mean average age at the time of interview was 26.6 years. In terms of ethnic background, 79 per cent of the adopted children were white in same-race placements, five per cent were African-Caribbean in transracial placements, 11 per cent were mixed race (white/African-Caribbean) with white adoptive parents, three per cent were Asian in transracial placements, and two per cent were mixed race (white/Asian) with white adoptive parents. When the numbers were large enough to permit testing, an adopted person's ethnic background was not found to be a statistically significant variable in the findings reported in this paper. In other words, in terms of educational achievement, adolescent problem behaviour and parent-child relationships, as reported by adopters, there were no statistically significant differences found between same-race and transracial placements, white and black adopted people (see Versluis-den Bieman and Verhulst, 1995).

Classification of pre-placement care

The study also provided an opportunity to compare some of the long-term outcomes of children who had been placed as babies and those who had been placed at an older age.

The quality of an adopted child's preplacement care was divided between those who were adopted as babies (six months and younger) and those who were adopted as older children. The majority of children adopted as young infants experience little, if any, adversity in the quality of their short pre-placement care other than that associated with the disturbance of being transferred from the care of the biological mother either directly to the adopters or indirectly via a short-term foster parent. The backgrounds of baby adopted children can therefore be regarded as non-adverse.

In contrast, children placed at older ages usually have suffered a history of either neglect, abuse or rejection from an early age. In most cases they have also experienced several changes of caretaker as they are variously looked after by friends, relatives, residential care workers and foster parents. Typically, often after several years of social work involvement, the children are placed for adoption.

However, there is a third group of adopted children whose life and care begin reasonably well. It is only later that their care deteriorates and they experience adversity. The most typical pattern is the child who lives with his or her lone mother for the first few years of life, unknown to social services and giving no cause for concern. The mother then enters a new sexual relationship and has more children. The first child's behaviour becomes increasingly difficult under these new social conditions. He or she suffers neglect, abuse or rejection at the hands of the step-father and/or the mother. Social workers become involved and the child experiences one or more episodes of foster care before finally being placed for adoption.

The research therefore recognised three types of adoption, each associated with a particular kind of pre-placement care:

- *Baby adoptions* in which children were placed before the age of six months with no adverse care prior to being placed;
- *Good start/late adoptions* in which children experienced non-adverse care for their first year of life or up until the time of placement, whichever was the shorter. Prior to being finally separated from their biological parents, these children experienced adverse care, usually in the form of abuse, neglect and/or rejection;
- *Poor start/late adoptions* in which children experienced more or less continuous adverse care during their first year of life or up until the time of placement, whichever was the longer.

On the basis of his or her known pre-placement care experience, each of the hundred adopted adult children was placed into one of the three categories (baby adoptions = 72, good start/late adoptions = 7, poor start/ late adoptions 21). We shall use these categories to see what impact, if any, the quality of pre-placement care has on some of the longer-term outcomes.

A word of caution is needed when interpreting the results. The parents interviewed volunteered their help. To this extent, they were not a random sample. Not surprisingly, given the method of collecting the sample, there were no examples of adoptions which had completely broken down during or prior to the child's adolescence. The 100 adoptions do offer the opportunity of making within-group comparisons. The numbers and percentages presented cannot be seen as representative of adoptions in general. However, comparisons between the three types of adoption are appropriately made. The *relative* differences between the three groups are meaningful. These within-group comparisons generate a number of strong and significant similarities and differences between the three types of adoption.

Education

Seventy-seven per cent of all the children had achieved at least one good grade CSE, GCE "O" level or GCSE qualification. However, as Table 1 shows, the distribution of maximum academic qualifications gained varied significantly between the three pre-placement care groups.

Table 1

Rates (%) of maximum academic qualifications achieved by type of adoption

Maximum academic qualification	Baby adoptions n = 72 %	Good start/ late adoptions n = 7 %	Poor start/ late adoptions n = 21 %
None	11	14	62
One or more CSE, GCE, 'O' level GCSE, 'A' level or Scottish Higher	54	57	33
Degree, PhD, MD	35	29	5
	100	100	100

$P<0.001$

Those adopted as babies and those who had a "good start/late adoption" enjoyed similar kinds of academic success, 89 per cent of those adopted as babies and 86 per cent of those who had a "good start/late adoption" gaining at least one basic educational qualification. However, the performance of the "poor start/late adoption" children was significantly weaker with only 38 per cent leaving school with an academic qualification.

Table 2

Comparison of parent-child relationships at 16 and type of adoption

Quality of parent-child relationships at 16	Baby adoptions n = 72 %	Good start/ late adoptions n = 7 %	Poor start/ late adoptions n = 21 %
Positive	83	71	38
Negative	17	29	62
Total	100	100	100

$P<0.001$

Parent-child relationships

One dimension and two benchmarks will be used to explore the quality of parent-child relationships. The dimension is the three different types of pre-placement care defined above. The benchmarks are: (1) the quality of *current* parent-child relationships; and (2) the quality of *past* relationships when the child was in his or her mid-teens (approximately aged 16).

What will be of particular interest is to see whether parents experienced any major changes in the quality of these relationships during this period.

Quality of parent-child relationships at 16

A direct question about the quality of relationships at this time tended to elicit reasonably clear and unambiguous answers from parents. Their evaluations were categorised as either positive or negative. Relationships were taken to be positive if parents spoke with warmth, pride, tolerance, understanding or pleasure about their child. For example: 'John was good at playing the trumpet and was a pleasure to have around. Yes, we got on well then.' Relationships were defined as negative if parents remembered adolescence as a difficult and tense time. Conflict and anger were nearly always cited as evidence of 'how bad things were'. For example:

> One Saturday night we got home from visiting some friends and we found Emma drunk. She began to get upset and angry and started calling me terrible names like 'barren bitch'. She said we didn't love her and she couldn't wait to leave home. It was a terrible time that went on for several years. Very, very stressful and dispiriting.

Table 2 shows the association between type of adoption and quality of parent-child relationship at 16 years.

Three out of five parents of children who had experienced poor quality pre-placement care reported that mid-adolescence was a difficult time. Many parents understood the reasons for their child's behaviour and to that extent could be quite forgiving. However, it did not mean that they denied being under considerable pressure and strain at this time. For example:

> Simon was badly beaten as a little boy by his step-father His mother

just gave up on him. It must have been very difficult for him and he found adolescence awfully hard. I felt for him but he couldn't half wind me up and upset me. I'd be in tears some nights when Graham [husband] came home from work.

It is possible to correlate the type of adoption with a variety of other adolescent difficulties including repeated shows of anger, referral to a mental health specialist (educational psychologist, child psychiatrist), and outbursts of problem behaviour. Not surprisingly, adolescent children who scored highly on these indicators were most likely to be in negative parent-child relationships.

The adjective most commonly used by parents in a negative relationship to describe their adolescent child was "angry". To the parent, their child seemed angry, confused and frustrated. Often, it was not clear to the parents why the child felt these emotions. In many cases, the anger was directed at the adoptive mother. For example:

Sarah got in a temper and would break things that I'd bought her as a present. Deliberately. She nagged me endlessly. Everything was my fault. I was rubbish. But she wouldn't leave me alone, even though I was "useless".

Eighty per cent of the parents of "poor start/late adopted" children described their adolescent child as "angry" compared to only five per cent of those who had adopted their children as babies. Similarly, 65 per cent of the "poor start/late adoption group" had been referred to a mental health professional at some time during their teens compared to only five per cent of children adopted as babies.

It was also possible to create an adolescent problem behaviour score. Each child was scored against ten problem behaviour measures: self-mutilation, eating disorder, excessive lying, truancy, exclusion from school, running away from home, alcohol problems and/or the use of drugs, theft from the parental home, offences committed outside the home, and violence against a family member (see Howe, forthcoming). Each child received a score from nought to ten. The mean score for all hundred children was 1.06 (i.e. an average of about one problem behaviour per child). However, the scores varied between each of the three pre-placement care groupings. Table 3 gives the mean adolescent problem behaviour score for each adoption type.

Table 3

Mean total scores of adolescent problem behaviour (out of ten) by pre-placement care experience

Measure	Baby adoptions n = 72	Good start/ late adoptions n = 7	Poor start/ late adoptions n = 21
Mean total problem behaviour score (out of ten)	0.13	0.95	2.62

P<0.001

The differences between the scores are statistically highly significant. The mean scores reveal that, with a few notable exceptions, most of the children (74 per cent) adopted as babies experienced no major problem behaviours according to their parents. In contrast, children in the "poor start/late adoption" group exhibited an average of 2.62 problem behaviours, although it must be recorded that eight out of 21 of these children scored *zero* on this measure. In other words, a significant minority of these children appeared to cope and behave well throughout childhood in spite of early life adversity. (For a fuller treatment of this topic see Howe, 1996.) The remaining 13 children with scores of one or more averaged 4.23 problem behaviours.

Eighty-four per cent of children from all three groups whose total problem behaviour score was *zero* enjoyed *positive* parent-child relationships during adolescence. In contrast, 61 per cent of children from all three groups who scored at least one adolescent problem behaviour had parents who felt that their relationship with their son or daughter was difficult and stressful at that time. Clearly, there is some circularity in this observation. Parents who are not having a good relationship with their child will describe problems, and those children with problems will have parents who describe them as difficult. Nevertheless, there is a strong correlation between the number of problem behaviours recorded for a child and (1) the quality of their pre-placement care, and (2) the quality of parent-child relationships at 16. Thus, "poor start/late placed" children were more likely to have higher problem behaviour scores and be in relationships with their parents which the latter viewed negatively.

Quality of current parent-child relationships compared to those at age 16

Overall, 76 per cent of parents described relationships with their child during adolescence as positive. At the time of the research interview (when the adopted child was aged at least 23 years), 93 per cent of parents reviewed the adoption positively and said that relationships with their child were good. In other words, 17 parents who found relationships with their son or daughter very difficult during adolescence now said that they got on very or reasonably well with their child.

As Table 4 shows, improved relationships were recorded in all three adoption groups. However, the biggest change occurred in the quality of parent-child relationships for the "poor start/late adoption" category. During adolescence only 38 per cent of parents felt that relationships with their child were positive. This figure jumped to 67 per cent for the quality of current relationships.

It has to be remembered that these are "within-group" comparisons. The actual figures quoted may not reflect the relative condition of adoptions in general. However, they do provide good evidence that many parents who experienced very poor relationships with their adolescent son or daughter might expect matters to improve as the child moves into adulthood. In a few cases, relationships did not recover. Contact was sometimes lost or hostilities remained. But if adopters were able to "stick with" their child through the severe difficulties met in adolescence, they were able, as one parent put it, "to come out the other side" and enjoy the pleasures of parenthood once again.

Table 4

Comparison of rates (%) of positive parent-child relationships at 16 and post-23 years old for each adoption type

Evaluation of adoption at age 16 and 23	Baby adoptions n = 72	Good start/ late adoptions n = 7	Poor start/ late adoptions n = 21
Positive parent-child relationship at 16	81	71	38
Positive parent-child relationship post-23 years	89	100	67

Parent-adult child rates of contact

It is also possible to pick up changes in the quality of parent-child relationships by examining the frequency of current contact. Parents were asked how often they were in contact, either physically or by telephone, with their adult son or daughter. Seven per cent of adult adopted children were still living with their parents. Forty-nine per cent were in touch at least once a week with another 36 per cent making contact at least once a month. Three per cent of adopters said they heard from their child less than once a month. This left five per cent who had no contact at all.

Interesting, though perhaps not surprising differences were also observed between the sexes. Table 5 compares the frequency of parent-child contact of sons and daughters.

Daughters were generally in more frequent contact with their parents than sons, though approximately equal numbers of both sexes were in touch at least once a month. Thirty-one per cent of adopted daughters had babies or young children of their own and in many cases this had increased the amount of contact they were having with their mothers. Even so, these subtle sex differences, no doubt mirrored in non-adopted populations, further refine the picture of parents' experiences of adoption.

Looking back

With their children now grown up and in most cases no longer living at home, parents concluded the interview by offering a long-term view of the adoption experience. Understandably, the quality of their current relationship with sons or daughters influenced the assessment.

Table 5

Comparison of the rates of contact with parents by adult adopted sons and daughters

Frequency of contact (visiting/telephoning)	Sons %	Daughters %
Still living with parents	8	6
More than once/week	29	69
Once every 1–4 weeks	51	22
Less than once/month	6	0
No contact	6	4
	100	101

Three perspectives emerged:
- *positive* reviews by parents who had enjoyed good relationships with their children both as adolescents and adults (76 per cent);
- *positive* reviews by parents who had *not* enjoyed good relationships with their children during adolescence but who now felt that relationships with their adult children were fine and much improved (17 per cent);
- *negative* reviews by parents who had poor relationships with their children during adolescence and which remained poor through into adulthood (seven per cent).

Each perspective is illustrated below using the parents' own words:

1 *Positive review of both past and present relationships*
- 'If I did it again,' concluded Doreen, 'I'd adopt four! Three wasn't enough!'
- 'Even the problems have been pleasures!' said Penny. 'They've given us so much happiness. We've been so lucky. It's been an absolute joy.'

- Maria is now in her thirties, with two children of her own, and Prue, her mother, still finds her a delight. 'She refreshes my life every time I see her. I'm very close to Maria. She comes round twice a week. I feel a very lucky person. Our lives would have been empty without the children.'

- 'I've had more happiness with the children than anybody has a right to expect,' reflected Alice. 'I think if you take children for what they are and not for what you want them to be – enjoy them for themselves – then that's what they want. They want to be wanted.'

2 *Positive review of poor past but good present relationships*

- Peggy, who had adopted five disturbed young children over a number of years, acknowledged that there had been very stressful and difficult times with some of them. But she felt positive about the outcome: *Seeing these children advance. I mean, there's times when you have problems and I find the stealing and the lying very difficult. But when you look at these children and think back to when they came and how damaged they were, and you look at them now – that's my reward!*

- After an adolescence of lies, stealing from home and shoplifting, relationships between Harriett and her parents, Val and Jim, broke down. She left home and lost contact with them. Several years later and out of the blue, Harriett got in touch. She said that she now had a baby and asked to come over and see her parents – 'Just like that, as if nothing had happened!' said Val. 'I said, "Of course you can." I was in tears by the time she arrived.' Val summed up her feelings: *Looking back over the last 30 odd years, at one stage we thought maybe we should never have adopted because we felt so desperate. Whatever we did with her we were rebuffed. But it now seems that now she's got her own family and children she seems to understand. I couldn't ask for a better relationship with her now. We bent over backwards to treat her and Philip [birth son] the same, but she never saw it that way. It never felt that way to her. Deep down, I'm sure she was tremendously insecure.*

- Marjorie had suffered some extremely tough times with her daughter

Amy, an intelligent, artistic but very difficult girl. Throughout adolescence there had been major problems. Amy had taken drugs, become pregnant, had an abortion, committed theft and fraud, been to prison and suffered violent relationships with boyfriends. Much of Amy's anger was directed at Marjorie who nevertheless continued to stand by her disturbed daughter. It was not until Amy was well into her twenties that her behaviour and emotions began to settle. She returned home and very gradually relationships with her mother improved. Marjorie was very philosophical about her experiences as a mother: *I feel wiser and humbler. . . I'm optimistic now. I think everything will be fine. Amy has taken me to places and led me down corridors of pain and joy and hope that I didn't know existed . . . You can't go through life and have experiences like that without being changed. I think life is a great leveller. I'd do it all again, yes. I would! Even Amy . . .*

3 *Negative review of both past and present relationships*
Parents who had either lost touch with their children or who were still experiencing strained and tense relationships were inclined to view the adoption more negatively.
- After years of upset and argument with her son, Larna said 'I feel empty now. I have no more to give.'

- Morag felt ambivalent:
My husband said the other day that Imogen had distorted our lives. I don't know whether I'd want to go through with it again but I'm not sorry I did it. I think that most of the time I know I'm fond of her and love her but there are times when I really want her out of the way . . . It's an ongoing problem and it's aged us both. We want out now. We're not young and we want it all to stop.

- Dale, after a very disturbed early childhood, was placed late with Millie and Rob. He left home at 16 years old, repeatedly got the sack as a trainee motor mechanic, and then started stealing cars and appearing in court. 'We felt we'd reached an all time low,' said Millie. *He's now 24 and we've had no contact with him for over a year now. He's never fitted into our family [four birth and three adopted children]. To be quite honest, I think he's a bit of a bounder. He always seems to have a big chip on his shoulder. Things would start off fine, but they would go wrong . . . I was always trying to reach him, but I never did.*

Conclusion

The quality of children's care prior to placement appears to have an influence on their subsequent emotional and social development (Howe, 1996). Adverse early life experiences leave many children feeling insecure, anxious and, in some cases, confused, angry or distant (Howe, 1995). Insecure and anxious children both demand parental attention and angrily *resist* it at the same time. Of course, the difficult and demanding behaviour which such relationships produce only makes matters worse. These children need emotional closeness and intimacy and yet they find it difficult to trust its continued availability. Such deep anxieties produce behaviour which is attention-seeking, demanding, awkward, fretful, possessive, ungrateful and conflictual. Although some of the "poor start/ late adopted" children had problem behaviours throughout the whole of their childhood, adolescence was a time when many parents experienced particular difficulties and upsets. Trying to "stay with" these angry and highly problematic children demanded a great deal from parents and some found it simply too hard and stressful.

Those who did manage to ride the storm (which could last several years) often found that their very insecure, hostile and angry children slowly began to develop an increased sense of security and self-confidence. They stopped fighting their parents and, seemingly for the first time, were able to accept their love without feeling confused, angry and anxious. In many cases, these feelings of security and acceptance seemed to be triggered by major relationship developments – meeting a caring, stable partner; having a baby; making contact with a birth parent. But in these cases, it was equally important for the children to feel that their adoptive parents were still available and willing to respond. It was at this stage that parents reported, much to their surprise, the beginnings of a much more intense, caring and reciprocal relationship with their grown-up children. Even the more detached, "avoidant" children began to explore ways of getting closer to their mothers and fathers.

There is no denying that many parents who adopt older, disturbed

children will find the behaviour of their adolescent ~s~
very demanding and extremely difficult. However
those parents who finally achieved more relaxed re
grown up children is to try and "stick with it" and ~ s.~
many also felt the need to make one final point. To help m~~
times of great stress, parents said that what is needed is support a~
advice from people who not only are experts in children's development
but also have a sophisticated and skilled understanding of the psychology
of adoption.

Acknowledgements

I am extremely grateful for the time and help given by the many adoptive
parents who allowed me to interview them. Their thoughts, observations
and reflections helped me appreciate a varied and complex experience. I
should also like to thank the Nuffield Foundation (Small Grants) who
helped support part of the research.

Note
*David Howe's research into adopted parents' perspectives on adoption
is expanded in his recent book* Adopters on Adoption, *published by BAAF
(see below).*

References

Borland M, O'Hara G and Triseliotis J, 'Placement outcomes for children with
special needs', *Adoption & Fostering*, 15:2, pp 18–28, 1991.

Fergusson D M, Lynskey M and Horwood L J, 'The adolescent outcomes of
adoption: a 16-year longitudinal study', *Journal of Child Psychology and
Psychiatry*, 36:4, pp 597–616, 1995.

Hodges J and Tizard B, 'Social and family relationships of ex-institutional
adolescents', *Journal of Child Psychology and Psychiatry*, 30, pp 77–97, 1989.

Howe D, *Attachment Theory for Social Work Practice*, Macmillan, 1995.

Howe D, 'Adoption and attachment', *Adoption & Fostering*, 19:4, pp 7–15, 1995.

Howe D, *Adopters on Adoption: Reflections on parenthood and children*, BAAF,
1996.

fowe D, 'Parent reported problems in 211 adopted children: some risk and protective factors', *Journal of Child Psychology and Psychiatry* (forthcoming).

Rushton A, Treseder J and Quinton D, 'An eight-year prospective study of older boys placed in permanent substitute families: a research note', *Journal of Child Psychology and Psychiatry*, 36:4, pp 687–96, 1995.

Thoburn J, 'Survey findings and conclusions', in Fratter J, Rowe J, Sapsford D and Thoburn J, *Permanent Family Placement: A decade of experience*, BAAF, 1991.

Versluis-den Bieman H J M and Verhulst F C, 'Self-reported and parent-reported problems in adolescent international adoptees', *Journal of Child Psychology and Psychiatry*, 36:8, pp 1411–28, 1995.

Section III
Openness in adoption

Throughout the early years of adoption in England and Wales (from 1926 until at least the early 70s), every effort was made to preserve the anonymity of adopters from birth parents. Adoptive applicants were able to conceal their identities on the court papers by the use of a serial number. Anonymity was only one-way, as it was considered impractical to deny the adopters information identifying the birth parents, but the two parties were kept firmly separate from each other. The baby was transferred through an intermediary (if only in another room in the hospital) and no contact between adopters and birth family (whether in person or by letter) was allowed thereafter. The thinking behind this policy was that adoption should be a clean break, allowing the child a fresh start in his or her new family. Towards the end of this period, some agencies were experimenting with exchange of letters and brief meetings between birth parents and adopters, events which often proved to be reassuring rather than unsettling to the parties. With hindsight, the trend towards more openness – beyond pre-adoption letters and meetings to varying degrees of post-adoption contact between the families – seems logical and inevitable, particularly with the adoption of older children, who included a fair proportion adopted from care. But moves in this direction were patchy and uncertain, with much anxiety about the effects on children and, notably among the judiciary, concern about the ambiguity of their legal position. This was uncharted territory, with no hard evidence to guide the debate.

The publication of a study by Triseliotis in 1973 entitled *In Search of Origins* provided policy-makers and practitioners with some much needed data. It had long been possible in Scotland for adopted children, once having attained adulthood, to gain access to their original birth certificates and thus to important information as to their birth parents' identities and whereabouts. This study demonstrated that, contrary to professional assumptions, adopted adults seeking information about their birth families, or contact with them, did so more from a natural interest and desire for knowledge than because of deep-seated pathology or discontent with their adoptive status. Reassuring to birth parents was the finding that efforts to trace and make contact were generally conducted responsibly and sensitively and not in a spirit of vengeance or malice. As a result of this research, adopted adults in England and Wales gained the right of access to their original birth certificates under the Children Act 1975. More recently, we have gained from the experience of open adoption in New Zealand, which forms the starting point for **Ryburn**'s article reprinted here. Influenced by Maori traditions, New Zealand has developed a form of inclusive adoption which allows children to maintain personal contact and part of their identity with their birth families. These ideas have had an important influence on British adoption since the late 1980s, reinforced by the fact that increasing proportions of children have had memories of their birth families and in some cases ongoing contacts when placed for adoption, unlike the typical baby adoptions of the 1960s and 70s.

Dutt and Sanyal (1991) provided a timely reminder that non-Western traditions are present in the UK too. Many black families have looked after children not their own on an open basis without excluding the child's original family. The writers argue for an adoptive process which embodies partnership between professionals and families, and which places emphasis on social ties rather than restrictive legislation. Their article foreshadows the theme of the next part of this collection.

Openness refers to a spectrum of relationships from open communication within the adoptive family via indirect contacts between birth and adoptive families to face-to-face contacts. Although openness often refers mainly to relationships with birth mothers, it may also involve brothers and sisters, fathers, grandparents and others. Indirect contacts and even one-off initial meetings with birth mothers have become commonplace in recent years, but continuing personal contact remains rare, whether by the adopters, the child or both.

The long-term consequences of such "fully" open adoption are not yet clear, though American research suggested that outcomes can be good, provided there is a shared approach by agency and adopters (McRoy, 1991). Early British evidence was reported by **Fratter (1989)**. Her sample was small – but then in the mid-1980s few placements entailed any degree of contact. Fratter interviewed adoptive parents in 22 families where there had been some degree of contact with birth parents after placement. In two-thirds of the families continuing face-to-face contact with one or both birth parents was continuing. As American experience has also shown, agency preparation had been important in helping adopters to see the potential value of openness. On the other hand, a number had initiated more contact than the agency had expected. In the majority of cases adopters thought the children benefited from the contact (e.g. by developing a better sense of identity or having fewer fantasies about the birth family). Most of the adopters also thought their attachment to the children was close and unaffected by the contact, even though proponents of the clean-break philosophy argued that children (and adopters) cannot handle two sets of parents (Goldstein *et al*, 1973). Six of the families did report significant tensions, with two believing the attachment process had been adversely affected. A key factor in the families with more negative experiences was that the birth parents had usually disapproved of the plan for adoption, although later examples cited by Ryburn (1994; 1997) suggested that contact can be sustained and useful, even when the adoption has been contested.

Fratter (1996) followed up her earlier study and met with adoptive parents four years later. She also interviewed about half of the children. All but one described contact with their birth parents as positive and their views nearly always corresponded with the depictions of their feelings given by the adoptive parents. This concordance of views incidentally indicates that adopters are likely to be reasonably accurate informants about their children, which reinforces confidence in studies like that by **Howe** (see section II) which have relied on adopters' testimony.

Research of this kind should move us on from the partisan "closed versus open" debate which generates heat without light. We need to know more about other viewpoints and participants in openness.

10 How adoptive parents feel about contact with birth parents after adoption

Joan Fratter

Joan Fratter is a senior social worker in Barnardo's Positive Options Project.

This paper was published in Adoption & Fostering, 13:4, 1989.

The material on which this article is based derives from interviews with adoptive parents in 22 families, undertaken towards the end of 1987 as part of the research for a Masters Degree at Cranfield Institute. The study was concerned with issues in family placement and contact and, in particular, the achievement of permanency for children in touch with birth relatives. Interviews were undertaken at the same time with representatives of 22 voluntary adoption agencies. Their experiences and attitudes in relation to family placement and contact are described elsewhere (Fratter *et al*, 1991).

The context

The research was begun at a time when practice in adoption was changing rapidly. Prior to the first UK Adoption of Children Act in 1926, arrangements for the care of children by others than their birth parents had been made informally within or between families or by the community exercising responsibility for its children (Heywood, 1978). "Kinship" and "tribal" adoption are still common elsewhere in societies which have resisted Western influence (O'Collins, 1984). However, in the fifty years following implementation of the Adoption of Children Act, arrangements for adoption were increasingly "professionalised" and the role of birth parents accordingly diminished. Legal adoption had been an adult focused service and it was not until the Children Act 1975 that the child's welfare became the "first consideration" (now section 6 of the Adoption Act 1976). The 1975 Act further endorsed the profession-alisation of adoption by prohibiting direct and third-party placements. In addition, the Act extended the grounds for dispensing with parental agreement to adoption. These provisions were designed to protect a child from an unsuitable placement and to facilitate the adoption of children whose parents were "unreasonably" withholding agreement.

After 1975 many agencies developed child care policies which viewed adoption as the only permanent form of alternative family placement for children unable to live with birth relatives. It was generally held that for both psychological and legal reasons, termination of contact by birth relatives was a prerequisite if adoption were to be achieved (for example, see *Terminating Parental Contact*, edited by Adcock & White).

Moving towards openness in adoption
However, when the House of Commons Social Services Committee began its enquiry into children in care in July 1982, the issue of contact between children in care and their families had become an important focus of concern. In 1983 an editorial in *Adoption & Fostering* observed: 'There is a well-founded suspicion that by controlling access to children in care local authorities can determine whether parents have the chance to rebuild their family.' The practice of terminating contact for children unable to live with birth relatives was challenged by the provisions of Schedule 1 of the Health and Social Services and Social Security Adjudications Act 1983 which gave limited rights to birth parents to appeal against restriction of access. In addition, changes in the age and circumstances of children needing permanent family placement led to doubts about the appropriateness of the closed model of adoption. Thoburn *et al* (1986) identified a group of children who 'will not allow themselves to be placed with substitute families if termination of contact with members of the natural family is a pre-requisite of placement'.

Thus, in planning for children, agencies were having to take into account the significance of their contact with their family of origin. Triseliotis (1985) suggested that 'adoption with a condition of access should be an option to take account of a few children's meaningful attachments to members of their biological family'. It became in-creasingly apparent during the early 1980s that in extending the range of children for whom adoption was deemed appropriate, practitioners had also to question the philosophy and practice underpinning the traditional model. In particular, the theory of a clean break with the past to enable a child to take on a new identity was being increasingly challenged.

Reconsideration of the traditional model of adoption was also a response to the growing awareness among practitioners, confirmed by research, of the importance of information and openness of attitude to an adopted child's emotional, psychological and social well-being. Descriptions of departures from the closed model in New Zealand and the USA demonstrated the potential benefit to all parties in the adoption triangle of greater openness in adoption practice. Howell and Ryburn (1987) describe how birth parents are able to choose adoptive parents through access to a family profile completed by the prospective adoptive parents themselves. The authors comment that 'the customary severance of all links between adopted child and birth parents is by no means necessarily in the best interests of the child, nor for that matter in the best interests of either birth parents or adoptive parents'.

In *Co-operative Adoption* (Rillera and Kaplan, 1985) there are accounts by adoptive parents, birth parents and birth grandparents of arrangements whereby birth parents can select adoptive parents during pregnancy and subsequently maintain contact.

The term "open adoption" began to be used to encompass any arrangement which departed from the closed model in which, typically, the social worker has a powerful role, acting as intermediary between birth parents and adoptive parents, and controlling the amount and nature of the information shared between the parties, while the birth parents and adoptive parents have limited opportunities for participation. In more open models, the parties can choose what information to share before and after placement, the birth parents may exercise a degree of choice regarding the adoptive placement, the two sets of parents may meet before placement, and subsequently, on a one-off or ongoing basis, maintain contact through letters via the agency or by face-to-face meetings. Open adoption arrangements may involve non-parental birth relatives, such as grandparents or brothers and sisters as well as, or instead of, birth parents.

Arrangements for continuing contact after adoption may be agreed informally between the parties or may be formalised by a written agreement or a condition attached to an Adoption Order (Adoption Act 1976, section 12 (6)).

Identifying adoptive parents for the study

The survey undertaken in 1986 by Thoburn and Rowe (1988) of 1,165 placements of children with special needs made by voluntary agencies between January 1980 and December 1984, provided useful information about permanent placements in the UK in which contact with birth parents had continued. The survey identified 33 adopted children who had been placed (in 23 families). With the co-operation of the ten voluntary agencies who had placed the children I was able to make contact with adoptive parents in 15 families, of whom adoptive parents in 11 families agreed to be interviewed. (Agencies did not think it appropriate for a variety of reasons to approach the adoptive parents in eight families.) Adoptive parents in a further 11 families were recruited to the study through the voluntary agencies (five families), through Parent to Parent Information on Adoption Service (PPIAS) (four families) and through a local authority social worker who knew of the research and introduced me to two families. Adoptive parents were invited to take part in the study if they or their adopted children had had some degree of contact with birth parents after placement.

The aim in interviewing this group of adoptive parents was to learn how they had experienced openness in adoption and, in particular, how they felt it affected their sense of entitlement and attachment and their child's sense of security and identity. Given that open adoption was increasingly being considered as one of the placement options available in planning for children, I also hoped to discover whether there were any factors associated with adoptive parents feeling satisfied with being involved in an adoption in which birth parents had played some role, however limited. (I had chosen not to include in the study adoptive parents whose contact after placement was with non-parental relatives as it seemed that, apart from the potential role conflict between birth parents and adoptive parents, other issues related to openness in adoption would apply both to parental and non-parental birth relatives.)

Profile of the adoptive families and the children

Among the adoptive parents in the 22 families were 20 married couples and two single women, one widowed and one divorced. One couple described themselves as having a "mixed-race marriage", in that one partner was "black West Indian" and the other white. All the other adoptive parents were white. Adoptive parents in 14 families had had no children born to them and adoptive parents in eight families had no other children than the one or two adopted children who were discussed in relation to this study. Only three of the families did not live in the south of England or East Anglia.

The 32 adopted children were a disparate group. All but two had special needs in that they had a disability or severe learning difficulties; at least one previously disrupted placement; a history of moves and changes of caregiver; lengthy periods in residential care; and/or had experienced deprivation or abuse. Their ages ranged at the time of the interview with their adoptive parents from two-and-a-half years to 20 years. There were 19 boys and 13 girls. More than two-thirds of the children had been living in their adoptive families for more than four years.

Twenty-two of the children were white and the remaining ten had a range of ethnic and cultural backgrounds, having one or both parents who were African-Caribbean, Indian, Sri-Lankan or Lebanese. Of these ten children, one African-Caribbean child was placed with an Anglo/Afro-Caribbean couple while the remaining nine were placed with white adoptive parents in six families.

Given the assumption in the literature that adoption with contact is likely to be most relevant for children coming into care at an older age (ten is usually suggested as a dividing line) it was a shock to find that only one child had been in that age group. More than half the children (17) had last been separated from one or both parents at the age of three years or under (indeed eight had been infants of up to 12 months).

There was considerable variation in the length of time children had spent in care awaiting placement. More than half had joined their adoptive family within two years of entering care for the last time, but one boy, placed at 14, had spent more than 13 years in the same children's home and four other children had been in residential care for periods of five years or more. However, 12 children had been placed with their adoptive parents when aged five years or under and only five had been aged 11–14 years at placement.

Eight children, six of whom had a physical disability and/or learning difficulties, had been accommodated at the request of their birth parents with a view to their being placed for adoption. However, the plan for adoption in respect of the remaining 24 children had been made when they were already being looked after by the local authority. Twenty-two were in some form of statutory care (pre-1989 Children Act provisions). It had been anticipated by social workers at the time of placement that the birth parents of 18 children (56 per cent) would not give agreement to adoption.

The adoptive parents were particularly generous in giving their time and sharing their experiences. I met 15 of the 32 adopted children included in the study during the course of the interviews. Only six took part to any extent in the discussions (it being the choice of their adoptive parents to include them).

The basis for adoptive parents participating in the study was that their children had been adopted with "continued contact with birth parents". However, as this was defined either by an agency worker or by the adoptive parents themselves (in the case of those who volunteered to participate through PPIAS), there was great variation in the range and extent of contact which was actually occurring at the time of the interviews. Inevitably there had been changes over time in the pattern of contacts. All the adoptive parents in the study had met one or both birth parents of their adopted children at least once, most before or during the introductions.

The nature and extent of contact

At the time of the interview only two adoptive families were having no contact of any sort with birth parents (although one adoptive couple was willing to exchange information and the other couple had recently requested, on behalf of their two children, a meeting with their birth mother). Adoptive parents in six families, caring for seven children, were maintaining contact by means of letter, telephone calls, gifts, photographs and cards. Adoptive parents in four of these six families had met birth relatives at least once since adoption and did not exclude the possibility of future meetings. Parents in 14 families had adopted 21 children who were having face-to-face contact with one or both birth parents. The frequency of such contact ranged from once every three to four weeks to once or twice a year. Three couples had adopted unrelated children and so each was in touch with two birth families.

There was wide variation in the degree of openness, as measured by the amount of contact between the adoptive parents, the birth parents and the child. The experience of adoptive parents ranged from one or two meetings with birth parent(s) with, subsequently, non face-to-face contact or the possibility of such contact, through to placements in which birth parents were welcome and regular visitors to the home of the adoptive family. Most adoptive families had a level of contact in between these two extremes.

A more significant measure of "openness", however, than the extent of contact with birth parents after adoption, was the attitude of the adoptive parents.

Openness of attitude

I felt that the adoptive parents in all but two of the families had an exceptional degree of openness of attitude which included: being able to appreciate adoption from the child's perspective; acknowledging the importance of the birth family to the child's sense of identity, and the difference between adoptive parenting and biological parenting and being able to express some sympathetic understanding of the feelings of birth parents.

The adoptive parents in these 20 families shared in varying degrees the generosity of spirit and the inclusiveness of the adoptive mother who said: 'When you love your children this must extend to their parents as well'. On the other hand, the "less open" adoptive parents in two families indicated some unease or resentment about their children's contact with birth parents which they acknowledged was not solely related to its impact on the children.

It became clear in the course of the interviews that agency preparation has considerable impact on prospective adopters with regard to openness of attitude. Adoptive parents in only four families had contemplated some form of contact continuing with birth relatives at the time of their approach to the agency. However, adoptive parents in 14 families had been influenced by agency values and practice, either in terms of becoming more open in attitude or in undertaking a placement with a level of contact which they would not otherwise have considered. It was striking that adoptive parents in 13 families had themselves initiated or chosen to maintain contact with birth parents after adoption rather than in accordance with agency expectations. This group of adoptive parents particularly valued the sense of being in control – of not being required to maintain contact because of a court order – but feeling able to be guided by the child's wishes and feelings. In fact there were no instances in this study of a condition of access attached to the Adoption Order.

Adoptive parents' feelings about contact

The majority of adoptive parents interviewed felt positively about having been involved in an adoption with some degree of contact with birth parents. There were 16 families who described benefits for themselves and their children, five who had experienced difficulties with some aspects of contact and one couple who conveyed unease about open adoption but without highlighting any specific concerns. Of the adoptive parents in 16 families who expressed a positive view, eight were currently in touch with birth parent(s) through non face-to-face contact, directly or indirectly, and eight had adopted children who were having face-to-face contact with one or both birth parents, and in six placements, with other birth relatives as well. Eight of these families had other children not adopted on an open basis and they expressed a preference for the open model. The six families who described some difficulties or reservations had adopted children who were maintaining face-to-face contact with birth parent(s) at a frequency of once to three times a year.

All the adoptive parents who described the experience of open adoption as beneficial were open in attitude, and in particular had a view of adoption as "a gift" rather than as "rescue" – they felt able to acknowledge that birth parents had parted with a precious part of themselves. Whether or not they had reservations about maintaining contact, none of the adoptive parents thought their attachment to the child had been delayed or impaired because of contact with birth parents. Indeed several adoptive parents felt that they had perhaps been able to develop a closer attachment to the child in the early stages because of their increased understanding about his or her circumstances and their respect for the birth parents.

With regard to their sense of entitlement, adoptive parents in 16 families had had the reassurance of knowing that the birth parents had given their agreement to adoption. All these families had had personal contact with the birth parents and had thus received approval. This was especially important for six couples for whom the benefit of continuing contact had been that the birth parents, who at the outset of the placement had been opposed to adoption, had eventually given their agreement because they were satisfied that the child wanted to be adopted and was settled in the family. Five of the 16 families had been either chosen by the birth parents, or knew that the birth parents were only giving agreement in relation to that specific placement. Adoptive parents in three families described ways in which contact after adoption had enhanced their sense of entitlement in that it had removed feelings of concern for, or guilt about, birth relatives.

While continuing contact had definitely or probably contributed to all but two of the birth parents who had initially been expected to oppose an adoption application giving agreement, adoptive parents in six families were aware of birth parents having conveyed some sense of disapproval or reluctance about adoption to the child. They had found this stressful. However, the adoptive parents felt that contact had at least provided some opportunity for them to judge the appropriateness of adoption for themselves and that without contact there would probably have been a contested case.

Impact on the adopted children

Adoptive parents were asked to assess the impact on the adopted children of openness. In all but one of the 22 families, the adoptive parents, including four couples who had described some problems associated with contact and the adoptive parents in four families whose children had severe learning difficulties, felt that their children had gained some benefit from face-to-face contact or other links with birth parents. The exception was an older teenager, placed at the age of ten after many years in residential care, whose ambivalent feelings and confusion were compounded by his awareness of his birth mother's disapproval (although she had given agreement to adoption). At an earlier stage in the placement, contact had been terminated but subsequently reinstated.

The areas discussed with the adoptive parents were the child's:

* sense of identity;
* understanding of the circumstances of adoption;
* feeling free to attach to the adoptive family.

The adoptive parents of the five children who had severe learning difficulties did not anticipate that their children would be directly affected by the emotional and psychological aspects of open adoption. These areas were therefore discussed in relation to 27 children.

With the exception of two older teenage boys placed as the ages of ten and 13 respectively, adoptive parents considered that their adopted children had benefited from the contact and/or links with birth parents in that this had contributed to their sense of identity, while not undermining their feelings of security. None of the adoptive parents expressed the view that continuing contact had affected the child's ability to attach and integrate within the family (although one adoptive father thought this may have been true for his daughter when she first joined the family at the age of ten).

In relation to their understanding of the circumstances of adoption, adoptive parents considered that continuing face-to-face or other forms of contact had been helpful for most children. Some had been freed from the sense of responsibility they had felt prior to placement about their entry into care, while for all but two of the children with face-to-face contact, there were fewer fantasies about birth parents. All the adoptive parents believed their adopted children would benefit from the fact that there would be no need for them to search in later years to achieve contact with birth relatives.

Adoptive parents were asked whether continuing contact had assisted the child to feel free to attach to a new family or had impeded this process. Where birth parents of children over the age of two years had indicated approval of the placements, adoptive parents believed that continuing contact had helped the child to attach to them without feeling disloyal to the birth family. The child had not been put in the position of having to choose between being adopted and maintaining contact with the family of origin. Furthermore, the child was reassured that the adoptive family accepted the birth family (and vice versa). The adoptive parents of six children believed that continuing contact was a condition of their agreeing to be adopted.

Of the eight children whose birth parents had either conveyed some disapproval of adoption, although giving agreement to the application, or had withheld agreement (one child) or opposed a freeing application (one child), only one was said not to have attached to his adoptive parents. However, his adoptive mother did not attribute this to contact but to his early damaging experiences and prolonged period in residential care.

The effect on birth parents of continuing contact

Adoptive parents in 13 families (including adoptive parents in three families who were each in touch with two sets of birth parents, having adopted unrelated children) felt able to comment on the impact of open adoption with contact on birth parents. They believed that birth parents in all 16 families had benefited in terms of their acceptance of their loss and their development of self-esteem through their involvement in a more open form of adoption. Some of these placements had been made in very difficult circumstances and the positive outcome for adoptive parents, and, in their view, for the birth parents was a tribute to the generosity and understanding of both adoptive and birth parents.

However, adoptive parents in the study who did not feel able to offer observations about the feelings of birth parents had described situations which would suggest that some birth parents had not been able to adjust to the loss of their child through adoption.

Placements in which adoptive parents were feeling positive about contact

For 24 children living in 16 families, the continued contact with birth parents, whether through face-to-face or other forms of contact, was described as positive in relation to the children's needs. The gains were indirect for the two children with Down's syndrome placed as babies whose adoptive parents felt that their own sense of entitlement and their understanding had been enhanced as a result of contact. Characteristics associated with the placements which adoptive parents viewed positively were:

- the child feeling free to attach to an extent which the adoptive parents found rewarding, and to become integrated into the family;
- the child being aware of the good relationship between the two families, seeing that they accepted each other and that the birth parents approved of the placement;
- the child having been helped by contact to achieve a sense of identity and an understanding of the circumstances leading to adoption;
- the contact with birth parents providing continuity and, in at least four placements, helping the child to make the transition to the new family;
- adoptive and birth parents negotiating arrangements directly and meetings taking place either in the home of the birth family or the adoptive family;
- the birth parent(s) fulfilling an appropriate role so that the child did not experience divided loyalties when maintaining contact with people important to him or her. (The role adopted was generally that of a non-parental relative, such as an aunt, uncle or a more distant member of the extended family.)

These factors contributed to adoptive parents feeling secure and in control. The ages of the 24 children ranged from two weeks to 14 years at placement but only three (excluding children with severe learning difficulties) were aged nine or over.

Placements in which adoptive parents expressed reservations or concerns

There were six placements (involving eight children) in which adoptive parents expressed some difficulties or tension arising from contact. In two cases these difficulties were in the past, in three cases current. In the sixth case general unease with aspects of open adoption was expressed. There were several contrasting features between these and the placements experienced positively in respect of contact:

- One adoptive couple had not attempted to build any relationship with their adopted son's birth mother. The adoptive parents in five other families described tension in their relationship with birth parents, either in the past or currently.

- The birth parents of six of these eight children had conveyed disapproval with the adoption plan and had given agreement only at a very late stage, or, in one case, had withheld agreement. Two birth mothers were described as having burdened the child with their own loss and sadness and were thought not to have relinquished the parental role in that they viewed continuing contact as a route to restoration.
- When asked about the impact of continuing contact on their children, most thought there had been some benefits. However, two were uncertain whether or not their child's attachment and sense of identity had been adversely affected.
- The children in four families met their birth parents on neutral territory with a social worker present. One adoptive couple negotiated directly with the birth parent to take their son to her home. In the sixth family, the social worker initially escorted the child to visit his mother and subsequently he made his own way.
- Six of the children had been separated from their birth parents many years earlier (five while under the age of five) and had then spent periods ranging from four to eight years in residential care.
- All had experienced some early deprivation or abuse.
- All the children had been more than seven years old at time of placement and six had been nine or older.

It is helpful to consider the problems described by these six families in relation to research findings about difficulties in the placement of older children in the UK, especially those with a long history of residential care. Hill *et al* (1988) reported that about one third of the 50 adoptive and permanent foster families in their study in Scotland 'regarded the child's attachment as less than they had hoped for'. Thoburn *et al* (1986) found that children needing contact with birth parents were less likely to be attached to new families whether they had contact or not. And in their summary of the survey through which children in this study were identified, Thoburn and Rowe (1988) stated that age was 'the only factor which seems clearly and consistently associated with breakdown'. (For children aged eight at placement the breakdown rate was 23 per cent and it increased to 40 per cent for children aged 12 to 14).

By contrast with the children whom adoptive parents described as not having attached or having difficulties regarding a sense of identity, there were three boys, placed at the ages of nine, 13 and 14 respectively, whose adoptive parents felt that adoption with contact had worked well. These three boys had fewer identified problems at placement than those adopted by the six families who had described difficulties, and their birth parents were supportive of the plan for adoption.

Practice issues

It is not claimed that this small group of adoptive parents is typical or representative of the wider population of adoptive parents. In addition, it is recognised that the picture conveyed by the adoptive parents was essentially a "snapshot", revealing how it felt at the time of the interview.

Nonetheless, placed alongside the studies available on open adoption from New Zealand and the USA, and UK studies about the placements of children with special needs (Wedge and Thoburn, 1986; Thoburn *et al*, 1986; Hill *et al*, 1988; Rushton *et al*, 1988), this exploratory study can certainly identify some directions for practice:

- Agencies in the past may have underestimated the potential of adoptive parents to develop an openness of attitude because of prevailing views about the necessity for a "clean break". In addition, there may be reluctance on the part of social workers to relinquish some of the power and control conferred by the closed adoption model. A more open adoption model allows birth parents and adoptive parents to participate and to choose what information to share and whether/how to maintain contact after adoption.

- Alternatives to the closed adoption model can assist adoptive parents to achieve 'some kind of kinship with the people who gave "their" child birth' (Rowe, 1971). The study demonstrates that adoptive parents who are willing to maintain some form of contact after adoption can be found.

- The number of children placed under the age of five who were having face-to-face contact with birth parents was unexpected, but they and all but two of the children placed under the age of nine, were described as experiencing no difficulties with contact. Adoptive parents had found that their children could have an attachment to two sets of parents.

- The placement of children and young adults over the age of nine tended to be more complex, mainly as a result of the children's difficulties of adjustment. And yet this is the age group of children for whom open adoption is most often suggested. Certainly open adoption with contact is no panacea for the unresolved feelings of children and birth parents. (However, there were some particularly successful examples of adoption with contact of older children.)

- The study highlighted ways in which birth parents can contribute positively both before and after adoption by conveying to the adoptive parents and to the children their acceptance of the plan for adoption and by maintaining an appropriate role.

- The openness of attitude with which adoptive parents embarked on the placement was significant in that an open attitude can maximise the benefits for the adoptive parents and the child of even limited contact with birth parents. Openness of attitude on the part of adoptive parents did not guarantee that they would experience an open adoption as satisfying, but it did seem to be a prerequisite of enhancing the benefits of contact for the child. This was particularly so with face-to-face contact.

- It was the experience of agencies that contact with non-parental relatives raised similar issues for adoptive parents to those where birth parents were having contact. However, with less potential for role conflict, contact with non-parental relatives was seen as more straightforward.

- While there is insufficient evidence from this or other studies to indicate that open adoption in which birth parents continue to have face-to-face contact after adoption should become the norm, there was general approval from the adoptive parents interviewed for the setting up of meetings between birth parents and adoptive parents; for birth parents having some opportunity to be involved in the choice of family and opportunities for contact to be maintained after adoption.

- The experience of more open adoption for the adoptive parents in the study was closely related to the attitude of the birth parents to adoption, the role they fulfilled and the relationships established within the adoption triangle. This highlights the importance of counselling for all participants and the need for the selection of adoptive parents to take into account the degree of openness which would be appropriate in any given situation.

The findings clearly suggest that a child's need for contact can be met within an adoption placement. The experience of agencies which have developed greater openness in adoption and of the adoptive parents in this study demonstrates that alternatives to the closed adoption model, although more complex for the participants, emotionally and practically, and more demanding of the agency, can enrich the lives of the adopted children, their adoptive parents and their birth relatives.

Joan Fratter re-interviewed adoptive parents in 18 of the 22 families in 1991 and found that the conclusions drawn from the interviews described above were broadly confirmed. She also interviewed 15 of the children and young people adopted by some of the families and five birth parents. They highlighted from different perspectives the benefits which contact with birth relatives can confer. The findings from these later interviews are described in Adoption with Contact: Implications for policy and practice, *published by BAAF in 1996.*

Since this paper was written, the provisions of the Children Act 1989 have been implemented and a court may make an order for contact in adoption cases under section 8. However, in general, courts are unwilling to impose a contact order on adoptive parents against their wishes.

References

Adcock M and White R (eds), *Terminating Parental Contact*, Discussion Series No 2, pp 14–24, Association of British Adoption and Fostering Agencies, 1980.

Adoption & Fostering, 7:1, p 3, House of Commons Select Committee (editorial).

Fratter J, Rowe J, Sapsford D and Thoburn J, *Permanent Family Placement*, BAAF, 1991.

Heywood J, *Children in Care*, 3rd ed, Routledge & Kegan Paul, 1978.

Hill M, Hutton S and Easton S, 'Adoptive parenting – plus and minus', *Adoption & Fostering*, 12:2, pp 17–23, 1988.

Howell D and Ryburn M, 'New Zealand: new ways to choose adopters', *Adoption & Fostering*, 11:4, pp 38–40, 1987.

O'Collins M, 'The influence of Western adoption laws on customary adoption in the Third World', in Bean P (ed), *Adoption: Essays in social policy, law and sociology*, pp 288–302, Tavistock, 1984.

Rillera M J and Kaplan S, *Co-operative Adoption: A handbook*, Westminster, Triadoption Publications California, 1985, USA.

Rowe J, 'The reality of the adoptive family', in Tod R J N (ed), *Social Work in Adoption*, Longman, 1971.

Rushton A, Treseder J and Quinton D, *New Parents for Older Children*, BAAF, 1988.

Short R (Chair), *Children in Care: Second report from the Social Services Committee, session 1983–84*, HMSO, 1984.

Thoburn J, Murdoch A and O'Brien A, *Permanence in Child Care*, Blackwell, 1986.

Thoburn J and Rowe J, 'A snapshot of permanent family placement', *Adoption & Fostering*, 12:3, pp 29–34, 1988.

Triseliotis J, 'Adoption with contact', *Adoption & Fostering*, 9:4, pp 19–24, 1985.

Wedge P and Thoburn J (eds), *Finding Families for 'Hard-to-place' Children*, BAAF, 1986.

11 Openness in adoption

Murray Ryburn

Murray Ryburn is Director of Social Work at the University of Birmingham and currently on a three-year leave of absence in New Zealand.

This article was published in Adoption & Fostering, 14:1, 1990.

Joan Fratter's article in the last issue of *Adoption & Fostering* (13:4) is important for several reasons, but not least for its significant contribution to the still very slight body of research on openness in adoptions. The research findings it describes confirm the well-established experience of many of us who have worked in the adoption field in New Zealand. I find it encouraging to think that in some respects our tradition may be able to inform practice here, so that colonialism need not be entirely a one-way exchange!

This article seeks to draw out some of the possible explanations for the way in which adoption without contact has been customary in this country, while *pakeha* (white) adoption in New Zealand has developed so that some degree of continuing contact is now the norm rather than the exception. It will also take a look at what changes may be necessary if it were to become a widely accepted way of managing adoptions here.

A restrictive view of kinship

Any answers to why closed adoption has developed can at best be speculative, but it seems nonetheless an important question to pose, for as adopted people have long been telling us, our identity in the future will be shaped by how we understand the past.

Traditional boundaries of kinship have been set by the degree of blood relatedness or consanguinity so that, for example, this has historically been the key determinant of the right to inherit both real and personal property. There was an obvious reluctance within such a tradition to include, within the bounds of family, children who were not blood related. Over a hundred years ago Engels (1972) referred to the restrictiveness of ideas of kinship when he wrote of the form of family as it had developed here and elsewhere as the 'monogamous family' where the emphasis was on the need to 'produce children of undisputed paternity'. It is noteworthy that as recently as last year the new Children Act (1989) deemed it necessary to make specific that "family" may include those who are not blood relatives.

It is not surprising that adoption legislation in the past was founded on a legal fiction – one which purported to extinguish all ties between a child and its birth family, so that the illusion was created that the child was a child of its adoptive family *as if by birth*. The development of the whole process which was called "matching" where every effort was made to eliminate the differences of heredity, is probably also witness to a desire to treat adoptive kinship as if it were birth kinship instead.

The Tomlin Report, which gave rise to adoption legislation, showed little real enthusiasm for changing the bounds of family kinship. However, the cost of relief under the Poor Law had risen appreciably following the war, as it did again after the General Strike, and adoption offered an easy way, as Kirk and McDaniel (1984, p 76) have pointed out, to transfer financial responsibility from the 'public purse to the private'.

First consideration

There are other factors, besides a wish to represent adoptive kinship as the same as birth kinship, which can help explain why adoption has developed as customarily excluding all birth family contact.

Adoption legislation is now founded on the "first consideration" principle, which differs little from the "paramountcy" principle in other legislation in imposing a legislative duty to promote first the best interests of children or young people. The assumption that the best interests of a child are readily separable from those of their birth families is seldom challenged. In attempting to establish the best interests of children, social workers have often, perhaps, sought to protect children from information relating to the circumstances of their births that was deemed stigmatising or potentially harmful to their sense of self-worth. Limiting the information given and excluding the likelihood of any further contact with birth families was one way of doing this.

In a climate where social workers rather than consumers were (and still are) expected to know best, the sort of advice recently offered me by one adopted person: 'only by knowing it all can I know who I am', usually went unnoticed. To some extent this has changed so that more comprehensive information is now usually given to adoptive parents regarding their child's background. However, there is still a widely held belief that information filtered through social workers, and given on a once only basis at the time of adoption, will be enough to answer all of a child's need for information as he or she grows.

Permanency planning
In protecting the best interests of children many social workers, particularly perhaps those now an age to be in management positions, have been greatly influenced by the permanence movement as it developed in the later 1970s and early 1980s. The permanency principle, in practice, often replaced the tyranny of drift with that of birth family contact. It did so in the quite unfounded belief (apart from the limited clinical impressions of some practitioners like Goldstein, Freud and Solnit, 1973, 1979) that children could only make secure new attachments when old attachments were severed. Research evidence, including Joan Fratter's, increasingly indicates that the reverse is in fact true. (See, for example, Thoburn *et al*, 1986.)

Identity formation
There has also been a reliance on a concept of identity formation which has emphasised the importance of a loving environment to the exclusion of what Triseliotis has called the need for 'a knowledge about one's background and personal history' (1983). This has perhaps been accompanied by a failure to appreciate that we all have a relationship with our past, whether or not this is informed by knowledge, and that a relationship founded in the real world of direct contact with birth families could be most likely, as Joan Fratter's study indicates, to help those in adoptions in setting a course for the future. Without such contact it can be very difficult for some adopted people to gain any realistic feel for their birth families, as this young woman describes:

When I first met my mother we just stood and looked at each other in disbelief. It was so difficult in that suddenly she was a real person and so I had to let go of all the sort of ideals of what my mother would be like. You know I had this picture of her – she'd be this all-perfect woman – and then there she was and it was just so hard to come to grips with her being a person.

Clean break theory

The termination of all birth family links has also been founded on the "clean break" theory, which is that adoptive parents will attach best to their children if there is no contact and that birth parents will come to terms with their loss more readily too. The "clean break" idea seems to rely more on proverbial wisdom like "out of sight, out of mind", than anything else. Adoptive parents face constant reminders, with or without contact, that their children were not born to them.

I really didn't have any thoughts about mothers until we actually got the children. We went to the hospital to pick up these gorgeous babies, but then we couldn't not feel that they had come from somewhere. And you can't divorce yourself from the person that brought your child into the world, no matter how hard you try.

The research of Winkler and Van Keppel (1984) and others indicates just how much relinquishing parents in adoptions without contact do not forget, and highlights the impossibility of grieving a living loss, as this birth mother described to me:

If I could have any information it would be better than nothing. Even to know that he died when he was three months old would be better than to have had 15 years of not knowing. It's intolerable.

The first New Zealand adoption law was passed in 1881. It contained no intention to extinguish the relationship between adopted children and their birth parents, but sought only to give legal protection to adoptive relationships. Children retained their birth names. There has in fact only been a relatively short period in New Zealand's adoption history from 1955 to 1985, when there was very restricted access to identifying information. This was largely in response to arguments of the 1950s and 1960s about the need to protect adopted people from the stigma of illegitimacy. Between 1881 and 1955 any party to an adoption could search the court records in respect of any specific adoption, and a copy of the Adoption Order, with information identifying birth parents was also made available to adopting parents (Griffiths, 1981). Full adult rights to birth records were restored to birth parents and adopted people in the 1985 Adult Adoption Information Act and there are now moves to extend access to information to siblings and adoptive parents. Of 8,500 reunions facilitated by this legislation in the past three years, there have been only six serious complaints. For more than a decade, before the recent legislation was passed, there had been an established and successful tradition of adoption reunions without the benefit of ready access to records. This tradition paralleled the growing openness that was to be found in adoption placements. It is worth noting that openness in adoption placements flourishes in New Zealand with the context of restrictive legislation that was passed in 1955, and it is a good example of how practice can lead, and need not be fettered by, legislation.

Maori tradition
New Zealand's adoption history is, however, much older than the *pakeha* history. The Maori have always shared the care of children among members of the wider family. Children of Maori parents have never been seen as belonging to birth parents alone – they have been seen as belong- ing also to the *whanau*, the extended family, the *hapu*, the sub-tribe, the *iwi*, the tribe, and ultimately to the whole Maori people. Maori parents who were just as likely to be married as single gave their children into the care of others for a variety of reasons. They did it, for example, to relieve stress on their own family unit, to provide companionship for someone living alone, to comfort a couple who were childless or mourn- ing the loss of a child. Perhaps the key reason, though, was to ensure the passing of knowledge and wisdom from one generation to another so that, for example, a grand-daughter may be adopted by her grandmother, or a grandson by his grandfather.

The idea of adoption as a way of caring for unwanted children was quite alien to this tradition. The gift of a child in adoption was made in consultation with the *whanau* and received in the spirit of *aroha* or life. The generosity of birth parents was recognised and acknowledged.

Perhaps the most important feature of all adoptions was that children grew up with continuing access to their birth families. The Maori model of adoption had, at its heart, twin beliefs. The first is summed up in an ancient proverb, '*nga taonga o nga tupuna tukua iho kia koe*' (the treasures of your ancestors must be passed on to you). Ancestral origins were the foundation of identity, both public and private. The second belief was that the *whakapapa*, the former generations, had a vital role to play in linking the past to the present and the future for the tribe as a whole. To break or to bury this connection inflicts a grave and irreplaceable loss on both the adopted person and the community into which the child is born. (see Rockel and Ryburn, 1988.)

Pakeha adoption

It is impossible to assess the influence that Maori adoption practice had on *pakeha* adoption in New Zealand. Certainly the Maori tradition was viewed as important and the Maori retained a parallel system in adoption outside *pakeha* adoption until after 1955. New children's legislation passed last year (The Children, Young Persons and their Families Act) with its emphasis on family, rather than social worker and court decision-making, certainly owes much to the Maori tradition. The value Maori people place on knowing about ancestral origins and their emphasis on inclusive rather than exclusive family and community relationships have doubtless influenced trends in *pakeha* adoption.

New Zealand has always prided itself on its reforming history in social policy, and when adoption practice began to become more open again, after the period of secrecy in the 1950s and 60s, it was especially in response to consumer demands for reform. (See, for example, Shawyer, 1979.) Today a philosophy of openness is pervasive in most *pakeha* adoption practice in New Zealand. This means that some form of continuing contact in adoption is very much the norm rather than the exception, and parties to adoption recognise that openness has potentially significant advantages for them.

In conducting extensive research interviews for a book on adoption (Rockel and Ryburn, 1988) a colleague and I found that those who were part of an open adoption confirmed the gains of openness experienced by those interviewed by Joan Fratter (*Adoption & Fostering*, 13:4).

Adoptive parents described feeling they had a much better yardstick for assessing their child's development so that they felt more confident in their parenting. They reported satisfaction at being able to see that their children's full information needs were met and felt that contact was very important to their children's sense of identity. They spoke of feeling confirmed by the knowledge that their parenting had the sanction of their child's birth parents. They also spoke of having been helped more fully to come to terms with the fact that they were parenting by adoption and not by birth.

Birth parents spoke of open adoption as providing tangibility to their loss so that, unlike the grief of a closed adoption where it was impossible, as time went by, to have any sort of image of their child to grieve, they could instead begin to come to terms with their loss and to resolve it. They spoke of the reassurance of knowing where their child was, how they were getting on, and of the comfort of knowing that if they met they would know each other. Birth parents also spoke of being able still to offer their child something in the future and reported how important it was to them that they knew that their children would have positive news and images of them.

Adopted people spoke of how having contact from very early on made it easy for them because they could grow up always knowing about their birth families and feeling comfortable with that knowledge. They spoke of the reassurance that came with hearing explanations directly from their birth parents and feeling closer to their adoptive parents as a result of birth family contact.

A new model of social work practice
What the spirit of openness has meant for adoption practice in New Zealand has been a need for social workers to find new ways of using their training, expertise and skill. Ways that do not accord greater value to their opinions than to anyone else's, so that professionals are not viewed as knowing better than the consumers of adoption policy and practice. What it calls for is a different model of adoption practice where social workers become less concerned with making "objective" assessments (something there is no evidence of our being able to do anyway) and become much more facilitators to a process.

Birth parent choice

This is partly reflected in the practice of allowing birth families choice in the placements of their children. Many New Zealand adoptions are adoptions of young children, and guardianship is often a preferred way of offering permanence to older children. Birth parent choice is a feature of virtually all agency adoptions and many private adoptions, which are still legal under the 1955 Act. Birth parents are given profiles of a number of possible placements for their child which fit, so far as is possible, the ideas they have about a suitable family for their child. It is worth noting that birth fathers, who have long been marginalised in the adoption process, are now much more actively involved.

The information, or profiles, on which an initial decision is made by birth parents is increasingly being supplied solely (as it was at the agency where I worked) by prospective adopters themselves. Thus it is not information as perceived and filtered through the eyes of an assessing social worker.

After making an initial decision, on the basis of the profiles, there will be the opportunity for the birth parents and the prospective adopters to meet. How and when this is arranged is determined by the wishes of the parties themselves and the social worker role is one of negotiation. At such meetings plans will be agreed for whatever continuing contact the parties wish to have. This will vary widely from extensive to quite limited contact, and is an agreement based on goodwill because the parties to the adoption perceive it to be in the best interests of all of them. The key feature of any such agreement is that it has a flexibility that will allow future negotiation for changed circumstances. In this way adoption parallels much more closely other sorts of relationships we have in life.

The possibilities for continuing contact that customarily exist in New Zealand would, I am sure, make for a far less adversarial system if they were adopted here. Parents who accept that they cannot effectively parent their children and still love them can, I believe, feel almost obliged to contest an adoption in the courts, in a system where they know that the complete severance of contact is likely. This may well seem to be the only way to try to salvage something of their self-esteem and to not lose forever a place in their children's lives.

Three other important qualities are brought to permanent placements by a system of birth parent choice. As one adoptive parent put it to me, 'I feel legitimated in my role of caring for someone else's child by knowing that I was chosen for him by his birth family'. While for birth parents, as this young mother put it during the course of the interview,

If I hadn't had a choice, I guess I would have felt that I'd lost every-thing for nothing but now that I've chosen her family I don't feel so helpless any more. I can see where she is and I've still got something through our contact that I can offer her as she grows up. And I don't have to worry about her because I know that she's alive and well.

Finally, with what you may consider is a fitting irony, the old idea of "choosing" takes on a new and different meaning. Children grow up feel-ing confirmed in their adoptive families knowing that they were indeed chosen for a particular family. They know, however, that they were chosen not by their adoptive parents, but rather their adoptive parents were chosen for them by their birth parents. What this also means is that there is, already established, the basis for a relationship upon which continuing contact can be built. It is a new sort of matching or linking that perhaps helps to avoid the sorts of dilemmas faced, for example, by this adopted person:

Any of us who are not adopted may have grown up in our birth families feeling quite different from our parents or brothers or sisters. When this is combined with the knowledge that we are adopted I think it can take on a different and potentially harmful significance. Know-ing, however, that your adoptive parents were chosen by your birth parents greatly diminishes, in my view, the likely significance that any such differences will assume. The knowledge that their adoptive parents were so chosen is one thing that most children and young people adopted in recent years in New Zealand now have.

Self-assessment by adopters

The other side of greater openness in adoption centres on the creation of the sort of educative environment that David Kirk (1964) was speaking about all those years ago in which adopters can be helped to decide for themselves if adoption is right for them. One agency's approach to this was described by myself and a colleague, Deborah Howell, in an earlier article in this journal (1987). It was founded on the belief that there is no evidence at all to suggest that social workers have any particular expertise to make accurate assessments which could have future predictive value concerning what placements will best meet the needs of children and young people. In the absence of such an expertise the whole notion of any sort of objectivity in assessment is a spurious one which leads social workers to assume a responsibility for "knowing best", which they can never discharge. The programme of self-assessment, set alongside a system of birth parent choice and openness in placements, represents an attempt to empower the parties to adoption themselves. It marks a radical departure from a model in which the social worker is expert, and re-shapes the social work task as one of negotiation and facilitation.

Could such a model work here?

The research of Joan Fratter indicates that openness in adoption can and does work well in this country. Perhaps this heralds a move towards the abandonment of a model which accords all power to social workers, and begins to empower and give responsibility to birth families and adoptive families. For this to happen on any large scale there will need to be an education programme that challenges first and foremost much current thinking among social workers and panel members. Ideally, such a programme will be led, as it was in New Zealand, by adoption consumers, people who are able to say, ' Thank you for trying to promote and protect my best interests, but I don't want the sort of protectiveness that you are offering. What I want, instead, is for you to hold the door ajar so that at some stage, whenever that may be, we can negotiate our own relationships in this adoption in the ways that we want to, in the ways that you take for granted in your own life and in a way that recognises that nothing stays the same.'

Such a programme will need to challenge many myths, such as the notion of objective assessment; the myth that birth family connections must be severed before new attachments can be made; the myth that love is a finite resource that cannot be spread between more than one family, without being diluted or diminished; the myth that adoptive parents cannot be found who can make, with our help as facilitators, as good an assessment as we can of their ability to parent someone else's child; the myth that adoptive parents cannot be found who can embrace the idea of continuing contact with their child's birth family; the myth that social workers can identify, better than birth parents, the best placement for their child; the myth that you can give a child information about their birth family without entering, seen or unseen, into a relationship with that family which will last their lifetime.

References

Engels F, *The Origin of the Family, Private Property and the State*, Lawrence & Wishart, 1972.

Fratter J, 'How adoptive parents feel about contact with birth parents after adoption', *Adoption & Fostering*, 13:4, pp 18–26, 1989.

Goldstein J, Freud A and Solnit A, *Beyond the Best Interests of the Child*, Free Press, 1979, USA.

Griffiths K, *Adoption: procedure – documentation – statistics, New Zealand 1881–1981*. Published by the author, 1981.

Howell D and Ryburn M, 'New Zealand: new ways to choose adopters', *Adoption & Fostering*, 11:4, pp 38–40, 1987.

Kirk D, *Shared Fate*, Collier–Macmillan, 1964.

Kirk H and McDaniels S, 'Adoption policy and practice in Great Britain and North America', *Journal of Social Policy*, 13 part I, 75–84.

Rockel J and Ryburn M, *Adoption Today: Change and choice in New Zealand*, Heinemann Reed, 1988.

Shawyer J, *Death by Adoption*, Cicada Press, 1979.

Thoburn J, Murdock A and O'Brien A, *Permanence in Child Care*, Basil Blackwell, 1986.

Triseliotis J, 'Identity and security in adoption and long-term fostering', *Adoption & Fostering*, 7:1, pp 22–32, 1983.

Winkler R and Van Keppel M, 'Relinquishing mothers in adoption: their long term adjustment', *Institute of Family Studies Monograph No. 3*, Melbourne, 1984, Australia.

12 'Openness' in adoption or open adoption – a Black perspective

Ratna Dutt and Arunda Sanyal

Ratna Dutt is currently Director of the Race Equality Unit, advising local authorities on race equality in social work. She has several years' experience in generic social work including working as a team manager of an ethnic minorities team in a London local authority. She has authored and co-authored articles and publications in the field of social work and black communities.

Arunda Sanyal is currently Acting Head of Children's Services with the London Borough of Tower Hamlets. She has several years' experience in generic and specialist social work including advising on policy and implementation of services to black and minority ethnic families.

This paper was published in Adoption & Fostering, 15:4, 1991.

Any debate or dialogue around services to black people must be seen within a context. In Britain where black people are discriminated against in every major aspect of their daily lives, where black children are racially abused in the streets and schools of Britain, the context must of necessity be racism. For racism affects all nlack people, affects all black and white relationships, and often results in white people having a distorted view of black reality.*

We share the view expressed by Harris (1991) that, 'In the light of racist values which exist in British society, the professionalism of white workers in general needs to be questioned at every level'.

Our contention is that the body of knowledge and the value system which form the tools of the white professional's practice are influenced and informed by racist ideology – an ideology that views black peoples, their experiences, their cultures as negative and weak. In spite of equal

---

* The term "black" is used to refer to people of African and South-East Asian descent wherever their country of origin. It includes people who have one black parent.

opportunity polices and/or race equality policies, white professionals have, to date, not been successful in really challenging the core of their knowledge and value base. The result is practice with black people that has no clear focus. The focus can change from vain over-reliance on cultural explanations, to underestimation of the effects of culture, to believing only policies will change practices, to believing self/race awareness will throw light on the problem. While the struggle goes on, practice with black children and their families continues to consistently fail those children and their families. The outcome of work in black communities is one in which a disproportionate number of black young people are locked up within the juvenile justice system; black adults are locked into psychiatric hospitals, and black children and young people are locked into the care system. There is enough evidence now to show that while the controlling aspect of social work practice disproportionately affects black communities, the caring and welfare aspects very rarely touch their lives. The outcome of white professionalism is one in which black professionals are devalued and their contributions marginalised or only given credibility when articulated in the writings of or voiced by white "professionals".

This devaluation results in black professionals not being heard or acknowledged and is nowhere as stark as within the debates around the placement needs of black children. These debates have pushed white professionals into demanding research and more research to prove that black children are best placed with black families – research which pretends to be both objective and value free. We suggest that social work research is neither objective nor value free and indeed is often used to maintain the status quo. We suggest that the outcome of any research in the social care field will depend on the hypotheses, the samples, methodology and analysis. We ask that the profession, and academics within the profession, examine the motivations that lead to such research, when conversely the same amount of energy and resources are not expended to ensure that every black child has a suitable black substitute family. We believe (Dutt and Ahmad, 1990/91) that,

> The black experience of research to date has generally been a negative one. It also has a long history. Stemming from "scientific"

research projects of the sixteenth century which "proved" black people were less intelligent than white people – based on data on brain, size, height, etc., to present-day research which informs us that black people are genetically more likely to be schizophrenic.

Research has frequently reinforced racist assumptions and stereotypes, which have viewed black people as having needs and as victims, without acknowledging their strengths.

Experience (and indeed research) has shown that research on black communities does not lead to change of a positive nature. It does not benefit black people, either with the process of research, nor in terms of service development.

Research has reinforced the notion of black people as objects of interest, but not from a value which is one of care or concern.

This is the context within which we examine concepts such as adoption and open adoption and how we view the white professional interpretation of these concepts. Before we move into that, however, we need to look at the process whereby the actions and practices of white professionals result in disproportionate numbers of black children in a system that often results in "no care".

The role of social workers involved in working with children and families is essentially to differentiate between "functional" and "non-functional" families and thereby ascertain the welfare of the child/ children in that family. This is arrived at by assessing and evaluating the quality of familial relationships, parental capability and the child-rearing practices the parents engage in. Based on this information, according to the assessors' interpretation, certain vital decisions are made such as: whether the child is at risk; whether the child needs protection, and whether they should be removed from home. In a society which views black people as inferior and in a profession which has focused on the weaknesses, and interpreted strengths as weaknesses, in black families, one must question the validity of such assessments. Assessments which, even when applied to many white families are fraught with problems, must by definition be highly problematic when applied to black families. It begs questions about:

- Definition of the child's best interest;
- The European concept of family;
- Whose definition of what is acceptable parenting and what child-rearing practice is right and acceptable?

"Open adoption" – a black perspective

We would like now to move the focus to the title of this paper, a black perspective on "open adoption". So what is a black perspective? Bandana Ahmad in her book, *Black Perspectives in Social Work*, suggests that a black perspective is . . . 'a statement against "white norms"; it is an expression of assertion that cannot be bound by semantic definition . . . The motivation that energises a black perspective is rooted in the principles of racial equality and justice. The articulation that voices a black perspective is part of a process that is committed to replacing the white distortion of black reality with black experience.' We believe that a black perspective in adoption or open adoption questions the status quo and white norms. We therefore feel it necessary to critically examine the white professional's perception of adoption, openness and the concept of the adoption triangle within openness. We believe that all these concepts, and practices which stem from these concepts, are fraught with problems and contradictions for all children. More often than not the problems and contradictions are highlighted and brought into focus when the subject is a black child. To start with the concept of adoption – the purpose of adoption is to find a permanent or secure home for children who cannot be cared for by their birth parents. It is a total transfer from one to the other. It is also a legal and artificial relationship between adopters and adoptees. This was apparently done to prevent birth families claiming back their children at a later date and to enable the adopting family to establish and feel secure in a new relationship. In other words, the assumption is that the new relationship cannot happen without doing away completely with the old. In this scenario the sympathy would appear to be more with the adopters than the children. Indeed, one of the objectives of the Adoption Law of 1926 was to enable white young middle-class, infertile married couples to have children by virtue of taking illegitimate white healthy babies. The babies were matched to the family in terms of general physical appearance. These ideas have persisted and still form the ideological basis of present practice.

By the 1970s the number of white healthy babies relinquished for adoption had declined to a low level. A number of factors contributed to this situation: the social acceptance of illegitimate babies, the access to family planning clinics and availability of contraceptives, acceptance of single parent families and public benefits. However, the demand for babies was still there and it was quickly realised that the black population was a likely source. This was the first time that attention focused on black healthy and attractive babies. They were adopted by white middle-class couples, whereas the older children and those with special needs remained in care in residential institutions. This was the beginning of transracial adoption. Professional thinking at this time began to change and practice seemed to become more child focused.

Research also confirmed that it was detrimental to children's welfare and development for them to remain in long-term institutional care, and that family placements were more desirable. Adoption was felt to be the best possible option and proved to be a viable practice. The idea was then sold to white prospective adopters.

However, the practice still continued within the same legal framework. Therefore, although in theory the service became more child focused it did not move away from the notion of total transplant from one family to another and a clean break from the birth families. Contact with or access to the children's family of origin were terminated. The justification for this was said to be in the best interests of the children. It was felt that the children would settle down better and attach more quickly to adopters.

False notion of "openness"

Current social work thinking is moving towards the idea and practice of "open adoption". This "openness" refers only to giving the child more information about his/her earlier life through the use of life story books, telling, post-adoption counselling and access to birth records. However, even given this flexibility, the adoption arrangements are still made within the existing legal framework, and the transfer from one family to another. It would seem that, in spite of changed thinking and new evidence around the whole subject of adoption, much of the fundamental principles remain static, very much creating the syndrome of "new wine in an old bottle". Within this kind of thinking the whole issue of power differentials is neither explored nor addressed. This creates a false notion of "openness" and equity among the three parties that are said to represent the adoption triangle, i.e. child, birth family and adoptive family. Furthermore it fails to acknowledge the power of the professional – a major party in this equation. The very way in which the three sides of the triangle are viewed as separate entities, isolated from each other, is problematic. Given that the substitute families are inside an ecological environment, and that of the birth family surrounds the children, it is difficult to envisage how it is possible to separate and remove the children in isolation and expect them to settle in an alien family environment. It is also difficult to understand the notion of openness in adoption when true partnership between all those involved in the triangle does not exist. An inextricable part of this partnership is the actions of the professionals who are supposed to act as catalysts and monitors of the process. If true partnership is to become a reality, and secrecy is to be a word of the past, and openness is to become a meaningful concept of the future, then professionals need to question the very basis of their beliefs and values.

Lessons from black communities

We suggest that lessons be learnt from the experiences of and functions within black communities. Adoption and fostering, contrary to white professionals' views, are not new concepts for black families. Black families have for decades looked after children who are not their own, and continue to do so now. The process is open and stems from the belief that where birth families are experiencing difficulty in caring for their children, then those children can be cared for by someone else. It is based on shared understanding, equal partnership and commitment. The children are fully aware of the arrangements and therefore do not feel insecure or undermined, and do not have to deal with any divided loyalties. Most Black families, whether they be African, Caribbean or

Asian, will have in their families or know of examples of families where children are "adopted" in the social, not the legal, sense.

Notwithstanding the fact that in this society the state, in the guise of a professional, intervenes in the process of adoption, it is possible to enter into a shared understanding and more equal partnership. For this to happen there needs to be a fundamental shift in social work thinking around this issue. We suggest that certain factors need serious consideration, such as:

- Assessment of what is meant by permanency;
- A different assessment process of permanent substitute carers and the role of those carers;
- Counselling of the substitute carers to enable understanding and importance of continuity;
- Involvement of birth families at every stage of their children's future plans;
- Involvement of children in every stage of their future.

It is worth remembering that the past, present and future are inextricably linked for all human beings and to pretend that one part can be forgotten for the sake of convenience denies reality.

The debate around same-race placement has, we believe, brought to the fore the importance of "roots" and "identity", vital to any meaningful debate on openness. This is an important contribution that black people in general, and black professionals in particular, have contributed to the development of "good practice" plans for children.

We conclude by suggesting that white professionals need to address the models and methods developed so far which interpret the world through the eyes of white Europeans only. We ask that they begin by examining their own values and beliefs that view "the other" with a distorted vision. We suggest that practice with black children/families will only improve when white professionals come to black communities with an understanding and objective view of black reality. The starting point is perhaps the valuing of black contributions and acknowledging that,

Everyone likes to give as well as to receive. No-one wishes only to receive all the time. We have taken much from your culture . . . I wish

you had taken something from our culture . . . for there were some good and beautiful things in it.

(Unknown Native American source)

References

Ahmad B, *Black Perspectives in Social Work*, Venture Press, 1990.

Dutt R and Ahmad B, 'Griffiths and the black perspectives', *Social Work and Social Sciences Review*, 2, 1990.

Harris V, 'Values of social work in the context of British society in conflict with anti-racism', in *Setting the Context for Change*, Northern Curriculum Development Project, CCETSW, 1991.

Section IV
Ethnic and cultural issues

This section looks particularly at two major concerns in contemporary adoption – transracial and intercountry adoption. They are linked by the one-way nature of the "traffic": children from poor families (often but by no means all black) moving to prosperous white families, either within their own country or across national boundaries and continents. Different views co-exist about terminology and ideas tend to change, but for present purposes we shall use the term black to refer to children from a diversity of minority ethnic backgrounds who share the common experience of racism. This is usually taken to include children of mixed parentage, who are disproportionately represented in foster and residential care (Bebbington and Miles, 1989; Barn, 1993). It is important and a legal duty, though, to take account of children's own views of their identity. **Tizard and Phoenix (1994)** suggest that most children of mixed parentage have a definite and positive sense of themselves which often embraces both sides of their background (see also Cooper, 1995). Banks (1995) found that preconceptions among both white and black workers did not do justice to the heterogeneous experience and identifications of mixed parentage children.

Up to the 1970s a "colour-blind" approach was common in which white adopters and professionals believed that it was a "good thing" to offer a new multi-cultural home for black children in need. This was seen as an advance on earlier practice when some white families had not wanted to foster or adopt a black child out of hostility or shame. However, as **Hayes (1987)** argued, transracial placements denied the richness and value of children's own race, culture and history. It has now become very widely accepted among practitioners that it is normally best for a black child to grow up in a family of similar background. This has, of course, always normally been the case for white children. Such matching enables black children to have continuity of heritage, learn how to deal with racism, and have daily contact with positive black role-models. This position has at times been much misunderstood and criticised by some politicians and sections of the media.

Small (1991) wrote of the development of transracial adoption as an issue in this country. He noted that inappropriate or negative stereotypes of black families by white practitioners had hindered both effective family support and the recruitment of black foster carers and adopters. Largely with the help of black practitioners, this position has now changed dramatically. Recognition of the strengths and values of black families and communities has substantially increased the availability of alternative care resources for looked after black children, although gaps remain. An important ingredient in this success has been to establish good links with community networks and groups, including those based on common religious beliefs (**Hayes 1987**; Barn *et al*, 1997; Singh, 1997).

A vexed issue which has dogged the debate about placements for black children concerns the nature and findings of research. **Small** argued that most studies have been flawed in their methods, while the questions and findings were biased. Many early studies did not include black researchers, hence risking that children would not be able to express themselves honestly. Also much of the research and theorising has been American, so it does not always apply to the different history and ethnic composition of the UK.

The first significant British study on the issue by Gill and Jackson (1983) produced mixed findings which have been repeated subsequently here and in other countries (Dalen and Saetersdal, 1987; Simon and Altstein, 1995; Rushton and Minnis, 1997). On the one hand, the sample of young black people brought up by white adopters generally had good relationships with the family, high self-esteem and were doing well academically. On the other hand, they mostly identified as white and had little connection with other black people or their own traditions. Although the outcomes seemed to be mostly positive, it should be remembered that unsatisfactory placements are unlikely to be included in research samples. Now that same-race placements have been the norm for some years, it is important to assess their outcomes, taking account of young people's identity and community integration.

As noted in the introduction, at the same time as transracial placements were rapidly decreasing in domestic adoptions, transcultural and often transracial placements arranged internationally have grown significantly. These can be seen as a humanitarian response to the needs of children with otherwise grim prospects, but there are major problems of exploitation from the perspective of relinquishing countries (Ngabonziza, 1991) and of adjustment for children and adopters in this country. In countries like Sweden and the Netherlands, virtually all adoptions over the last two decades have been intercountry. Careful systems and regulations have been set up to guard against placements of children who could be cared for in their own countries. Adopters receive special preparation for the particular issues involved in caring for a child with a different linguistic and cultural background, and often a history of health and attachment problems (Verhulst, 1990; Selman, 1991).

In contrast, central and local government in the UK were ill-prepared for the growth in intercountry adoptions, which followed high profile media attention to children in so-called "orphanages" in Romania, China and elsewhere: few of the children were in fact orphans (Reich, 1993; Watts and Dickens, 1996). **Selman and White (1994)** described how the British system seemed to satisfy nobody. Would-be adopters felt unsupported by the authorities and had to "go it alone". Partly as a result, many children came into the country "through the back door", i.e. without proper permission but with immigration officials turning a blind eye. Professionals were dismayed at such a lack of proper regulation. As a short-term remedy, the Government produced regulations which required local authorities to provide reports when requested. A White Paper was introduced in 1993 aiming to overcome some of the difficulties, particularly by accrediting and requiring existing agencies to develop effective services. As we have seen, four years later no corresponding legislation has emerged. If and when this comes, **Selman and White** proposed that a small number of specialist agencies should be approved to deal with international adoptions, rather than dispersing responsibility among many who will not have adequate experience and skills in this area.

13 Placing black children

Mary Hayes

Mary Hayes was a Specialist Adoption and Fostering Officer, Derbyshire Social Services Department, when she gave this paper at a BAAF seminar on placing babies for adoption in March 1987. She is currently Director of the Meaningful Employment Needs Domestic Support (MENDS) project in the USA.

This paper was published in Adoption & Fostering, 11:3, 1987.

In terms of preparing black families to foster and adopt children, black families are no different from white families. However, in order to be successful, black families respond to and will interact more freely with the social worker who reflects their image. Whenever I speak to groups made up predominantly of white people about the issues and needs of black children requiring substitute care, it becomes a necessary prerequisite to delve into some of the history of black people in Britain and to highlight some misunderstandings which are brought about by ignorance or lack of knowledge of black families and our culture. Additionally I like to emphasise the attitudinal changes which are slowly beginning to happen throughout England. Attitudinal changes are happening because the level of awareness and understanding that Britain is a multiracial society is beginning to sink in.

However, the misplacement or transracial placement of black children into white families – never the other way around – is not considered by the black community throughout Britain to be an appropriate demonstration of attitudinal change. It is common knowledge to social services departments that throughout Britain black children without permanent families generally outnumber all other children in need of adoption or fostering. It is also common knowledge that transracial adoption has been accepted by white social work practice for over 20 years in Britain. This paper will attempt to address both of these issues and highlight some effective recruitment techniques used in the USA.

The underlying justification of transracial adoption is that the acceptance of black children into white families demonstrates British society as opening its doors or exemplifying tolerance to other races and an understanding of their culture. Perhaps this is true, but in a very small percentage of placements. This acceptance in the majority of transracial placements blindly dismisses any possible value of black culture for the child involved. The black child, being treated as white, with no emphasis placed on the richness and value of her or his own race, fails to acknowledge these facts. This denial of colour, race and culture is often brought about by fear, fear on the part of the white substitute parents, fear of appearing discriminatory, fear of "drawing attention" to the child, fear of recognising obvious differences.

All of these fears need to be recognised, all of the differences need to be addressed and dealt with. The child recognises them whether she or he talks about them or not. The denial of black culture and history reinforces the negative images so many people have about black people, our history and our culture and this is insidiously passed on to the black child. Again, when white social workers are seen placing black children in white families, society's already negative opinions of black families are reinforced.

The media consisting of radio, television, newspapers, literature, theatre and film in Britain reflect white ideals. Even in 1987 positive images of black people are still greatly lacking. In fact, until very recently the media have done a powerful job of perpetuating and reinforcing negative stereotypes of black people. The impressions of the isolated black child about his or her race, while viewing television or reading bad press, are not positive. Unless the black child's carer is intelligent, aware, willing and able to talk to the child about some of the richer aspects of black life, black people, black culture, the child will be raised in relative isolation and ignorance. Children will grow up believing all that they have learned, heard, seen; never having their impressions challenged; never having learned anything positive about their culture. They will go out into the real, unsheltered world having internalised their racism or oppression, believing all the negative things about black people, and they will be seen by society as the same as those they themselves reject and fear because of untruths or hidden knowledge. The confusion these young people have to deal with, often alone (alone because they are no longer seen as "one of us" in the real world, alone because they never had any contact with black people and/or reject black people through their own internalised racism) presents great difficulty and often prevents them from coping. In order to be accepted, they frequently go to the wrong group, black or white, and many end up in trouble.

Social services departments across the country have begun to recognise the damaging effects these inappropriate transracial placements create. Derbyshire County Council therefore has a policy on same-race placement which has the approval of the black community.

Those who favour black families for black children put strong emphasis on the history and culture of black people. This history is passed on to the black child. For example, the treatment of black groups in Britain and the negative images of black people cannot be separated from the overall context of historical relationships within the Commonwealth countries of Britain. It was British colonial "theft" which created the practice of separation and inequality between black and white people at the beginning of the Industrial Revolution. Greater wealth and cheaper labour were the slogans of the day. At the outset Britain developed a highly superior attitude, which prevails to this day, proclaiming black people to be innately low in intelligence, culture and morals, but useful nevertheless as free labour, thus justifying the practice of rigid separation. In order to deny our many accomplishments, all of the black inventors, scientists, artists, and writers were denied recognition and robbed of their status. Those who fought for their land, their rights, their dignity, were quickly eliminated or beaten into submission. The long-range effects of the historical denial of black accomplishments is reflected in the attitudes of the majority of white British people today.

Because Britain is a racist society, the majority of white British people are themselves racist. Social workers do not belong to a special category just because they are in the "caring profession". In fact, individuals in this profession, who resist examining their attitudes, challenging their often long-held beliefs in lieu of learning more truthful ones and putting into practice the corrected knowledge of other races, should start thinking about whether or not social work is the right career for them.

Recruitment of black families

Until very recently virtually no effort was being made to recruit black families to foster or adopt black children. When local authorities finally became aware of the outrage felt by the black community, pressure was brought to bear in order to right the overwhelming wrongs done to black people. Attempts by local authorities to recruit black foster parents have begun to scratch the surface of the vast store of recruitable black substitute parents. In fact the attempt is slow in many areas to even scratch at the surface. This is mainly because social services departments are still using white social workers to communicate with black families in the hope of recruiting them – an ineffective process. To begin with, black people are suspicious of white social workers and with good cause. The black communities blame social services for destroying black families by removing our children and placing them into "care". The successful recruitment of black foster parents is something which must be approached by black social workers, if the department truly wants positive results.

There are a number of constructive ways to recruit black substitute parents:

- Personal involvement with the local black church. Get to know ministers and lay preachers.
- Notices put into Sunday bulletins.
- Speak to Church women's groups, possibly show them the *Black and in Care* video (available from 20 Compton Terrace, London N1 2UN).
- In Chicago, a large black church sponsored a fashion show in conjunction with the local residential homes. Both church members and the children in care modelled clothes. Without putting any emphasis on the children in need of homes, they were seen by potential substitute parents. It was done in such a way that no-one knew who was who.
- In Detroit, the black television anchor woman featured each week "A child in need" on state-wide television. The result was almost 100 per cent success with more potential substitute parents coming forward.
- In Cleveland, Ohio, the Sunday paper featured "A child is waiting" – again 100 per cent success with more potential substitute parents coming forward. Black people respond to the needs of black children provided they know they are needed and are being requested to help.

188

If you put an advertisement in your local paper stating the need for homes for black children, black folk do not read the advertisement unless it is accompanied by a photograph of a black child or a black social worker. They naturally think the plea is to white foster parents. Most of us feel that news in the white press is for and about white folk, unless it is to highlight a crime committed by one of us. Thus if a photograph does not accompany the advertisement, it often does not register.

- Black radio stations offer another form of positive communication. Have a black social worker engage in dialogue with the master of ceremonies or disc jockey, or arrange to have a phone-in programme where members of the black community can speak to a black social worker and have some of the myths dispelled in the open over the air.

Despite all these advances in recruitment methods, not enough emphasis is placed on finding black families to adopt black children in this country. Why is this? Is it because there are too many white couples waiting for a first or second child? Couples whose needs should be met? What about the needs of the black child? The continuing exercise of transracial placement further perpetuates the myth that black families do not adopt.

If a small agency of five black social workers can successfully place 100 black children into black families in less than nine months, the only obstacle preventing large white agencies from accomplishing at least that is lack of commitment. If the black community is educated to appreciate the adoptive needs and then approached it will respond. The successful recruitment of black substitute families is something which must be approached by black social workers, if the department truly wants positive results. Black social workers offer understanding and familiarity with African, Caribbean and Asian culture, history, lifestyle, languages and the binding strength of the black family.

In addition, if the child is of mixed parentage, that child should not be placed in a white home. That child will at some point in life be viewed as black by the world, and, if given the right environment, she or he will view her or himself as black in the right, positive way.

When coming forward for recruitment as substitute parents, most people have some fears about not being accepted. Black people's fears are even stronger because most of us know how we are viewed by the white establishment, so it is important to have continuous contact with your prospective black clients. Older or single black women should not automatically be turned away. If they are, you will miss the chance to recruit some of the best substitute parents available. Don't be put off if the husband or boyfriend is not always available. If he has told you 'my wife and I want to do this' or 'she wants to do this so it's OK with me', accept that. He may not attend any of the training sessions – don't worry about it. You can be sure that in their household mum does most of the raising (which is not very different from what happens in most British households).

As for assessment forms, a firm, informative relationship needs to be established before starting the formal assessment. I have also found that I do not record all of the personal information I collect. Whose business is it why Mrs A got a divorce? It was eight years ago and she has done a splendid job raising her four children alone. Most black people see white social workers as insensitive to their parenting skills. And who needs to know that Ms B's three children all had different fathers, and she never married any one of them? Slavery left its mark on us in many different ways. The important point is that these single black women are doing a great job of raising their children alone and have love left over to care for one or two more. So who are we to stand on our British and professional morals and misjudge these wonderful resources?

Too many black children have been inappropriately placed. Let's not be colour blind any longer and let's not have the next generation of black children think that we did not care enough to try.

14 Ethnic and racial identity in adoption within the United Kingdom

John Small

John Small was Assistant Director of Social Services with the London Borough of Hackney. He has a BA (Hons) in Applied Social Work and the Certificate of Qualification in Social Work from Bradford University. He has worked as a generic social worker in three London boroughs, and in Jamaica as a Children's Officer and Assistant for Day Care Services.

He was also Project Director for New Black Families, the first black adoption agency in England. He is the founder and first President of the Association of Black Social Workers and Allied Professionals and served for six years as a Council member of the Central Council for Education and Training in Social Work. He is International Editor for the 'Journal of Multi-Racial Social Work', City University of New York, and in recent years has published extensively on ethnic sensitive practice and the transcultural mode of social work.

This paper was published in Adoption & Fostering, 15:4, 1991.

Transracial adoption became a contentious issue in the United Kingdom in the early 1980s and the debate has centred around issues relating to race and ethnicity. This has been largely due to the black community* becoming much more conscious of the plight of black children, and the level of expertise and confidence which has developed among black professionals, as reflected by New Black Families Unit (Small, 1983) and the Association of Black Social Workers and Allied Professionals (ABSWAP) (Small, 1987). The debate has been often controversial and

---

*The use of the term "black" emphasises the common experience of African-Caribbean and South Asian people who are the subject of racism and their collective will to struggle against it. There are many other groups who experience varying degrees of prejudice and discrimination such as Turkish, Chinese, Greek Cypriots and Moroccans, but not usually to the same degree as some other minority groups such as the Jews and the Irish. It is not intended to exclude any individual or groups but in this paper, race and ethnicity are considered as they relate to the more visible groups.

the evidence contradictory. Proponents' and opponents' views have been amplified by the media and analysed by academics. Race and ethnicity in adoption have brought to the foreground political, social, psychological and, more recently, legal issues. There are very little empirical data available to guide policy and practice. The Department of Health, the Children Act 1989 and the courts have confirmed that race and ethnicity are important factors in the placement of black children in substitute families. In this article I will identify the importance of race and ethnicity and outline the various positions. Available evidence is examined both from the perspective of the proponents and the opponents.

Competing perspectives
The opponents and proponents of transracial adoption are identified through their world views, their ideas of what society should be like and the relationship that they think should exist between the majority and the minority communities as opposed to the needs of the child, which should be their primary concern. There are three major competing perspectives which have influenced the debate. Firstly, and most dominant is assimilation versus separation. In the former, children are seen as children, the "colour blind" approach. It proposes that no significance should be given to race and ethnicity, that there are several ethnic groups living among a majority group and, although not homogenous, they believe that they share a common ethnic identity, "human identity". This is supposed to epitomise a truly harmonious, multiracial society (Deny, 1983; Rex, 1967, 1970). Transracial adopters can show a commitment to this idea by adopting black children, but racial and ethnic identity is incidental and marginal to the process. The converse is the fear of the idea of separation between the races. This is rooted in the view that were the child to develop a sense of racial and ethnic identity, this would have adverse consequences and would result in a breakdown of the adoption, and that a separate community would develop where blacks and whites would co-exist in disharmony and there would be little interaction.

The sense of racial and ethnic identity is very strong among various groups and there is little evidence that this will not continue into the future. The characteristics of ethnic groups may change but the child's colour will not. A society based on rigid separation is a contradiction, since the groups must interact. The fears embedded in this are unreal and should not affect the quality of care offered to a child.

The second competing perspective is diversity versus unity. Britain is seen as an ethnically diverse society with positive advantages in diversity where racial and ethnic differences are accepted and appreciated by society. The converse, however, is that diversity is seen as a threat to integration, assimilation and a harmonious multiracial society.

The third is the pluralist view which encourages all groups to actively participate in society within a framework of common shared values and accepting the need for individual racial and ethnic identity. The ethnic majority cannot expect to remain as they are, irrespective of the presence of various minority groups, nor should the ethnic minority communities expect that all the elements of their culture and lifestyles should remain unchanged. There should be a sensitive balance between a shared common identity within society and a distinctive identity of minority groups. The need for a balance imposes obligations on both sides and this is vital to the maintenance of plurality. The group must be allowed to maintain the elements of their identity which are considered to be essential to their distinctive nature (Smith, 1974). Small (1986) has shown how these world views have resulted in a typology of transracial adopters and has outlined the characteristics which they should have, but to date there is no research to identify whether there is any link between the characteristics and success or failure in transracial adoption.

Race, ethnicity and identity
Transracial adoption has had a short but contentious history and has been centred around the question of whether a white family in a racist society*

---

* A racist society is defined as one in which power and authority are largely concentrated in the hands of the white population and where this power and authority are used to reward or punish a group or individual on the basis of the race, ethnicity or colour of that group or individual. Where an individual uses such power and authority in this way it is individual racism and where it is used within the context of organisational process it is institutional racism. An individual action may reflect the conditioning process that the individual has had in the society or be a symptom of the nature of an organisation. The organisational structure may reflect the ideas of the individuals who put the organisation together. The organisation may have been put together at a specific time to respond to the needs of a particular group of people. Consequently, it may not be able to respond to the "newcomers" or, indeed, it may be resistant to change.

can provide the environment which will advance the psychological well-being of the black child. In this context, racial and ethnic identity is seen as a process which should create conjunction between the child's perception of self, the immediate environment and society, thereby producing equilibrium. In this regard, the child should be psychologically satisfied with the self as being of a specific racial and ethnic group and this is accepted and positively reinforced by those with whom the child interacts. A healthy racial and ethnic identity must, therefore, be one with which the child is happy, and which is accepted by the adoptive parents, extended family and society rather than rejected or related to negatively. In short, there should be harmony with self.

For analytical purposes, psychologists have maintained a clear distinction between personal and social identity. ' . . . personal identity refers to those intimate and private aspects of the person which are central to the person's sense of autonomy and uniqueness. It is the fulcrum of the person's sense of continuity and consistency across different social contexts . . . ' and, 'Social identity refers to the public self which is derived from the person's membership of different social groups and categories and occupancy of various social roles'. However, from a developmental perspective, social identity merges with personal identity over time (Hunt, 1976). There is a mass of evidence to confirm the part played by the expectations of "significant others" in terms of approval and disapproval of certain aspects of behaviour (Braginski, 1976; Seeman, 1959; Milner, 1983). Miller (1963) has used the term "subjective public identity" to refer to the "deepest inner self" which emerges out of the learning process and therefore affects self-image. Role psychology, Interpersonal Theory, Social Learning and Object Relations Theory, along with Freudian psychology, have been used to explain how racial and ethnic identity are affected by the internalisation of the anxiety concerns of the child (Small, 1984). As the child develops awareness of self by the process in which interaction takes place, the child's self is defined. Although Tizard and Phoenix (1989) in a review of the literature and research suggest that the process is "illusive" and "problematic", nevertheless research evidence has shown that all societies emphasise some aspects of the characteristics of individuals and assign social identity accordingly. It is also accepted that some "objectively assigned" identities are more central to self than others. In the UK at present, society does not present all racial and ethnic identities as equally desirable (Hughes and Hughes, 1952). It is generally known that, in this society, black people are seen in a negative way and that this affects adults and children, but children are usually more profoundly affected.

Research evidence in the United Kingdom

Race and ethnicity as variables in adoption have been largely ignored, irrespective of the fact that adoption has always fascinated researchers and there are volumes of research on adoption generally. There is also very little research on transracial adoption in the United Kingdom. We do not know how many black children are in care, what proportion are fostered or adopted, nor the proportion that are placed in transracial settings. We do not know the outcomes of children beyond teenage years who were transracially adopted. In the absence of extensive research evidence in the UK, research findings in the USA have influenced most profoundly the methods and research in this country. This is particularly so with the work of Simon and Altstein (1977), Fanshel (1972), Howard (1984) and Grow and Shapiro (1974). In 1972, Fanshel studied 100 children of Indian background where only 10 per cent of the children were found to be experiencing difficulties. Grow and Shapiro's (1974) study of 125 transracially placed children found that only 23 were experiencing difficulties which compared well with white children who were adopted by white families, but was severely criticised by Chimezie (1977) for not addressing the issue of racial identity. Simon and Altstein (1977) used postal questionnaires to 204 families and 133 responded. The findings compare favourably with white children in white families and Kim (1978) studied 406 Korean children aged 12–17 years where it was found that the children had little concept of Korean identity.

In the UK, the first follow-up study was the British Adoption Four-year Project (BAP) where homes were found for 53 black children with 51 couples. In some of the families, race and ethnic identity did not feature as prominent factors. The Rowe and Lambert (1973) study of 2,817 "children who wait" found a significant number of black children waited longer for placement. The Soul Kids Campaign (ABAFA, 1977) sought to recruit black families and 11 children were placed with new families. Although modest in outcome, the project identified a range of factors which were militating against black families. In 1980, New Black Families (Small, 1982; Arnold, 1982) demonstrated that black families could be found for black children. Bagley and Young (1979) followed up 31 black children aged 7–14 years, 27 of whom were of mixed parentage and who were adopted by white families. They found that about half of the children identified themselves as white and there was a positive relationship between racial awareness and self-image. The most recent research is Gill and Jackson (1983). They studied 36 transracially placed children aged between 12 and six years old and found that they had no contact with the black community. Their coping mechanism was based on denying their racial background and they had not developed a sense of racial identity. ' . . . The children saw themselves as "white" in all but skin colour', and part of the reason for older black children not being adopted by white families ' . . . may be that older black children may, by the time a placement has occurred, have already internalised a definition of themselves as being black and this definition may jeopardise the possibility of integration and emotional identification within a white family . . . '. As a result of the cases which came to light in relation to transracially placed children, ABSWAP was founded and the Association took up the issue of race and ethnicity which resulted in a call for radical transformation of such policy.

The validity of current research evidence: the opponents' view
The opponents have argued that the available research does not emanate from separate sense data only, but from patterns of experience which are already affected by interpretation. It is argued that the findings are already "theory laden" because facts are interpreted and the language is generally selective, abstracted and symbolic; that concepts used are not given to us by nature, they are constructed by the researcher and there are background assumptions to these concepts. The subjective life of most minority people, it is argued, follows very different patterns in this society than that of the majority. Consequently, obvious interpretation by the researcher could be totally erroneous because 'facts do not proclaim their own meaning'.

Karl Mannheim (1986) has maintained that the social process permeates even "perspective of thought", that is, the manner in which one views an objective, what one perceives in it, how one construes it in thinking and the principles by which knowledge should be criticised are themselves socially and historically conditioned. As a consequence, instruments are culturally biased and when applied to children they are almost always resisted, therefore their validity must be questioned. In addition, social workers' records and reports along with teachers' evaluations all have in-built biases and thereby impose their own limitations.

It is also argued that research in transracial adoption activated the most deep-seated feelings and attitudes about race and ethnicity, beliefs and practices, and the feelings of the researcher and the respondent may, unconsciously or consciously, carry more weight than the data. Simon and Altstein (1977) have told us that the parents are usually the most informed but they are the ones who are the most emotionally involved and likely to be most biased in favour of their children and themselves. Cicourel (1964) has suggested that research instruments must be constructed in such a way that the subjective meaning of the everyday life of the subject be incorporated in them to prevent the researcher from determining the answer that is desired, and to prevent a situation where researchers follow footsteps in the sand only to discover that they made the footsteps in the first place.

Race, ethnicity and the law
The 1989 Children Act requires local authorities to pay due regard to race, culture, religion and the linguistic background of the child:

> *A child's ethnic origin, cultural background and religion are important factors for consideration . . . in the great majority of cases, placement with a family of similar ethnic origin and religion is most likely to meet the child's needs as fully as possible and safeguard his or her welfare most effectively.*

For the first time courts have handed down judgements which seem to recognise the importance of race and ethnicity in family placements. In one such case, a child of mixed parentage was in a short-term placement with white foster carers for a period of 17 months. The foster carers applied to adopt the child and were rejected by the local authority. The foster parents took the matter to court and the High Court accepted the view that race and ethnicity were important factors and that the child should be placed with a black family. The case went to Appeal and the order was upheld. In another case, a black child was placed at three weeks old with a white family. The foster carers applied to adopt the child and the local authority along with the guardian *ad litem* opposed the adoption. At the hearing, care and control was given to the foster carers with "reasonable access" to the father. These two cases have reinforced the policy objectives of same-race placement by some local authorities, which is considered to be an important part of their equal opportunities policy. However, in determining what is best for the child, race and ethnicity feature among many other factors.

Race and ethnic reality
The black experience is unique, but nevertheless white norms are used to measure the black person. In respect of the black child there are issues of language, race, colour, ethnicity and attitude which must be success-fully resolved at every stage of the child's development through the life cycle (Erickson, 1968). There is a duality, the "private" and the "public self", a survival skill which is transmitted by black families. Adaptive techniques must be developed at every stage of the life cycle to deal with those struggles and stresses arising from the process. Duality is such a technique which has consequences for the child's ego (Devore, 1983) and these adaptive techniques are not within the construction of reality by white families.

Challenge: conflict and change
There is currently a divergence of views among professional groups, and perhaps among some parts of the black community, as to whether transracial adoptions should take place.

There is a dominant view that transracial placement jeopardises the identity needs of black children and this is supported by the findings of Gill and Jackson (1983). It is against this background that ABSWAP concluded in its report to the House of Commons Social Services Committee in 1983 that,

> *Transracial placement as an aspect of current child care policy is in essence a microcosm of the oppression of black people in society; the most valuable resources of any ethnic groups are its children. Transracial placement poses the most dangerous threat to the harmonious society to which we aspire. It is in essence "internal colonisation".*

This, regrettably, was seen as a purely political position, fashioned around the black child while not really addressing the issue of race and ethnicity.

The Association argued that it was as a result of the shortage of healthy white babies that transracial placement came about, with serious consequences for the children who were placed. These are identified as:

- failure to develop a sense of black identity;
- failure to develop survival skills;
- failure to develop cultural and linguistic attributes to function in the black community;
- development of negative self-image/self-esteem; and
- the development of a white identity which would cause profound difficulties in the real world.

Race and ethnic identity: its preconditions

Race and ethnic identity, as distinct from personal identity, direct our attention to two pertinent factors:

- the structure and dynamics of the family, and
- the position of the child within the family.

In the case of the former, racial and ethnic identity become synonymous with the acceptance within the family of the child's race and ethnicity, and the extent of acceptance and integration without the need to effect a change in the child's identity. There is little or no conflict about the child's race and ethnicity and this is likely to continue over time. In the case of the latter, there is a state of well-being in the child as far as race and ethnicity are concerned. This analytical separation allows us to understand how the dynamics of the family can, but should not, be separated from the ability of the family to nurture the child's identity through the developmental stages.

The central question is what conditions must be met to enable a positive sense of racial and ethnic identity in the black child (Small, 1989)? The preconditions appear to be that:

- the family must be secure in itself to deal with the conflicts in society and the social pressures that will inevitably arise;
- the family must be in a state of equilibrium where race and ethnicity are concerned;
- the child must have positive feedback about him/herself;
- the family must accept that it has been transformed and there are new core values to be internalised by its members; and
- the family must have a network outside to act as reinforcement to its newly-found values.

Racial and ethnic identity will, therefore, depend on the extent of positive racial awareness and the quality of interaction within the family framework which is controlled by consistency, continuity and predictability. The extent to which these factors are present will determine the relative stability of racial and ethnic identity.

Children of mixed relationships

The issue of race and ethnicity as they relate to children of mixed relationships has been of interest to sociologists from the 1950s when it was postulated that these children would have divided loyalties and identity problems. This problem approach was taken by Hill (1965), Richmond (1954), Barber (1955) and Little (1950), but Collins expressed the view that the identity of children of mixed relationships would depend on the composition of the immigrant community and its relationship with white society. Durojaiye (1970) found that those children tended to choose friends of similar mixed relationships, while Bagley and Young (1984) found a process of positive identification among the group of children studied. The research in this area is very limited despite the evidence that in some local authorities this group of children constitutes a significant percentage of the overall number of children in care. We do not know what percentage are placed for adoption, at what age, or the outcome of such placements.

Factors likely to affect racial and ethnic identity

There are a number of factors which will affect racial identity:
- the multiracial nature of the family;
- the conflicting views about integration and assimilation;
- the changing nature of society;
- the influence of family members and friends;
- the ability of the family to "ward off" external negative forces;
- the relationship between majority and minority ethnic groups; and
- the view of and attitude towards black families.

The strengths of black families

Sadly, black families are still being projected as pathological, and children who are placed transracially tend to internalise these views. There must, therefore, be a shift from concepts of social pathology to social health by recognising the strengths of black families which, in a round-about way, will have a positive effect on the self-image of black children (Milner, 1983; Small, 1989; Hill, 1972). Discriminatory practices must be addressed in a coherent and practical way over a significant period of time. Addressing these issues will require a profound cognitive shift; a deconstruction and reconstruction of ideas about the strengths and weaknesses of black and ethnic minority families, and a view of these families as partners as opposed to clients. The process will require re-examination of concepts such as:
- "the immigrant", "culture", "racial identity", "ethnicity";
- "assimilation", "adoption", "separation", "attachment";
- "matriarchal and patriarchal families", and a recognition of the strengths of black families such as:
  - strong work orientation
  - strong achievement orientation
  - strong religious orientation
  - strong kinship orientation
  - ability to organise self-help and to accept help
  - ability to split into separate units and cope with the disruptive effect of migration
  - survival of the family irrespective of the destructive forces which have been directed towards black families

- ability to cope with uncertainty/separation/attachment
- adjustment to stress/alienation/racism
- adjustment to new family roles and the elasticity of the black family.

What appears to have been overlooked within the debate are the variables within the process which cause a specific form of identity to emerge out of a complex network of "simultaneous action and reflection". In the case of racial and ethnic identity, it appears to be determined by the child's perception of the parents' expectations, which is guided either consciously or unconsciously by the objectives of the parents. It is, therefore, of paramount importance that we strive to understand the process by researching into the factors which contribute to a positive or negative racial and ethnic identity.

References

ABAFA, Soul Kids Campaign, London, 1977.

Association of Black Social Workers and Allied Professionals (ABSWAP), *Black Children in Care*, p 12, 1983.

Arnold E, 'Finding black families for black children', in Cheetham J (ed), *Social Work and Ethnicity*, Allen & Unwin, pp 98–111, 1982.

Bagley C and Young L, 'The identity, adjustment and achievement of trans-racially adopted children: a review and empirical report', in Verma G C and Bagley C (eds), *Race, Education and Identity*, Macmillan, 1979.

Bagley C and Young L, 'Policy dilemmas and the adoption of black children', in Cheetham J (ed), *Social Work and Ethnicity*, Allen & Unwin, 1982.

Banton M, *The Coloured Quarter*, Cape, 1955.

Banton M, *Race Relations*, Tavistock, 1967.

Banton M, 'It's our country', in Miles R and Phizaklea A (eds), *Racism and Political Action in Britain*, Routledge & Kegan Paul, first edition, 1984.

Braginski B, Braginski D and Ring K, *Methods of Madness: The mental hospital as a last resort*, Holt, 1969, USA.

Chimezie A, 'Bold but irrelevant', in, Grow L C and Shapiro D (eds) in

'Transracial adoption', *Child Welfare*, 56, pp 75–86, 1977.

Cicourel A V, *Methods and Measurements in Sociology*, Free Press, 1964, USA.

Collins S, *Coloured Minorities in Britain*, Butterworth, 1957.

Denny D, 'Some dominant perspectives in the literature relating to multiracial social work', *British Journal of Social Work*, 13:2, pp 149–74, 1983.

Devore W, 'Social casework', *The Journal of Contemporary Social Work*, Family Service Association of America, 1983, USA.

Durojaiye M, 'Patterns of friendship choice in an ethnically mixed junior school', *Race*, 12:2, pp 189–99, 1970.

Erickson E H, *Identity, Youth and Crisis*, Norton, 1968, USA.

Fanshel D, *Far from the Reservation: The transracial adoption of American Indian children*, Scarecrow Press, 1972, USA.

Gill O and Jackson B, *Adoption and Race: Black, Asian and Mixed-Race children in white families*, BAAF/Batsford, 1983.

Grow L C and Shapiro D, '*Black children, white parents: A study of transracial adoption*', Child Welfare League of America, 1974.

Hill C, '*How Colour Prejudiced is Britain?*', Gollancz, 1965.

Hill R, *The Strengths of Black Families*, Emmerson-Hill, 1972, USA.

HMSO, *The Children Act: Guidance and Regulations*, Vol 3, 1991.

Hughes E and Hughes H M, *Where People Meet*, Glencoe Free Press, 1952.

Hunt R G, 'Role and role conflict', in Hollander E P and Hunt R G (eds), *Current Perspectives in Social Psychology*, fourth edition, Oxford University Press, pp 282–88, 1976, USA.

Kim D S, 'Intercountry adoptions: a study of self-concept of adolescent Korean children who were adopted by American families', University of Chicago, unpublished PhD Thesis, 1976.

Little K, *Negroes in Britain*, Routledge & Kegan Paul, first edition, 1984, revised 1998.

Mannheim K, *Ideology and Utopia*, Routledge & Kegan Paul, pp 259–262, 1986.

Maximé J E, 'Some psychological models of black self-concept', in Ahmed S, Cheetham J and Small J W (eds), *Social Work with Black Children and their Families*, Batsford/BAAF, 1986.

Miller D R, 'The study of relationships: situation identity and social interaction', in Koch S (ed), *Psychology: A study of science*, Vol 5, The process areas, the person and some applied fields, McGraw Hill Book Company, pp 639–737, 1963.

Milner D, *Children and Race*, Alan Sutton, 1983.

Milner D, *Children and Race: Ten years on*, Ward Lock Educational, 1983.

Rex J and Moore R, *Race, Community and Conflict: A study of Sparkbrook*, Oxford University Press, 1967.

Rex J, *Race Relations in Sociological Theory*, Routledge & Kegan Paul, 1970.

Richmond A, *Colour Prejudice in Britain*, Routledge & Kegan Paul, 1954.

Rowe J and Lambert L, *Children Who Wait*, Association of British Adoption Agencies (now BAAF), 1975.

Seeman M, 'On the meaning of alienation', *American Sociological Review*, 24, pp 783–91, 1959, USA.

Simon R J and Altstein H, *Transracial Adoption*, John Wiley, 1977, USA.

Small J W, 'New black families', *Adoption & Fostering*, 6:3, 1982.

Small J W,' The crisis in adoption', *International Journal of Social Psychiatry*, 30:1 & 2, 1984.

Small J W, *Social Work with Black Children and their Families*, op cit.

Small J W, Paper presented to conference, 'Implications of the transcultural mode of social work education and training', Friends House, March 1986, unpublished.

Small J W, Foreword in *Anti-racist Social Work*, Dominelli L (ed), Macmillan Education, 1988.

Small J W, 'Towards a black perspective in social work: a transcultural exploration', in Langan M and Lee P (eds), *Radical Social Work Today*, Unwin Hyman, 1989.

Small J W, 'Transracial placements: conflicts and contradiction', in Morgan S and Righton P (eds), *Child Care: Concerns and Conflicts*, Hodder & Stoughton: Open University, 1989.

Smith M E, *The Plural Society in the British West Indies*, Sangster/University of California Press, 1974, USA.

Tizard B and Phoenix A, 'Black identity and transracial adoption', *New Community*, 5:3, pp 427–37, 1989.

15 Not such mixed-up kids

Barbara Tizard and Ann Phoenix

Barbara Tizard is an Emeritus Professor at the Thomas Coram Research Unit, University of London, Institute of Education. Ann Phoenix is a Senior Lecturer in Psychology at Birkbeck, also University of London.

This paper was published in Adoption & Fostering, 18:1, 1994.

The number of young children of mixed black and white parentage is increasing. (To avoid ambiguity, in this article we use the term "black" to refer only to people with two African or African-Caribbean parents, while we refer to people with one white and one black parent as being of mixed parentage.) The 1989 Labour Force Survey found that of people of 'West Indian' origin who were married or cohabiting, 27 per cent of men and 28 per cent of women had white partners. A disproportionately high number of mixed parentage children enter care, and there has been much debate as to whether they should be placed with black or white carers. Much of the argument centres around the identity needs of the young people, and whether white carers can adequately help them to develop a positive identity and deal with racism.

However, there has been very little research about the identity of mixed parentage children, both those in the care system and those living with their own families. The research briefly reported here is concerned with the identity and experiences of racism of young people of mixed parentage living with their own parent(s). (A fuller account of the study can be found in Tizard and Phoenix, 1993.) Such a study is clearly relevant to the issue of whether mixed parentage children in care "need" to develop a particular kind of identity, and the extent to which identity problems are influenced by the colour of their carers. It is also important to know how social class influences both the young people's identity and their experiences of racism, since the adoptive families with whom children in care are likely to be placed tend to be middle class.

In our study we interviewed 58 15–16-year-olds of mixed white and

African-Caribbean or African parentage, together with 98 white and 87 black young people. Because we wanted to explore the way in which the influence of race and gender is mediated by social class half our sample of mixed parentage young people (55 per cent), mainly from middle-class families, were located at independent schools in London and the home counties; the rest were attending multiracial comprehensive schools in London. We found our sample by asking head teachers if they had young people who fitted our criteria, and if we could interview them. Eighty-eight per cent of the mixed parentage students lived with their white mothers, and 60 per cent lived with their black fathers as well. While some looked black, others looked of Indian origin, or were recognisably of mixed parentage, and nine looked white – perhaps of southern European origin. One of the project directors was white, the other black. The great majority (78 per cent) of the interviews with the mixed parentage students were carried out by the black project director and another black woman.

Constructions of racial identity

We explored with the young people how they defined their racial identity, what their feelings were about it and the extent to which they felt an affinity to black cultures, and to black and white people. In answer to the question, 'Do you think of yourself as black?' only 39 per cent answered 'yes', and 49 per cent 'no', while the rest answered 'sometimes'. (Thirty per cent of the black students and 16 per cent of the white students said that they thought of people of mixed parentage as black.) Those who did not think of themselves as black offered descriptions of themselves as brown, mixed, half-and-half or coloured. None said they thought of themselves as white, but 10 per cent (six) said that they sometimes felt white, or that they felt 'more white than black' (five of the six looked white). However, while categorising themselves in these ways spontaneous comments during the course of the interview suggested that their racial identities were sometime too complex to fit the categories well. Some described themselves at different times as black and mixed, others were aware of having a different racial identity in different situations, while some resisted colour labels. One girl, for example, who had said that she included people of mixed parentage as black, when asked later whether she regarded herself as black replied:

No, I don't think of myself as black, exactly, I think of myself as half-British, half-Jamaican, though essentially I feel myself to be British because I was born here.

Forty-three per cent of the young people of mixed parentage, more often those from working-class families, referred to people of mixed parentage as "half-caste", as did 67 per cent of the black students and 61 per cent of the white students. A quarter of the mixed parentage sample described themselves as of mixed race. No-one used the term "mixed parentage".

Defining oneself as black was strongly associated with holding more politicised views of racism, for example, describing racism as the behaviour of white people only (Banks, 1992). It was *not* associated with feeling positive about their racial identity, or with affiliation to black cultures, or with living with a black parent. (Some black parents had taught their children to think of themselves as "mixed", while the more politicised of the white parents had taught them they were "black".) Appearance was also an influence – of the nine young people who looked white, only one thought of themselves as black.

There were important reasons why the majority of our sample did not regard themselves as black. Most (but not all) of their closest attachments seemed to be their mothers, who were usually white. To regard themselves as black often seemed to them a form of betrayal, or at least rejection, and they preferred to think of themselves as "half-and-half". As one girl put it:

I wouldn't call myself black . . . Lots of people have said you might just as well call yourself black, but I feel that it is denying the fact that my mother is white, and I'm not going to do that.

Moreover, many had been encouraged by one or both parents to value, acknowledge, and be proud of, both their black and white inheritance. And some of those attending multiracial schools had discovered that black people did not always accept them as black; about a fifth of our sample had met with exclusion, hostility and verbal abuse from black children. For those who had been brought up to think of themselves as black this was a disturbing and confusing experience.

While 51 per cent of the sample had when younger wished to be another colour, at least at times, only 14 per cent did so now. From their answers to this and several other questions about their attitude to their mixed parentage, as well as from spontaneous comments throughout the interview, we assessed 60 per cent as having a definitely positive racial identity. That is, even if in the past they had wished to be another colour, they were now proud of their mixed parentage and saw many advantages to it.

I'm proud of my colour, you get the best of both worlds. You're not one colour, but two, and I think that's nice.

I'm comfortable with both black and white people, which I know a lot of people aren't. And I'm accepted by both because I have a white family and a black family.

If you look at it superficially it's a disadvantage, because you are a piggy in the middle, but I think if you look at it deeper, it's a definite advantage, because you're not trapped in any group ... and I think you see things in a clearer perspective, because you're not in the actual centre of the turmoil, you can see things from outside, and you can look at it more objectively.

However, 20 per cent still wished to be another colour, or expressed some unhappiness or, rarely, confusion about their racial identity. We labelled this group as having a "problematic" rather than a negative identity because all but one expressed contradictory feelings. One girl, for example, said:

When I started to mix with boys I just felt different, because in my class I'm the only coloured person ... I felt actually at a disadvantage, because everyone is weighing up what they look like and I'm different. I think I'll always go through life being a bit different, but sometimes it'll be an advantage as well as a problem ... I suppose I'm pleased I'm neither black nor white, as well as upset because I'm different.

This feeling of being different from both black and white people undoubtedly troubled most of the "problematic" group. However, some of those with a positive identity regarded their difference as an interesting advantage.

The remaining 20 per cent we classed as intermediate. While not wishing to be another colour, they were not definitely proud of their colour or inheritance, often saying it was not a matter of being proud.

These racial identities, while less often positive than those of the black students, are much more positive than those attributed to people of mixed parentage in the past. Factors likely to have contributed to this change include changing social attitudes to "mixed marriages", the admiration currently shown by both black and white youth for the appearance, especially the ringlets, characteristics of many mixed parentage girls, and the high status of black youth cultures among sectors of white youth. The attitudes of the young people to their inheritance are also much more positive than those reported by social workers and clinical psychologists (e.g. Banks, 1992). This difference reflects, we believe, the fact that ours was a community sample, rather than one drawn from social service or clinical referrals, where problems of all kinds can be anticipated.

Having a "problematic" or "intermediate" racial identity was not related to living with white adults only, but it was related to having mainly white friends, and white girl or boy friends, and attending mainly white schools. These factors also strongly influenced the extent to which colour was central in the young people's lives. At the end of the interview we asked them to rank in order a number of possible influences on their identity, which we defined as "their sense of who they were". A third put colour among their first four choices (compared with two-thirds of the black group), while 39 per cent did not include it at all. We also explored this issue less directly by asking about the extent to which they believed colour impinged on a variety of aspects of their lives. About half (48 per cent) thought, for example, that their school experiences would have been different if they had had more black teachers, and 50 per cent thought that their lives in the future would be easier if they were white. Those young people for whom colour was more central tended to be those with more black friends, and those who reported more experience of racism.

It was clear that the racial composition of the neighbourhood and the school they attended had a major impact on the young people's racial identity. If they attended predominantly white independent schools in white areas they may have had no black friends (over a quarter of the whole sample did not) and no allegiance to, or much knowledge of, black youth cultures. Despite living with a black parent some felt uncomfortable with black people, uneasy with young black males in particular, and not attracted to black people of the opposite sex. One girl in this situation, who lived alone with her black mother in a white neighbourhood, said:

> *The only time that I have ever actually been with any coloured people that are really black is through my mother, and usually they are people that I don't really know, so I feel more comfortable with white people . . . whenever I think of myself as married, I never think of myself as married to a coloured person . . . it's probably because I don't know that many black people.*

However, two-thirds of the young people felt comfortable with both black and white people, and had both black and white friends, although because of the schools they attended their close friends were twice as likely to be white as black. The majority (68 per cent) said they would prefer to live in a racially mixed area, and 75 per cent had no colour preference for a marriage partner.

Cultural allegiances
As the young people themselves were aware, tastes in such things as clothes and music make a definite statement about identity. Half of the mixed parentage students, compared with 83 per cent of the black students, and 26 per cent of the white students, preferred black youth music (hip hop, soul, ragga, etc) to all other, while about a quarter dressed in black youth styles and listened by preference to black radio stations. Young people from working-class families attending multiracial comprehensive schools were those most likely to be attracted to black youth cultures. Links with African and Caribbean culture were more tenuous, although half had visited their black parent's country of origin. A fifth said they thought of themselves as either half Nigerian, or half West Indian, or in a few cases as Nigerian or West Indian, etc, but a large

majority (73 per cent, compared with only 59 per cent of the black students) said they thought of themselves as English or British. However, about two-thirds of young people in all racial groups who lived in London said that they felt 'more of a Londoner than anything else'.

Experiences of racism

The great majority of the young people, 85 per cent, said that they had both observed and experienced racism. Name calling in the primary school, which had been deeply wounding, was the most common form of racism reported by a quarter of the sample. Racism was most often experienced by boys and by working-class young people. It seemed to be rampant in boys' schools, but a third of the young people, especially those in middle-class girls' schools, said there was no racism at all in their present school. None showed any awareness of the concept of institutional racism, and 79 per cent defined racism as discriminatory behaviour from any racial group to any other.

It is often said that only black parents can help black children to deal with racism. However, we were surprised to find much less communication about racism in both black and mixed families than we had expected. In only about half the families, according to the mixed parentage young people, had there been any discussion about race or racism with them, or overheard by them, or any discussion of the parents' experience of racism, or any communication from them to the parent(s) about their own experience of racism. Only 57 per cent said that their parent(s) had given them advice on dealing with racism. Of less direct forms of communication, 50 per cent said their parents(s) had taught them to be proud of their colour, and rather more – 65 per cent – had talked to them about famous black people. In the black group these proportions were slightly, but not substantially, higher. Many had also observed, whether admiringly or critically, their parents dealing with racism, but the black parents did not seem to come in for more admiration, or criticism, than the white parents. In general, the young people admired non-violent, effective confrontation with racists, but many had not yet mastered this coping technique themselves. We found no evidence that those living with a black parent coped differently, or received different advice, from those living only with a white parent.

Diversity in racial identities

It should by now be clear that the racial identities of our sample of mixed parentage young people differed widely, and that the main influences on them that we were able to show were social class, type of school, gender and the degree of politicisation of the young people. Those from working-class families reported more personal experiences of racism and were more likely to describe racism in their schools. They were also more likely to adhere to black youth cultures, and to have links with Caribbean culture, and to like African or Caribbean food. The young people from middle-class families tended to have white friends, to speak in a middle class speech style, enjoyed Italian or Chinese food most, read *The Independent* or *The Guardian*, and preferred pop or classical music.

Girls experienced and observed less racism than boys. Being a mixed parentage middle-class girl in a predominantly white school was thus a very different and easier experience then being a mixed parentage boy in a working-class school and area. On the other hand, having a black identity, or a positive identity, was not related to gender and social class. A black identity was associated with holding politicised views, so that middle-class young people attending independent schools, without black friends or links with black culture, might still regard themselves as black if they had become politicised.

But having a black identity was no guarantee of having a positive racial identity – young people with a "mixed" identity were just as likely as those with a black identity to feel positive about their colour and proud of their inheritance. Problems with racial identity were not significantly associated with the colour of the parents the young people were living with. Banks (1992) has described the problems of mixed parentage children living with single white mothers who were racist. We considered that a few of the single white mothers in our study were racist, but there were more who were supportive of, and positive about, their children's racial mix, more so than some black parents. We suspected, although we had no systematic evidence about this, that all aspects of racial identity were influenced by the relative strength of the young people's positive or negative feelings towards their black and their white parents and step-parents.

Issues for adoption and fostering

Our study was obviously small, and unrepresentative in that more than half the sample came from middle-class families and were girls. But for those very reasons we think it is relevant to the issue of transracial or same-race placement. Adoption studies such as Gill and Jackson's (1983) caused alarm by showing that the children (many of mixed parentage and in middle-class families) did not identify strongly with black people or black culture and had mainly white friends. But we found similar characteristics in children, especially girls, living with an unpoliticised middle-class black parent in a white suburb, and attending a school with very few other black students.

Whether or not one agrees with their parents' educational decisions (which they believed would in the long run benefit their child) such families are a growing part of our multiracial society. All identities are, in any case, subject to change. Many of the young people in our study described the ways in which aspects of their racial identity had changed during their childhood and adolescence. This process of change is likely to continue as they encounter new experiences on leaving school.

We also found no evidence that the colour of the parents influenced any aspect of the child's identity or ways of dealing with racism, and we are therefore sceptical about the importance given to this factor in selecting carers. Of course, we do not want to imply that any white (or indeed, black) person would be an adequate foster or adoptive parent for mixed parentage young people. The parents in our sample, unlike most foster and adoptive parents, had formed a relationship with a person of another colour and brought up their child. Many, though not all, felt positive, even enthusiastic about their child's dual inheritance. People with racist views, or those who feel unenthusiastic about one half of the child's inheritance, are unacceptable as carers. But our findings suggest that the colour of the parents is likely to have less impact on the child's development than their attitudes to race and racism, their choice of school and their social class.

It is not easy to suggest how carers can help young people with identity issues, since so much depends on values and judgements. Young people who felt comfortable with their racial identity, and at ease with both black and white people and cultures, were more likely to be attending multiracial schools. On the other hand, their academic attainments may not be so high as those in independent schools. Young people from families where there was more communication about racism seemed to deal with it more confidently, but a few parents bored or alienated their children by what the child saw as excessive concern, while other parents felt it not in the child's best interests to dwell on racism. The parents' own example of dealing with racism seemed to be an important influence, although children were critical of behaviour that was ineffective or counter-productive. Those young people who felt their parents supported them in dealing with racism, as with other issues, and valued their dual inheritance, seemed to have a more positive attitude to their identity. However, influences from school, the peer group and the media also played an important part.

Since this paper was first published, there has been a burgeoning of interest in "mixed parentage". The resulting debates support our findings that, although there continue to be disputes over terminology, many people of mixed parentage are now choosing to identify themselves as "mixed" or "bi-racial". At the same time, there has been an increasing recognition that racism is not a unitary process, but that racisms are plural. These developments pose challenges to the conceptualisation of black and white people as binary opposites and make it clear that "race" and "racial meanings" are not static, but are social processes (i.e. that they are racialised). While it is difficult for social policy and social work practices to keep in line with theoretical developments on "race" and racisms, it is clearly important for complex notions of racialisation to be applied in general social work practice, including in relation to "transracial adoption".

References

Banks N, 'Mixed up kids', *Social Work Today*, 24:3, 1992.

Gill O and Jackson B, *Adoption and Race*, Batsford, 1983.

Tizard B and Phoenix A, *Black, White or Mixed Race?* Routledge, 1993.

16 Mediation and the role of "accredited bodies" in intercountry adoption

Peter Selman and Jill White

Peter Selman is Head of Department and Senior Lecturer in Social Policy at the University of Newcastle upon Tyne. Jill White was formerly Development Officer at BAAF.

This paper was published in Adoption & Fostering, 18:2, 1994.

The Hague Convention and the role of accredited bodies

Chapter III of the Convention provides for a system of Central Authorities and also outlines the role of "accredited bodies" in fulfilling duties in respect of particular adoptions (Duncan, 1993). Two articles are of particular importance:

Article 9 states that:

'Central Authorities shall take directly or through public authorities or other bodies duly accredited in their State all appropriate measures to:

a) collect, preserve and exchange information about the situation of the child and the prospective adopters . . .

b) facilitate, follow and expedite proceedings with a view to obtaining the adoption;

c) promote the development of adoption counselling and post-adoption services . . .'

Article 10 states that:

'Accreditation shall only be granted to . . . bodies demonstrating their competence to carry out properly the tasks with which they may be entrusted.'

Independent adoptions

At present, the vast majority of British couples adopting from abroad make all the practical arrangements themselves or through individual lawyers (Humphrey and Humphrey, 1993; IBA, 1991). A central issue at the Hague was whether such "independent" adoptions should be allowed. *Article 22* allows for the continued involvement of individuals such as lawyers in the mediation of intercountry adoption, providing that *both* receiving and sending countries are agreeable.

Duncan (1993) has pointed out that the acceptance of such independent intermediaries within the Hague Convention was necessary to make possible the ratification of the Convention by the USA. The British Government seems in principle to insist on agency adoption, in line with policy on *domestic* adoption, but not to have addressed the question of whether an "agency" adoption can leave all the practical arrangements to the prospective adopters. There would seem to be at least a need for approval to be sought, as in Sweden, for the proposed method of mediation and this presumably is envisaged as part of the 'authorisation to proceed', proposed in the White Paper. However, the experience of Sweden and the Netherlands seems to be that such "independent" adoptions fall far short of a true agency adoption in terms of safeguarding the child (Selman, 1993).

In their report to the Hague Conference, Defence for Children International (1991) sees a spectrum of intercountry adoptions ranging from full *agency* arrangements in both sending and receiving countries to *independent* adoptions where a couple arrange for a home study and then travel to the country of origin to directly locate a child. The proposals in the White Paper appear to envisage arrangements which will fall somewhere in the middle, with a clear agency role in approval and procedures relating to immigration and nationality, but the actual task of finding or identifying a child left to the prospective adopters and no clear guidelines on preparation and counselling.

The strongest safeguard for the child is where there is agency to agency involvement in all stages of adoption (Van Loon, 1990; para 140–141, p 150). The Hague Convention clearly encourages sending countries to work through approved agencies, as is already the practice in Korea, Thailand and India (Van Loon, 1990; para 66–68, p 72), but in many South American countries private adoptions remain common (Van Loon, 1990; para 69, p 74). Likewise in receiving countries, there is great variation in the proportion of agency adoptions, from Norway and Finland, where independent adoptions are prohibited, to Italy and Switzerland where less than 20 per cent of adoptions are handled by agencies.

Evidence from the USA (Landau, 1990; Pierce and Vitello, 1991) and Germany (Textor, 1991), and recent revelations about adoptions from El Salvador (*World in Action*, 29 November 1993) show that independent adoptions do carry the greatest risk, and that this is still affecting British adoptions today. Van Loon (1990; para 178, p 192) has also expressed concern about such adoptions 'with their inherent risk of failure because of insufficient preparation and susceptibility to child trafficking'.

There is evidence that most prospective adopters would welcome more help in making practical arrangements (IBA, 1991) and that many would choose to go through an agency in Britain if there were one, although some, given the choice, might still prefer the adventure of doing it themselves (Humphrey and Humphrey, 1993).

The development of adoption agencies in Sweden and the Netherlands

The role of adoption agencies in other countries has been described in an earlier article (Selman, 1993). When intercountry adoption commenced in Sweden in the aftermath of the Korean War, most adoptions were "independent". Parents went out to Korea and other countries to find a child they could adopt, just as British couples went to Romania a few years ago. In the mid-sixties, the Swedish Government, acting as 'a clearing house and post office for applications' (Andersson, 1991), entered into a bilateral agreement with South Korea, rather as the British Government has with Romania. In 1969 the Adoption Centre (AC) was founded by Swedish parents who had already adopted from abroad and developed a more comprehensive service for would-be adopters, including preparation courses (Andersson, 1986). Other voluntary agencies were to follow.

The Adoption Assistance Act of 1979 provided for the approval of such organisations to act as mediators. Organisations have established links with overseas agencies and can offer an informed service to guide parents through the complex process of adopting from abroad. In seeking authorisation they must show that they have such links and demonstrate a thorough knowledge of the laws and procedures of the countries in question (NIA, 1985, 1991).

A similar process occurred in the Netherlands. Early adoptions were largely private but later voluntary adoption agencies were formed by groups of parents and in 1975 the Netherlands Intercountry Child Welfare Organisation (later to become Worldchildren) was formed under the supervision of the Ministry of Justice with a view to it eventually being responsible for *all* intercountry adoptions. This never happened and soon other new agencies arose, while independent adoptions continued. Since the 1988 Act on Intercountry Adoption, agencies have to be licensed by the Ministry of Justice following criticisms of the variability of standards. In granting a license, the interest of the adopted child is seen as the primary consideration (Hoksbergen, 1986, 1991; Bunjes, 1992). Larger agencies make all the necessary practical arrangements as well as being involved in preparation and post-adoption support. For example, Worldchildren allocate a social work professional and a procedural administrator to each set of applicants (White, 1993).

The need for adoption assistance in the UK
In its response to the Adoption Law Review, BAAF (1993) noted that the present system in the UK has major gaps which 'effectively require the adopters, at some point, to "go it alone" to identify the child they might adopt'. This contrasts sharply with the situation in the Netherlands and Sweden outlined in the previous section. The question that must be addressed is whether the mediating activities carried out by the Dutch and Swedish agencies should be a responsibility of agencies in this country or whether they can be left to prospective adopters.

In the White Paper, the Government notes that accredited bodies would be authorised to arrange adoptions, but does not indicate whether they would expect this to involve direct links with sending countries as opposed to completing home studies and forwarding reports to the Department of Health.

It seems to us that there are a number of key tasks, in addition to the approval of prospective adopters, that must be carried out and which could properly be allocated by a Central Authority to accredited bodies:
1 Establishing and maintaining links with agencies in other countries, especially in *sending* countries, and building up information about routes into ICA for children from those countries.

2 Facilitating contacts with relevant authorities, for example, embassies in sending countries.

3 Establishing common standards in the preparation of adopters and developing preparation courses.

4 Developing an exchange service to optimise matching of available children with approved prospective adopters.

5 Making practical arrangements for adopters to travel to the sending country and bring back the child placed with them.

6 Ensuring that maximum information is provided on the child's background and that links with the sending country are maintained to enable information to flow back to those countries.

7 Assisting in establishing volunteer post-adoption groups utilising the experience of those who have already adopted from abroad.

8 Helping those adopted from abroad to trace their origins when they reach adulthood.

Some of these tasks are primarily about standard setting and a national co-ordinating role, which might be retained by the Central Authority or allocated to another national body as in the case of the Swedish National Board or Bureau VIA in the Netherlands (Selman, 1993; van Tuyll, 1994). Others are clearly appropriate for adoption agencies, whether national or local.

The provision of adoption assistance
The White Paper (DoH, 1993) identifies three possible types of "accredited agency" which might be expected to take on such work.

Local authority social services departments
The White Paper states that ' . . . local authorities would be accredited agencies' (Section 6.22, p 16). The existence of well-developed services for *domestic* adoption offers one area of potential for developing a high quality service for *intercountry* adoption, especially as the Government has indicated that in overseas adoptions local authority social services departments will have a 'statutory duty to provide or arrange for . . . assessments and an explicit power to charge for them' (section 6.33, p 17).

There would seem to be an implicit authority to 'prepare and arrange' such adoptions (section 6.21, p 16), but it is hard to see how this could effectively be done by *all* local authorities. Even if a majority felt able to offer counselling and assessment, it would not be feasible to have a situation where local authorities formed links with sending countries, most of which would prefer to work with just one or two *specialised* agencies, recognising that this gives the closest control over the process of ICA.

One or two might feel, in the light of the volume of local interest, that they *could* extend their activities in this direction; others might seek to establish a local consortium as in Greater Manchester (Humphries, 1993) or to contract out work to a voluntary agency. BAAF (1993) has suggested the development of 'some kind of intercountry adoption exchange'. What is clearly *impracticable* is for all local authorities to offer a full service. What is clearly *unacceptable* is for mediation activities to be left with non-accredited bodies or to individual applicants, as occurs at present.

Existing voluntary agencies
The White Paper states that ' . . . the Government considers that at least one voluntary adoption agency, able to build up skills and experience in this complex field, would be a valuable addition' (section 6.22, p 16). Such agencies have often developed expertise in arranging placements for children with special needs, which could be invaluable in preparing prospective adopters for intercountry adoption. One of the *national* voluntary agencies would be in a strong position to develop a service available to all citizens. However, none has come forward yet, almost certainly because of the strong resource implications.

An alternative is for *local* activity by voluntary agencies, as exemplified by Childlink's relationship with the London Boroughs (see Childlink, 1992; Selman, 1993), but at present their contracted role ceases on completion of the home study, although post-placement advice is often given. However, while agencies such as Childlink might be well placed to provide mediation services, the setting up costs of launching such a major new development would be prohibitive, even if the new service might eventually prove self-financing (Hesselgrave, 1994).

Clearly, voluntary organisations cannot afford to take speculative risks. Given the need for such services to be developed in relation to fulfilling properly the UK's obligations under the Hague Convention, there is perhaps some room for arguing that central government resources should be allocated to provide at least pump-priming finance.

It is clear that no voluntary agency should take on board such work *without* adequate resources. However, dependence on *local* initiatives alone will make it hard to ensure even access to support throughout the UK.

New specialist agency dedicated to ICA

The White Paper says that 'the Government will continue to encourage those with appropriate insights and skills to enter the field of inter-country adoption on a full agency basis' (section 6.22, p 16).

If such an agency were to emerge it is possible that its origins, like other European agencies, would lie in existing parents' organisations such as STORK [now AFAA]. However, it must be recognised that services elsewhere in Europe have evolved in very different contexts; for example, in the Netherlands a comprehensive family counselling service is nationally accessible at any stage after an adoption. We would argue that the current situation in Britain is very different and that the role of the parents' organisations should rather be to work closely with existing statutory and/or voluntary agencies to develop services for intercountry adoption. It is unclear how effective lines of communication are between the parents' organisations and the Department of Health in exploring this area.

If a specialist agency were to emerge, a major problem would be funding, even if a lot of the work were to be done by (volunteer) existing intercountry adopters. This would be further exacerbated by the absence of any existing professional staff. Many of the smaller European agencies run on the basis of almost entirely using volunteers. Would this be acceptable in the UK? Would it even be *possible* under existing regulations for the approval of adoption agencies? Furthermore, even where agencies make a substantial charge for their services, a govern-ment subsidy may be required for financial viability, as is the case in the preparation courses run by VIA in the Netherlands.

There are other issues which would have to be resolved such as whether the agency would concentrate on mediating activities (as in Sweden and the Netherlands) or also do home studies; whether a number of country-specific agencies would be preferable to one dealing with many countries; whether a placement-only agency could be truly child centred and avoid pressures to seek out babies for placement (Selman, 1991, pp 169–175).

Even if an agency were to operate only in relation to one or two countries and to concentrate on mediation there would be a need for major investment in setting up a high quality service. Without such investment, in both professional and administrative staff, a specialist ICA agency would find it hard to maintain standards expected in relation to domestic adoption.

The crucial lesson to be learned from looking at the experience of Sweden and the Netherlands is that skilled mediation offers control over the actual process of intercountry adoption, and so is the best prospect for eliminating child trafficking and safeguarding the interests not only of children, but of birth and adoptive parents. If Britain is not to establish a separate specialised agency, it is essential to ensure that the work such an agency might do, both in placement and in post-adoption support, is carried out within *our* agency system. This will entail going well beyond the services currently provided, and indeed beyond those envisaged in the White Paper.

Post-adoption services for ICA – a neglected area

In the Netherlands there has been a growing awareness of the risks of intercountry adoption and of a number of problems emerging in adolescence, where the availability of skilled help may be essential (Hoksbergen, 1987, 1991). This was a factor in the development of the preparation courses run by VIA (Bunjes, 1992; van Tuyll, 1994). Previously, all information about the experience of ICA was dealt with at the home study stage as in the UK, but this was felt to preclude the opportunity for intensive input at an earlier stage. It is interesting to note that an estimated 30 per cent of course participants considering adoption from overseas do not proceed to adopt (White, 1993).

Such concerns have also led to calls for better post-adoption support and there are clearly important lessons to be drawn from post-adoption problems in families created through ICA, which can be fed back into the preparation courses. Indeed, the two services are combined by the agency WAN (Werkverband Adoptie Nazorg) in the Netherlands. World-children also makes extensive use of adopters to run locally based groups for prospective adopters to help them cope with the waiting time involved in an intercountry adoption and in post-placement support groups. This highlights the absolute need for co-ordination of practice developments nationally at all stages of the adoption process. The needs of children adopted from abroad who wish to find out more about their origins will also have to be addressed on a national basis by, for example, developing adequate central record-keeping, if the UK is to discharge its Hague responsibilities.

A possible way forward

The White Paper proposals represent a major step forward in regulating intercountry adoption in the UK and will hopefully put an end to "back-door" entry.

What seems to us to remain unresolved is whether there is an assumption that the actual linking of prospective adopters and child will continue to be a responsibility of the parents in conjunction with organisations or individuals in the sending countries and whether such adoptions can be described as "agency" adoptions in the full sense of the word.

One problem about the development of mediating activities is the uncertainty over the extent of ICA in years to come. It seems unlikely that the UK will see absolute numbers as high as those experienced by countries such as Sweden and the Netherlands (500–1,000 per annum in recent years and over 1,500 per annum in the mid 1980s) and there is no prospect of a comparable level *per head* of population which would mean over 10,000 adoptions a year.

The BAAF intercountry adoption survey (BAAF, 1991) estimated that a total of 715 adoptions in 1990–91 involved children from overseas. However, estimates are no substitute for facts when planning services and government attention needs to be given to the proper collection and publication of adoption statistics in this area lamentably lacking at the moment. If the numbers are closer to current DoH estimates of around

200 per year, the need for the work to be done by specialist bodies is even more evident.

It is clearly vital that the UK Government recognises the need for appropriate bodies to carry out the crucial tasks we have identified above. Although there appears to be *some* acknowledgment of this in the White Paper, there has been no recognition of the unavoidable costs of meeting our obligations to children adopted from abroad and to the families who adopt them. Indeed, the paper states that implementation of its proposals must be 'cost-neutral' (DoH, 1993, 7.4, p 18). To move forward, at least pump-priming resources will be needed to enable organisations with invaluable expertise in this area to develop the necessary services in a coherent fashion.

Given the particular context of the UK, support might most fruitfully be given to establishing a central co-ordinating body for ICA, perhaps through an appropriate voluntary organisation. Such a body could also be encouraged to offer mediation on a national level, together with development of more local consortia and an intercountry adoption exchange service (BAAF, 1993). Failure to do so will perpetuate a haphazard and patchy service which at best will not discharge the UK's duties under the Hague Convention honourably, and at worst may expose children adopted from abroad to unnecessary risk.

Little has changed since the publication of this article in summer 1994. The election of a new government has delayed further plans to introduce a new Adoption Bill and done nothing to reverse its predecessor's decision to end funding for the Overseas Adoption Helpline, although the Helpline continues its work as an approved charity with independent funding. The UK has still not ratified the Hague Convention. Despite progress by the Department of Health in negotiating bilateral agreements (e.g. with China, Romania, Belarus, and Peru and potentially with the Philippines, Paraguay and Bolivia) and the accreditation of Doncaster Adoption and Family Welfare as an agency for ICA, in practice we still do not have an agency which extends its remit to mediation.

Meanwhile, Sweden has ratified the Hague Convention and passed new legislation, the Intercountry Adoption Intermediation Act 1997, which requires adoptions from abroad to be mediated only by associa-

tions authorised by NIA, unless a child is related to the adopters or there are "special reasons", in which case alternative procedures must still be approved by the Swedish National Board (NIA, 1997).

References

Andersson G, 'The adopting and adopted Swedes and their contemporary society', in Hoksbergen R, *Adoption in Worldwide Perspective*, Lisse, Swets and Zeitliger, 1986, The Netherlands.

Andersson G, *Intercountry Adoptions in Sweden – The experience of 25 years and 32,000 placements*, paper presented at International Conference on Adoption, Edinburgh, 1991.

Andersson G, personal communication, June 1993.

BAAF, *Intercountry Adoption: A Survey of Agencies*, BAAF, 1991.

BAAF, *The BAAF Response to the Review of Adoption Law*, BAAF, 1993.

Bunjes L, *Foreign Adoption in the Netherlands: General information and preparation*, Maarssen, The Netherlands, 1992.

Childlink, *Intercountry Adoption Procedures for Referrals – Applications – Assessments*, London, Childlink, 1992.

Defence for Children International (DCI), *Preliminary Findings of a Joint Investigation on Independent Intercountry Adoptions* DCI, 'Terre des Hommes', ISS, 1991.

Department of Health, *Adoption: The future* Cm 2288, HMSO, 1993.

Duncan W, 'The Hague Convention on the protection of children and co-operation in respect of intercountry adoption', *Adoption & Fostering*, 17:3, 1993.

Hesselgrave C, personal communication, February 1994.

Hoksbergen R, 'Thirty years of adoption practice in the Netherlands' in Hoksbergen R (ed), *Adoption in Worldwide Perspective*, Lisse, Swets and Zeitliger, 1986, The Netherlands.

Hoksbergen R, *Adopted Children at Home and School*, Lisse, Swets and Zeitliger, 1987, The Netherlands.

Hoksbergen R, 'Intercountry adoption coming of age in the Netherlands: basic issues, trends and developments', in Altstein H and Simon R J, *Intercountry Adoption: A multinational perspective*, Praeger, 1991, USA.

Humphrey M and Humphrey H, *Intercountry Adoption: Practical experiences*, Routledge, 1993.

Humphries M, personal communication, 1993.

International Bar Association, The *Intercountry Adoption Process from the UK Adoptive Parents' Perspective*, IBA, 1991.

Landau E, *Black Market Adoptions*, F. Watts, 1990, USA.

NIA (Swedish National Board for Intercountry Adoptions), *Adoption in Sweden*, Solna, Sweden, 1985.

NIA (Swedish National Board for Intercountry Adoptions), *Legal Provisions Concerning Adoption*, Solna, Sweden, 1991.

NIA (Swedish National Board for Intercountry Adoptions), *Legal Provisions Concerning Adoption*, Stockholm, 1997.

Pierce W and Vitello R, 'Independent adoptions and the "Baby Market" ', in Hibbs E, *Adoption in International Perspective*, Madison, IUP, 1991.

Selman P, 'Intercountry adoption: what can Britain learn from the experience of other European countries?', in Room G (ed), *Towards a European Welfare State*, pp 151–86, SAUS, 1991.

Selman P, 'Services for intercountry Adoption in the UK: some lessons from Europe', *Adoption & Fostering*, 17:3, 1993.

Textor M, 'International adoption in West Germany: a private affair', in Altstein H and Simon R J, *Intercountry Adoption: A multinational perspective*, Praeger, 1991, USA.

van Loon J H A, *Report on Intercountry Adoption*, Hague Conference on Private International Law, April 1990.

van Tuyll L, 'Intercountry adoption in the Netherlands: compulsory preparation classes for new adoptive parents', *Adoption & Fostering* 18:3, 1994.

White J, *Adoption in the Netherlands*, BAAF, 1993.

Section V
Post-adoption support

During the heyday of "closed" baby adoptions, it seemed there was no need for any further involvement of adoption agencies once an adoption order was granted. Bringing up the children was thought unlikely to pose major problems. Previously childless adopters usually wanted nothing so much as to merge with the population of parents in general. They did not want further interference or reminders that they were different.

The major changes in adoption patterns and processes we have noted so far have combined to make the notion of the clean break untenable, so that needs and demands for contact with services after adoption have become increasingly recognised. These needs arise from each party in the adoption network. Since 1930 in Scotland and the 1980s in England and Wales, adopted young adults have been able to request information about their families and potentially seek contact. The publicity which followed the opening up of access to records in England and Wales led to an upsurge in interest, accompanied by a need and legal requirement for counselling (Haimes and Timms, 1986; Lambert *et al*, 1991).

The growth in placements of children from care has meant that increasing numbers of adopters have wanted access to advice and help to deal with some of the emotional, behavioural and educational difficulties they encounter with their children (Phillips and McWilliam, 1996). Agencies like BAAF and Barnardo's have offered consultancy for those who have adopted transracially, so they can better maintain the children's positive sense of their origins and identity.

The needs and wishes of birth families were for a long time ignored, but now their rights are being acknowledged, albeit imperfectly. Birth mothers' deep sense of loss, guilt and lifelong interest in the welfare of their children have been amply documented (e.g. Howe *et al*, 1991). The increasingly common practice of initial meetings and "post-box" communication, as well as the rarer face-to-face contacts, often require an agency to act as an intermediary.

As a result of all these issues, both statutory and voluntary agencies have developed a range of post-adoption services over the last ten years (Triseliotis *et al*, 1997). Some cater for specific purposes; others offer an integrated service. One of the pioneers was the Post-Adoption Centre in London. **Sawbridge (1988)** described how this was mainly set up to assist adoptive families, but was also open to enquiries from birth parents who came to make up a significant proportion of referrals. In the late 1980s, adoptive parents' requests for help mainly centred on how to:
- communicate with children about adoption;
- parent black children;
- deal with aggression in adolescence; and
- develop relationships with "unreachable" children.

Many adopted people wanted assistance with searching out their birth parents. Some black adoptees expressed anger, sadness and bewilderment about unconscious racism in their adoptive families of a kind which has often not been represented in research samples. Birth mothers had a tremendous need to talk, especially with others in the same position. They wanted to express their grief and reduce their sense of isolation. Some wished to trace the children they had lost years before.

Feast (1992) described a more specialist counselling service, again in the voluntary sector, for adopted adults wishing to have access to their birth records. Nearly all of those referred wanted to trace their birth families once they had viewed their records. Among their reasons for seeking to trace were a desire for factual information (e.g. about appearance and heredity), concern for the birth parents' well-being, a need for reassurance about the circumstances of the adoption, and a desire for a real relationship with birth family members. As other studies have shown, with few exceptions, interest in information and contact with birth families did not signify rejection of the adoptive family (Lambert *et al*, 1990).

The views of adoptive parents about a support service was ascertained by **McGhee (1995)**. BAAF's Scottish Centre provided a one-off consultation to adoptive parents who were currently experiencing difficulties. The families were often quite well supported by family and friends, but still wanted specialist help. A majority of the adopters felt they gained reassurance, insight or a fresh perspective. They were also given information about counselling and support groups available for longer-term help. In many areas, a range of more continuous supports is now available for adopters from local authorities and/or voluntary agencies. Besides the national support group (PPIAS), these include local groups, workshops, newsletters and respite care, as well as referral to psychological and psychiatric services if required (Magee and Thoday, 1995; Triseliotis *et al*, 1997).

Logan and Hughes (1995) conducted a survey of users of a post-adoption service in the North-West of England set up to assist birth mothers whose children had been adopted. Often the women had longstanding emotional and mental health problems, for which individual help was needed. Many did not necessarily want direct contact with their children, but they did yearn for knowledge of their children's welfare and progress.

A group of parents who face particular difficulties are those whose children are adopted against their wishes (Ryburn, 1994). This has been a growing population since the permanency movement led local authorities to be much more active in seeking to end contact and request courts to dispense with parental agreement in order to facilitate the adoption of children. The parents often have strong emotional needs, yet can get little help from local authorities towards whom they often feel bitter. **Mason and Selman (1997)** evaluated a project established in the North-East of England to assist parents in this position. They reported 'the fact that they had lost the battle to keep their children had not lessened their desire for contact' (p 29). The parents valued highly the opportunity to meet with others like themselves, gain a sympathetic hearing and obtain specific advice about the law and procedures from project workers. This helpful project had to close when funding was not renewed.

17 The Post Adoption Centre – what are the users teaching us?

Phillida Sawbridge

Phillida Sawbridge was Director of the Post Adoption Centre from its inception in 1986 to her retirement in 1994. Here we present the 20th Hilda Lewis Memorial Lecture which she gave at the BAAF Medical Group seminar on 'Post Adoption help for families: who, when and how?' in London on 19 October 1987.

This paper was published in Adoption & Fostering, 12:1, 1988.

I did not have the privilege of knowing Dr Hilda Lewis personally, but ever since I started working in the field of adoption, her name has been familiar to me. I turned to Margaret Kornitzer for more information about her, and got a pen-picture which could not be bettered. She said, 'In the early days of the Standing Conference of Societies Registered for Adoption (SCSRA) (how many people recognise that name as the fore-runner of *BAAF*?), medically speaking, Hilda Lewis was "It". Her standing and her approach were early factors in the success of the Standing Conference, and she needed no stepping stones to knowledge or understanding – she was there already.' What greater tribute could one pay?

For those who may not know much about her, Lady Lewis was born Hilda Stoessiger in 1900. She graduated with Honours at the London School of Medicine for Women and became honorary physician to the Princess Louise Kensington Hospital for Children in London. In 1932 she was appointed Medical Officer to the Maudsley Hospital and two years later she married Aubrey (later Sir Aubrey) Lewis.

Later Hilda Lewis became an adviser to the Caldecott Community and made a study of the background and behaviour of the children there, published in 1954 as *Deprived Children: The Mersham experiment*. This was part of her life-long interest in the problems of children deprived of care from their natural parents. It was her interest in this field which led to her involvement from the start with the SCSRA and to her becoming psychiatric adviser to the Children's Society. She died in 1966.

As I was thinking about this lecture, I tried to visualise Hilda Lewis and I wished I had been present last year when a picture of her was shown on the screen. I was then reminded of a story told by Dr Fred Stone at the ABAA Seminar in 1969 in Scarborough. He described how he had asked a little adopted boy to draw his birth mother. The child managed it all, from the feet up, until he got to the head. He then broke down in sobs, saying, 'I can never see her face'.

Now, for me not to be able to visualise Hilda Lewis' face is not a tragedy, much as I wish I had known her in her lifetime. But the sadness inherent in every adoption is precisely that: adopted people cannot see, or remember, the face of the mother who brought them into the world – the first face that most babies learn to recognise and from which they learn about loving and being cared for.

Fortunately, most babies being adopted are placed very quickly, and another mother's face is the one they learn to recognise and love. But as adopted people grow older and begin to understand about relationships and the implications of a mother parting with a child, most of them realise – and have to learn to live with – the sorrow, the loss that is one aspect of adoption for all parties.

Before you start thinking you are in for a sad session, let me hasten to say that I am focusing on pain only as doctors do, appropriately, I hope, in a Medical Group seminar, with a view to understanding it better and, where possible, easing it. I also think there has been a tendency to view adoption as an easy and happy solution to three parties' problems: a mother cannot bring up her baby, a couple cannot have a baby, a baby needs a home. Transfer the baby and everyone's needs are met. At one level that is, of course, true, but what that fails to acknowledge is the pain, anger, impotence, frustration and grief of the mother; the probable pain, anger, impotence, frustration and grief which the childless couple had gone through in learning about and accepting their childlessness; and the grief of the child, however young, in losing the mother. While all these feelings may not be uppermost at the time of the placement for adoption, they will almost certainly resurface to hit the people concerned sometime during their lives.

That is what the Post-Adoption Centre is all about. We are there to try to help people when all those complicated feelings do surface.

The need for continuing support

The Centre opened in September 1986 as an independent charity, funded for three years by a private trust. The staff gradually built up to a full-time director and two full-time administrative secretaries, plus five part-time counsellors. It is open to anyone who is personally or professionally involved with an adoption.

I like to think that Hilda Lewis would have approved of the idea of this Centre. She was one of the first to recognise that the making of an Adoption Order was not the end of the matter for the participants, even if it is for social workers or other professionals. In an article in the BMJ in 1965, she referred to a proportion of adoptive parents who may 'continue to need support for many years, especially in the matter of when and how to tell the growing and inquiring child about his [sic] adoption'. She collaborated with Margaret Kornitzer in writing the first version of the leaflet called *If you are adopted* (price 6d, post free at the time of publication!) for adolescents and their parents, recognising that this was a prime time for wanting further explanation. She would probably not have been surprised to learn that this Centre had come into being, arising mainly out of the perceived need of adoptive families for support.

Perhaps she would have been less surprised than some of us at the distribution of enquiries and concerns. Although the work with adoptive families is probably the most time consuming, and they are the ones we are most likely to take on for a series of sessions, they represented only 21 per cent of the total enquiries or requests for help in the Centre's first year of operation. Forty-four per cent were adopted adults and 15 per cent were birth parents. The balance were other relatives, most often brothers and sisters, sometimes grandparents. As the workers trying to understand and help all parties, we sometimes feel like the pig in the middle or, more accurately, like the apex of a pyramid reaching down each side of the triangle. From one side the basic concern we are hearing is: '*Is it just because she's adopted?*' On the second side it is: '*I just need to know, to feel whole*'. On the third side: '*The sadness and the guilt have never gone away*'.

I would like now to look a little more closely at these concerns as they are brought to us and at what we can learn from them, both to inform future practice and to find ways to help. I would stress that the people we see are a self-selected group, who come because they do have concerns. Many more do not come because adoption is not raising particular issues for them. It is important to remember that.

I will start with the adoptive parents, since that was really the starting point of the Centre, growing as it did out of a more acute awareness of their needs than of those of the other parties. One interesting fact is that very few of the parents adopted children with special needs: almost all adopted apparently normal, healthy babies or sometimes toddlers.

Adoptive parents

Adoptive parents have come to us with a range of concerns, but in broad terms they fall into four main groupings. The first are those who want help in "telling" or "explaining" as it is perhaps better called. It may surprise you that this area of concern, recognised by Hilda Lewis, still remains over 20 years later. So much more is done these days to prepare adoptive parents and help them explain adoption to the child. But I think that, vital and helpful as good preparation is, there is a limit to how much can be absorbed in advance. Also, there is a big difference between discussing something in the abstract and being confronted with doing it with a real live child whom you love and want to protect from anything that might risk hurting her or him. When your son or daughter asks: 'Why did my first mummy give me away?', finding a way to answer not only the overt but the hidden questions is highly challenging. It is also not easy for infertile parents to have to open up the old wounds again, and find a way of explaining their childlessness which sufficiently conveys their sadness and longing for a child, but does not overburden the adopted child with it. On top of these considerations, adopted children these days have frequently suffered traumatic experiences before placement, whether by several abrupt changes of caretaker, by neglect, or by actual physical or sexual abuse. How much of that should parents impart to the child, and at what stages? How much does the child remember or half remember? The dilemmas are often insoluble. As one mother wrote:

I think adoptive parents need support and reassurance which is not available from the adoption societies once the baby is placed. You are

235

very much on your own unless you happen to know anyone else with adopted children. You are frightened of ruining the child's happiness by saying too much or not saying enough – making them feel too special or not special enough. As with all aspects of their lives, we want to do the best for them.

To these people we have offered two things: individual counselling to one or both parents, whether face to face, on the telephone or by letter. (A good deal of our work is done on the phone or by letter because, although we were originally expecting only to serve London and south-east England, we receive enquiries from all over the country. There is clearly a widespread need and people do not know where to turn.) We try to help people examine the issues, look at what makes explaining so hard and work out comfortable ways of handling the matter. In addition, we have run several series of workshops called 'How do I find the right words?', in which groups of parents can explore these issues together and test out different approaches. These have proved very popular and we are now also running workshops for social workers, training them to be able to run such events themselves.

The second sub-group of adoptive parents consists of white parents who have adopted black children. Some are wanting advice from our multiracial team about how to prepare the child for the racism he or she will undoubtedly encounter, and how to be better parents to a black child. Some come when there are already problems in the family and they are not sure how far racial differences are a factor, or else they know they are and want help in understanding the issues better. These are multi-faceted problems of incredible sensitivity and, partly to help with them, our black colleagues have set up a Black Advisory Group on post-adoption issues. This group has set itself a number of tasks in relation to the adoption of black children, whether by white or by black parents, and we expect our practice and understanding to benefit, as it already has from the initial one-day workshop which launched the group. We are also engaged in a continuing programme of racism awareness training, which we white workers particularly need to help us avoid the pitfalls of denial, or of resistance to acknowledging the black individual's experience. Since there is a large element of education in the kind of counselling we are doing, we have to be prepared to keep supplementing our own knowledge and understanding.

Most of the help we have offered in this area has so far been on an individual or family basis, but we plan to offer group support both to parents and to young people involved in transracial adoptions, since isolation is often a key factor.

The third sub-group of adoptive families is those in which the child, or more often teenager, is showing real aggression towards and rejection of the parents, who are at their wits' end. Sixteen-year-old Donna is a typical example. Adopted as a baby, she had been a highly rewarding child until she was about 14. Then she suddenly started to truant from school, steal from home, stay out late, often refuse to talk to her parents, and constantly throw at them that they were 'not her real parents'. Some adolescents do seem to behave like that, but for adoptive parents there is the added dimension of being made to wonder if they did have a right to this child, or if she would have been better off with other parents.

Ideally we would like to see the whole family together and also talk to Donna on her own. Sadly, she had flounced out of the home before her parents came to us, and their concern was whether and how to try to exercise any further control or even maintain contact. Donna was living with her boyfriend, whom they considered a very bad influence, and only came home when she needed money. In several long sessions with both parents, we tried to help them feel better about themselves as parents and as people, to put what happened in perspective, and to work out what they wanted to do, what it was realistic to try to do, and how to accept what they couldn't change. As in all settings, the problems of teenagers are the toughest to handle, and we haven't found any easy answers – and often not even got within sight of the teenager concerned.

The fourth sub-group of adoptive families represents those where a child, usually of primary school age, is causing concern because she or he is "cut-off", "unreachable", or else displaying behaviour which indicates all is not well – lack of concentration at school, stealing, lying or fantasising, malicious destruction, and so on. With some of these, we will offer to undertake family work. We draw on family therapy and other techniques, and try to adapt what we do to the needs of the individual family.

On several occasions it has been a real team approach, with one person working with the child, one or even two with the adults, and everyone coming together at intervals to try to integrate what is going on. The perennial question is, 'How much of this is due to adoption?'. While this is unanswerable, it is obviously something we have to keep trying to weigh. Often a child really is preoccupied by thoughts and fantasies about adoption, and frequently, in this particular group of children, the self-image of the child is very poor. While most adopted children apparently can happily accept that they were "chosen" and "special", and not dwell too much on the painful decision their birth mother had to make, there are some who feel deep down that there must have been something wrong with them to have been "given away". These children, even if they cannot articulate it, lack a sense of self-worth, however much loved and nurtured by their adoptive parents. They seem to live on an emotional tight-rope, half expecting a further rejection, perhaps seeing it where it does not exist, and unable to let themselves relax and accept the love that is on offer.

After an initial interview or maybe after several sessions of work, we refer a few of the families elsewhere, often to the Maudsley Hospital Children's Department for an assessment. Dr Stephen Wolkind, the Consultant Child Psychiatrist there, is one of our consultants, and we have been able to plug in to their services in a very useful way. Many parents are reassured by being given a full psychological assessment of their child, together with the taking of a comprehensive background history. It may be found that there is a problem like dyslexia, for which help can be offered, and which makes the behaviour more comprehensible. If not, at least such possibilities have been ruled out, and attention can be focused on either the actual handling of the child, perhaps through behavioural techniques, or on trying to give help with whatever emotional problems have been identified.

Nature versus nurture?
One of the interesting questions that arises for me from our work with this small minority of adoptive families is this: if one believes in the reversibility of early trauma – as I do, or I would not have been involved in the family placement of older children for so many years – then what

is it that makes some children apparently unable to cast off its effects? Put the other way round, what are the ingredients of a subsequent good experience of family life or of nurturing which enable so many children to overcome the loss of first parents, the effect of one or maybe two or three moves at an early age, or even worse experiences, while others seem scarred by them for life? I never seem able to escape the perennial nature/nurture dilemma. Are the scarred ones people who were born with a personality which could not cope with grief, loss or pain so early? Or was their subsequent experience not sufficiently healing to enable them to recover? Or have later problems perhaps nothing to do with early distress? I personally find too many apparent associations to believe that last alternative, but I haven't had any answers to the others. If I had, I suppose I could solve all the dilemmas of placing agencies! But perhaps, as the work of the Centre proceeds, we may begin to formulate a few new ideas on this age-old but knotty question, and we hope that the research we are involved with might have something to say on the matter.

A healthy counterbalance to the small number of distressed or disturbed adopted young people is the much, much larger percentage of adult adoptees who approach us for help or advice in finding out more about their origins. Our experience is that these are normal, healthy individuals of all ages from 18 to their 60s who simply want to know more about where they came from, why their mother could not keep them, what she is doing now and what their genetic inheritance is. This last may be less of a reason for searching now that medical forms give information on parents.

There is a lot of social pressure on people to identify and acknowledge their roots and origins. Most people's first question about a new baby is, 'Who does she look like?' (The fact that Winston Churchill, with some truth, said all newborn babies looked like him is beside the point!) At school, children make family trees. In placing older children we consciously build on identifications. We publicise photographs of children waiting for families, and are pleased when applicants find a family resemblance. The research report on Kay Donley's agency in Michigan, Spaulding for Children, was called *Chaos, Madness and Unpredictability or Placing the Child with Ears Like Uncle Harry's*. This refers to a couple who felt drawn to a child and adopted him just because he had the family ears. But if you are adopted and don't have Uncle Harry's ears, or any real resemblances to anyone in the adoptive family, isn't it understandable that you might want to seek out a blood relative to see who you do look like? I don't see that there's anything pathological about that.

"Searching" adoptees

If many of the searchers, maybe most, ultimately hope for some kind of relationship with their birth mother – and it is usually with the mother, at least at first – this need in no way imply a denigration of the parental relationship they have, or had, with their adopters. They know it is different, but the person who bore them does have a special place in their lives. If they can work out how she can fill that place alongside all the other existing relationships each has, then there is no reason why she can't be comfortably accommodated. It is only when any of the parties involved wants to cross the boundaries into a different role, or feels so threatened that they try to set up barriers, that complications or even disasters ensue. Our experience refutes the early findings of John Triseliotis that "searching" adoptees are almost by definition the product of unsatisfactory adoptive homes, or else have fairly major personal problems. They are only a minority.

Many of the searchers only begin their enquiries after their adoptive parents are dead. Nearly all say, 'I didn't want to hurt them'. They understand better than anyone how painful and difficult the explaining is for many adopters. Some know their birth parents hold information they would dearly love to have, but they are prepared to spend months on painstaking research rather than open up such a difficult subject with their adoptive parents, which has clearly become taboo.

The implications of this for both preparation and support of adopters is obvious, but we also have to remember that we are talking mostly about couples who adopted 20, 30 or even 40 years ago. However, much as practice has changed and improved, I don't think we can be complacent. If quite recent adopters are coming thankfully to our workshops for help with explaining, we have to assume that the task is little easier now than before, in spite of increased information, and that some parents will deal with it by creating the no-go area that the older generation did.

One group of adoptees whose need to search might especially be understood is those who have been transracially adopted. We have not worked with many, but those we have seen probably typify many more who have not found their way to us. What counselling has uncovered is a great deal of emotion about the adoptee's experience of unconscious racism within the family. There is a mixture of anger, sadness and bewilderment, and an awareness of being black without understanding what that means except in appearance. The adoptees have usually been struggling with a negative self-image, and a determination to discover themselves through finding the lost parent, who is usually black, whether that is the birth mother or the putative father. Sadly for some, the black parent or parents may have returned home to another country, and this renders doubly difficult the already hard task of tracing.

What then about the people being traced – the birth parents on the third side of the triangle? How do they respond and feel? Perhaps the greatest area of new ground we have broken at the Centre has been in the services we have offered to parents who have relinquished a child for adoption. In the past, it has been customary to see them through to legal adoption and then say, 'Now get on with your life and put all this behind you'. Most of them have tried to do the first part, but the "putting behind" is quite a different matter, and few have had any help at all in doing it. Twenty or 30 years later, some of them are still carrying around the pain, the guilt and the anger of what they feel they were forced to do by parental or societal pressure, and their lives have been deeply coloured by it.

Supporting birth parents
We set up a group for such mothers, and by the third meeting the numbers had grown to 24 so we had to divide up into smaller groups. We believe this is only the tip of the iceberg. Not one of these women had ever met another who identified herself as having relinquished a child for adoption. Their need to talk was overwhelming and the emotion filling the room was almost tangible. The two of us running the group were like limp rags at the end, so how each mother was feeling is hard to imagine. They ranged from a young woman who gave up her baby only four years ago, and who is finding it almost impossible to overcome her sense of loss and to get her life back together again, to several women in their 50s who had been traced by a son or daughter. These birth mothers

were happy in feeling the wheel had come full circle, although they too mourned the missing years, and the meeting had by no means solved every problem.

We feel there is a large potential client group of such parents who really do need help and support for longer than the three months following relinquishment. An Australian study (Winkler and van Keppel, 1984) showed that mothers who received counselling and support for a considerable time after the adoption coped markedly better in life than did those who received little or nothing. Among these latter, there was a high incidence of mental and physical illness, and other indications of continuing lack of adjustment.

One birth mother we have worked with, now aged 39, gave up her son for adoption 23 years ago. He had recently traced her, and when she received his letter, sent on to her from an address where she had formerly lived, she panicked. She had married unhappily and been divorced, not told her second husband about the child (feeling that telling her first husband had contributed to the poor relationship), and now felt it would be catastrophic to have contact with this son.

She came to the Centre for counselling, and after she had had time and space to get all her confused feelings off her chest, she began to see that she need not assume anything about what contact might bring. She could in fact remain in control and not go any further than she wanted to. She began to realise how much it would mean to her to know how this son had fared in life, and she ended by going off to write back to him. She suggested they correspond for a time to get to know each other a bit before seeing if both felt a meeting would be appropriate. Over a period of weeks this is what happened, and during that time she got up her courage to tell her husband. He was wonderfully understanding and supportive and the eventual outcome was a meeting between mother and son, followed by a visit to the mother's home to meet her husband. This mother is now trying to persuade her son to tell his adoptive parents what he has done, and is most anxious that they should not feel threatened by her appearance on the scene.

That is not always the way. Another mother who was found by her 28-year-old daughter when she was in her late 40s, viewed it as the outcome she had longed and prayed for all those years and engulfed her daughter in an overpowering and smothering love. The adopters were jealous and hurt, but the birth mother had not resolved the deep bitterness she had felt ever since being refused help to keep her baby, and she felt it was now her turn as a parent. The daughter was apparently going along with this in the early days, but frankly I foresee problems ahead. Be that as it may, I cannot help feeling that more work with this mother in the beginning would have avoided her harbouring the long-standing bitterness she still feels, and which is guiding her actions and attitudes.

Tracing can bring other difficulties. We are aware, for instance, of more than one example of the dangers of a sexual relationship developing between a still young and attractive mother and her adult son who may remind her of his father. Such attraction can also be felt by brothers and sisters who meet as adults, not having grown up with the incest taboos between them. None of these new relationships is simple and there are no blueprints for any of them.

Emerging issues

Now that I have outlined some of the concerns and feelings of the three main parties to an adoption, I should like to begin to pull the picture together by highlighting some of the issues we see emerging. This first year of operation has given us a unique opportunity to observe and begin trying to evaluate some of the consequences of adoption work over the past few decades, and to try to identify what can be learned for current practice.

I have touched on adopters' concerns over explaining adoption, on the challenges of transracial placements, the tribulations of some teenagers, the "blocked" younger child and the effects of early trauma. I have mentioned some of the factors involved in adult adoptees' search for birth parents, openness of communication and the feelings and needs of birth parents. Underlying some of these are other themes, for instance, infertility. I feel Hilda Lewis would have a sense of *déjà vu* here. In the past, infertility had to be proved before parents could adopt, and many childless couples are still turning to adoption as a way of founding a family. I remember only too well trotting out the all-important phrase in reports on prospective adopters: 'They have "come to terms" with their infertility'. Can people? Most people do in one way or another learn to live with losses of all kinds, but that doesn't mean the feelings engendered by the loss won't come back to hit them at various stages. For example, as teenagers mature sexually, infertile parents can feel very threatened or inadequate.

Discovering which of the parents is infertile has sometimes shed light on a perplexing picture of unbalanced relationships, or on particularly defensive reactions in one partner. There is nothing new in this – I recall being taught such things when I first trained as a social worker. But there are fashions in social work as in psychiatry and medicine, and sometimes what we or our predecessors knew gets submerged or forgotten in the excitement of discovering new and different aspects of the work.

Another theme we have been conscious of is again one that was a by-word in adoption in Hilda Lewis' time: "matching". It was probably partly due to transracial adoptions that the attitude to matching changed, and adopters were more or less expected to take whatever child came next on the list, rather than be selected for comparability of colour or background. At the Centre, we are realising how much it helps children's confidence and sense of belonging in their family if they can identify similarities with parents. It is also a factor in developing a smoother relationship with birth parents if the adoptee seeks them out as an adult.

Finally, although there are many more underlying themes I could dwell on if time permitted, I want to highlight the one I believe applies to all parties and which is somehow the key to the whole situation: that is, the weighing of gain and loss. I began by referring to the pain each person feels, and this is because, for everyone, there is some loss involved. What workers in this field have to try to do is help people balance the loss with the appropriate gain. It is significant that we have most neglected those who stand to lose most and gain least – the birth mothers. If a sense of the loss seems overwhelmingly uppermost at times, we must also remember that, for probably years on end, the gains have predominated throughout the childhood of most adopted people. There is no absolute remedy for childlessness, for the loss of a child or for the loss of parents. *But adoption still gets as near as it is possible to substituting maximum gains.* If I seem to have emphasised "loss" more, it is only because that is the nature of our work. But even those who come in distress usually emphasise how positive the overall experience is or has been. Having problems doesn't invalidate a whole experience.

Building better services

In conclusion, I would like to emphasise the need for better services for adoptive and birth families. We have a golden opportunity in the forthcoming implementation of section 1 of the Children Act 1975. This requires local authorities to offer a comprehensive adoption service, in collaboration with voluntary agencies, including the availability of counselling for all parties. Once again, it is an extra requirement on local authorities for which no extra money is being made available, so one sees that the Government's commitment is hardly whole-hearted. Nevertheless, there are some things that can be done without requiring too much in the way of extra resources. Services to relinquishing mothers must clearly be improved, and this could mean less demand later for psychiatric and other interventions. Likewise services for adopters, in terms of the availability of counselling or groups to help with issues like explaining at different stages of the child's life; and most especially, services for the parents of turbulent teenagers.

This is an improvement which many parents of non-adopted children would welcome, as few people know where to turn when adolescence becomes really disruptive. But over and over again, parents tell us that adoption has either been over-emphasised or ignored by those trying to help them, or that they were being forced into a theoretical mould rather than being really listened to in the way they wanted.

We are struggling to learn what a really good and helpful service is, and as we do so, we are increasingly conscious that this kind of follow-up is vital to a proper understanding of where placement practice should be going. We hope to keep sharing the lessons we learn. It is perhaps symbolic that the first formal occasion to do so should be in honour of a woman who understood the issues so well, and so much in advance of her time.

References

Winkler R C and van Keppel M, *Relinquishing Mothers in Adoption*, Melbourne: Institute for Family Studies, 1984, Australia.

18 Working in the adoption circle – outcomes of section 51 counselling

Julia Feast

Julia Feast is Project Leader of The Children's Society's Post-Adoption and Care: Counselling and Research Project, London. When she wrote this article in 1992 she was a post-adoption counsellor with The Children's Society and a guardian ad litem and Reporting Officer with the Inner and North London panel.

This paper was published in Adoption & Fostering, 16:4, 1992.

The Children's Society has been involved in adoption since 1935. It used to be one of the largest adoption agencies and during the 1960s placed over 6,500 babies with new families. However, like many other adoption agencies during the 1980s it moved away from placing babies to finding homes for children who were deemed difficult to place.

At the time of writing The Children's Society had six family placement projects throughout England and Wales which provided services for local authorities placing children who had special needs and required a permanent substitute home. All these projects provided post-adoption services, and part of their work was to provide counselling to adopted adults who wished to have access to their birth records under section 51 of the 1976 Adoption Act.

This article was written not only to share the results and outcomes of my work with adopted adults during a three-year period from July 1988 to July 1991, but also to explore some of the many issues and challenges raised in this area of work.

Services offered
The Society offers an ongoing service to adopted adults including statutory counselling, providing information from the Society's records and advice and support for as long as it is needed. Advice is offered on

WORKING IN THE ADOPTION CIRCLE

how to conduct a search for the birth family and an intermediary service is provided when members of the birth family are located. We also offer a counselling service for the birth and adoptive families.

Before contacting an agency, the adopted adult will often have considered some of the emotions she or he may experience when they begin their journey in search of information and their birth families, for example, happiness, elation, hope, attraction, compassion and fear. They may not have considered the more negative feelings, however, and attention therefore needs to be given to emotions such as sadness, resentment, guilt, jealousy, anger and bitterness. A typical example is given below.

Brian was 28 years old when he found his birth family. He discovered that his parents had married and that he had full siblings. After the initial feelings of elation and compassion he felt towards his birth parents for having no choice but to place him for adoption, some weeks later he felt an enormous sense of loss that he had not been brought up by them, and felt resentment towards his brother and sister who had.

These emotions are not only experienced by the adopted adult, but also by the birth and adoptive family members. It is important to provide a service for them too, although inevitably this has resource implications.

Means of referrals
From July 1988 to July 1991 I received a total of 165 referrals. One hundred and thirty-two were from adopted adults who requested access to their birth records, 33 were from adoptive and birth parents and people who were not adopted, but who were brought up in the Society's care.

Of the 132 adopted adults, 106 people approached the Society directly. Sixteen were referred after being counselled by the General Register Office (GRO) and ten after receiving counselling from the local authority.

These statistics show that many people bypass the General Register Office and the figures produced by the GRO therefore may not reflect the true number of adopted people who come forward for information. This may be a common occurrence with other adoption agencies.

Characteristics of those referred

Out of the total of 132 adopted adults 84 were women and 48 were men. Eleven out of the 132 who received counselling were of mixed parentage and transracially placed. This is a small number but may reflect the fact that until the 1970s and 1980s black children were often not placed for adoption, but remained instead in the care system. They, like children with a physical or mental disability, were considered hard to place – 'Black children, for the most part, remained outside the scope of adoption services' (Ladner, 1977, p 60). Figure 1 shows the age at which people first approached The Society for counselling. It can be seen that women tend to come forward earlier than men, although the peak for both genders is still the 26–30 age group (e.g. 37 females came forward between the ages of 18–25, whereas males totalled 12).

The peak age of 26–30 often relates to other life events – marriage, birth of children, death of adoptive parents. Some feel simply that they have reached a stage in their lives where they need to explore their origins and obtain some answers to their questions.

As it seems that 26–30 is the most common age for adopted people to begin their quest for information from their birth records, this may help agencies predict their workloads for the coming years. Adoption placement apparently reached its peak in the 1960s, which suggests that many adoption agencies and local authorities may experience an influx of referrals as these adults reach their late 20s and 30s.

Tracing

One hundred and twenty-six people made a decision to trace after they received information from their records. Only six people made a decision not to go any further. Some of the reasons given for this were that they felt disloyal to their adoptive family, that they were afraid of disrupting their birth families' lives, and ultimately that they were afraid of being rejected.

Not all of the 126 who initially decided to trace have taken their search forward. Reasons given included having no time to trace because of family commitments; being unable to find the person sought, particularly when the surname is a common one such as Smith. For others, the time is just not right. Some people do not take their search forward immediately, but return to the agency at a later date for advice and support.

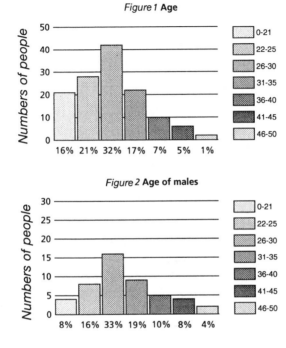

Figure 1 **Age**

Figure 2 **Age of males**

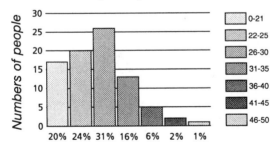

Figure 3 **Age of females**

Table 1

Stages of readiness for information and tracing

Feelings	Circumstances
Not safe to know or to ask.	Insecurity of adoptive parents who give limited information about birth family. Negative attitudes towards birth mother in records/by adopters. Feels resentful about adoption. Awareness of potential for unpleasant information in birth records. Waiting for death of adoptive parents – strong feelings of loyalty.
Safe to know, but no apparent need to find out more.	Given information by adopters. Loyalty/sensitivity to feelings of adopters. No events in life stimulating need to know more.

Readiness to seek information or use counselling

Safe to know and a desire to know more. Does not want to trace or wants to put the decision to trace on hold.	Passed a life event (e.g., birth of child or marriage) and wants to know more. Loyalty and sensitivity to feelings of adopters or practical difficulties prevent him/her. Need to digest information received. Does not wish to disrupt his/her own or birth families' lives. Afraid of facing rejection.

Readiness to trace or be traced

Safe to know, and a desire to know more than is in records, or need to have direct contact. Feels ready to trace.	Desire to know that birth parent is alive and well. Wants to let birth parent know s/he is well and reassure about the adoption. Curious to know who s/he looks like. Birth parent is no longer a fantasy but reality. Would like to develop friendship. Curious to know about siblings. Wants to know about family's medical history.

In Table 1 I have hypothesised that the relationship between feelings, circumstances and the adopted person's readiness to trace.

Figure 4
Tracing

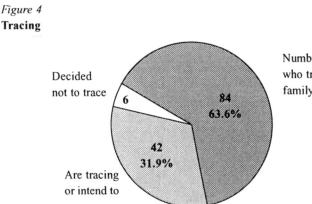

Figure 4 shows a breakdown of the decisions people took after receiving information and shows that 63 per cent have located their birth families.

Normally the birth mother is approached in the first instance. In the three years to July 1991 we had received only three outright refusals for contact from birth mothers and one refusal from a birth father. Decisions are often related to current circumstances, for example, partners against contact or children who don't know about the adoptee.

Once people have contacted the birth family, decisions are then made about how they should progress. Discussions and negotiations take place with the parties concerned to explore some of the options, for example, exchanging letters and photographs, a personal meeting or telephone contact. Whichever approach is chosen, it is directed by the parties themselves. Most who decide to have a personal meeting prefer to do so without the intermediary being present and usually away from starchy office conditions. Sometimes, the initial approach has been made through another family member (e.g. grandparents or aunt or uncle) and satisfactory contact can be maintained while the birth parents consider whether they want to have contact with the child they relinquished for adoption.

Maria, aged 18, approached the Society for information. The records indicated that her birth grandparents knew of her birth and after a few months of searching, her maternal grandmother was located. The grandmother was delighted to hear that Maria wanted contact and was sure her daughter, Angela, would be equally pleased. However, Angela refused to have anything to do with Maria. The grandmother decided to meet Maria. Her relationship with Maria has flourished and Maria was able to fill some of the gaps in her knowledge. Maria was content not to push Angela in any way and made no further approaches to her. A year later, however, Angela approached The Society needing to talk about Maria and her earlier request for contact. Angela decided to write to Maria and they have now met.

This example illustrates that even when the initial response is "no", it may not be so forever, and also that other members of the birth family may be able to retain a link for the adopted adult.

Out of the 84 people who have made contact with birth families, four found their birth father first and 28 have located both birth parents. Few people initially come for information about their father, and it is often not until they see the putative father's name that it appears he becomes a significant person.

James, now 35 years old, was counselled eight years ago and following his search he had a successful reunion with his birth mother, Rita. However, in 1991 he returned for further counselling as he wanted to find his father. He did not feel able to talk to his birth mother about this and the records stated that the putative father had no knowledge of James. However, James still felt he wanted to find him. Within a few weeks James' birth father, Derek, was located and an approach was made. He was happily married with four other children. He had always known about James and had still kept the photographs given to him by Rita. He was relieved to know that James was well and was very pleased to have contact. All his family were aware of his child.

This highlights the point that information given at the time of the adoption is not always correct and it is essential to consider this during the counselling process.

From my experience, when people are determined to find their birth families they are often successful. For the majority, even when the reunion is short-lived, the outcomes and long-term effects have been good. By finding birth family members and gaining up-to-date informa-tion they can fill in the missing pieces and build a full sense of identity.

Prior to receiving information and searching, we encourage people to explore some of the risk factors. Before taking any action, they have to consider the effects on their self-esteem. It can be enormously helpful for them to know that their birth parents demonstrated concern and made enquiries up until their adoption, and that the decision to place them for adoption was not easy. However, they must also consider how they will feel if they are faced with another rejection. What will this do for their sense of self-worth? Those who have embarked upon a search may have to cope with feeling disloyal, secretive, excited, elated – while at the same time being sensitive to other people's feelings. It can be a real balancing act for the adopted adult.

Many adopted adults who have come forward for information feel they are unable to tell their parents for fear that they will be hurt. The majority of them have been happily placed and maintain regular contact with their adoptive families. Hence for some, contact with their birth family is maintained under a shroud of secrecy, perpetuating the secrecy which has existed in adoption in the past. Many have not been able to raise questions about their adoption, partly because it is not a subject which is freely discussed, and because they sense their parents' hurt.

Betty was 35 years old. A bright successful person who had always been curious about her adoption. She had always known she was adopted, but it was a closed subject. She knew very little about her background and after receiving full information from her birth records said, 'For all these years I feel that I have been sitting in a candlelit room and now someone has switched the light on'.

Betty's adoptive parents, like many others during the 1950s, were probably told that their child would not be curious '. . . provided that he has not grown up with the idea that his adoptive parents do not love him, or that there is some mystery about his origins, he will not dwell unduly on these matters or want to get in touch with his natural parents.' *(What shall we tell our adopted child?* Information leaflet issued by the Standing Conference of Societies Registered for Adoptions).

The counsellor and the agency

So what can we learn from the adopted people I have seen during a three-year period, bearing in mind that this is a small percentage of the total number of adoptions made?

The counsellor needs to consider some of the dilemmas with which they may be faced when undertaking section 51 work. They need to prepare the adopted person for all the happy or sad outcomes, as well as addressing some of the issues which may arise from the relationships they form with their birth family. Genetic sexual attraction is one of these issues. In the sample of 84 adopted people who have had reunions with their birth family, I am aware of four experiences of genetic sexual attraction. It may not be a common occurrence, but it is important for counsellors to acknowledge that genetic sexual attraction can happen and consider the implications of such feelings. Hopefully, by discussing this the people it involves will then feel able to talk freely to their counsellors if it happens to them.

John was aged 28 years when he received birth records counselling. At the time he had been married for six years. He received a positive response from both his birth parents and their families. He became very close to one of his half-sisters, Susan. They enjoyed the same sense of humour and had a lot of interests in common. He began to feel uncomfortable when he became aware that he was continually waiting for Susan to phone him, and noticed that his heartbeat raced on hearing her voice.

The feelings he experienced were those he would normally expect to have for a girlfriend or lover. Fortunately, John's counsellor had raised the subject of genetic sexual attraction with him, so he felt able to talk his attraction through without feeling that it was a taboo subject. He was able to understand how easy it was for his feelings to become confused; she was his half-sister, but they had not lived together so the natural boundaries which usually form around this relationship did not exist. Fortunately, John was able to work through this confusion and has developed a deep friendship but non-sexual relationship with his sister.

Although John was able to resolve his sexual feelings, there are situations where genetic sexual attraction has had profound effects on the people it involves.

Another important dilemma which adoption agencies need to resolve is the nature and amount of information which is given to the adopted adult from the agency's case records. Questions need to be raised: Is the birth father's name given even if there is nothing to indicate that he knows about the child? What are the possible repercussions? When acting as intermediaries should we be using cover stories when making the approach? Should we just be approaching the birth parent(s) direct?

How open should we be and to what extent do we give out third party information? For example, if we don't tell them their birth parent had suffered from depression what could be the implications? The following case study illustrates the way in which information about a birth parent's depression may help prepare the adopted adult for further sadness.

Debbie was just 18 when she came for information. She was very happily adopted but never asked any questions about her original parents. Her parents did not raise the subject either because she had shown no curiosity. Prior to receiving information from her records, she had decided to tell her parents and they were very supportive. The records described Debbie's birth mother, Clare, as being lethargic, and depressed after parting with her. Debbie embarked on a search for both of her birth parents. She traced her birth father, David, within a matter of days and he was delighted to hear about her and told the counsellor that when she was born she weighed 7lbs 2¼ ozs – he had clearly never forgotten her. He had apparently lived with Debbie's mother for nine years after her birth, but they subsequently separated and Clare married someone else. Clare had never got over giving her daughter away and suffered from depression since the birth. Last year she committed suicide. This inevitably was a shock to Debbie, but knowing her mother had appeared depressed after her birth helped prepare her for the possibility that she may not be well now. Was the description of Debbie's mother not hers to have, and did it not help her to consider the possibilities of what she might find?

After many months when her relationship was established with David, she asked us to approach the maternal grandparents. They were absolutely thrilled and had recently looked at her adoption papers and wondered how they could find her as she was their only blood relative. Debbie's outcome has been sad but also very positive for all involved. Through all this, she has become more open and much closer to her adoptive parents.

Openness and the right to information

Openness is a word which is often used in adoption today, and for the people I have seen it is an essential ingredient if they are to build a full sense of self-identity. Openness is not just confined to the adoptive placement, but also to agencies which hold the records. It is essential that we protect the birth parents who gave information, but at the same time we have to pose the question, does the adopted adult have a right to this information?

Agencies need to consider how much information they are prepared to give, and if they withhold information they must be clear about the reasons for doing so. This is a difficult area particularly as until 1975 the information held by agencies was for their viewing only. The birth parent therefore had the assurance that the information they gave at the time of placement would always remain confidential.

The report of the Adoption Law Review working party recommends the right of birth parents to register a veto on the Adoption Contact Register so that they cannot be traced, as well as supporting openness and recommending that agencies or guardians *ad litem* compile packages of information for adopted people. While attempting to meet different interests, these recommendations can produce starkly different consequences for the adopted adult keen to trace birth parents.

For the 132 adopted adults I have seen, information is very important. It can enhance proper understanding of the reasons for their adoption. To know the difficulties their birth parent(s) had to encounter can help remove the feeling of being rejected.

Agencies fear that giving last known addresses of birth parents to the adopted adult will mean they will turn up on the doorstep and disrupt people's lives. My experience has been that as long as the positive and negative aspects of approaching the birth family have been fully explored, the adopted adult in 99.9 per cent of cases will opt to use the counsellor or a partner as the intermediary.

Inevitably, there will be the rare situations where it is very clear that the adopted person is unstable and that their motives for finding the birth family are questionable. In these circumstances, the agency may feel it is essential to keep the search for the birth family under their control and withhold last known addresses.

Post-adoption and section 51 counselling should not be viewed as low priority work for which little training or support is needed. Counsellors may face many dilemmas and difficult situations. They are often meeting people who may be exploring their feelings about their adoption for the first time, and they may have to deal with raw unresolved feelings. The counsellor needs to be skilled and knowledgeable in order to provide a comprehensive service both to the adopted adult and to other members in the adoption circle. It is important to understand the mechanics of searching and the likely outcomes to help the adopted adult make informed decisions.

Conclusion

The 1975 Children Act acknowledges that adopted people should have the right to have access to information about their origins. This change in law has not only been a positive move forward for adopted adults, but also for family placing agencies too. It has given adoption agencies and local authorities the opportunity to have access to the consumers. By listening to and taking note of the experiences adopted people have had, we can make improvements in the services we provide today.

Hopefully, the recommendations of the Adoption Law Review Consultative Document will lead to a more responsive, flexible service and establish what information can be given to adopted adults.

Making a decision to obtain information from birth records can present the adopted person with difficult decisions and painful emotions. How disappointing and frustrating it is when they then receive limited or restricted information.

We need to prepare prospective adoptive parents about the importance of giving information, and provide an environment where discussion about the adoption is acceptable. Existing adoptive parents need to be reassured that if their child needs information about their origins, this is not a reflection on their parenting, but rather a need for the adopted person to fill in gaps in their knowledge. We need to recognise the challenge this presents for adoptive parents, but my experience has shown that when adoptive parents have made the courageous step to support their child in their search, it often enhances and deepens their relationship.

The Adoption Law Review consultation now taking place is a good opportunity for agencies to look at their practices and policies. They can take this opportunity to implement changes which will not only help the children being placed for adoption today, but will also ensure that today's adopted adults, who have previously been given little or no information about their birth families, achieve a full sense of identity.

In 1997, The Children's Society received funding from the Nuffield Foundation to undertake a major large-scale study about "adopted people's search for identity and reunion". The results of the research will be published in 1999.

19 The agenda for post-adoption services

Janette Logan

Janette Logan is a lecturer in social work at the University of Manchester

This paper was published in Adoption & Fostering, 19:1, 1995.

Contemporary adoption practice is at a crossroads. The proposals outlined in the White Paper *(Adoption: The future*, DoH, 1993), alongside developments already taking place in practice – particularly concerning issues of openness and contact – present all involved in adoption, either personally or professionally, with new dilemmas and challenges. The "cost neutrality" basis for changes in legislation, however, appears to suggests that such changes can be *easily* accommodated at *no additional cost* to agencies. Such an assumption is not only naïve but also questions whether post-adoption issues are taken sufficiently seriously, thereby minimising the needs of the adoptee, adopter or birth parent.

This article is based on the findings of research designed to evaluate a voluntary post-adoption service (Hughes and Logan, 1993). While the research focused initially on the experience and needs of birth parents, the findings raised a number of important themes for all involved in the adoption process, whether adopter, adopted person/child, birth parents or adoption and post-adoption workers. In contrast to the Government's "cost neutrality" approach, the research demonstrated that the costs involved in adoption and post-adoption can be considerable, both in human and financial terms.

There were three stages to the research: a record survey (n = 101), a postal questionnaire (n = 39) and in-depth interviews (n = 30). Of the 30 randomly selected birth parents who were interviewed, 28 were women, the vast majority of whom had parted with their child over 20 years ago. Most had given birth as young, unmarried women, often still at school and living at home with their parents. All those who responded to the questionnaire or who were interviewed were white British. We had no way of identifying the race/ethnic origin of the full sample of 101 as this information was not recorded.

The themes identified in our study fell broadly into the following areas:

- the long-term impact of relinquishment on birth parents;
- the complexity of issues of openness and contact at the time of adoption and in post-adoption arrangements;
- the need to make adoption and post-adoption services sensitive and accessible to people from black and minority ethnic groups; and
- the development of post-adoption services.

The impact on birth parents

Historically the needs and experiences of birth parents have been neglected; they have persistently been denied a voice in the adoption and post-adoption process. A number of popularly held misconceptions (particularly about birth *mothers*) may have contributed to this marked omission in research, literature and practice. First, the misconception that they parted with their children in a voluntary capacity – most birth mothers felt they had no real choice; secondly, the misconception that the birth mother had no emotional ties to her child, as parting occurred before real bonding could take place. Birth mothers have historically been condemned both for transgressing society's norms regarding sexual behaviour and single parenthood and for failing their children as mothers by placing them for adoption. Seen in this context, birth mothers have failed to conform to social expectations and feel they have been punished.

A "conspiracy of silence" has shrouded the legitimate needs of birth families and legitimised the absence of services which might help them to adjust to the loss of a child. The research findings demonstrated that the memory and feelings associated with relinquishment persisted throughout life, often at considerable cost to their own emotional and psychological well-being. Feelings of guilt, loss and low self-esteem were commonly reported some 20 or 30 years after the adoption.

A significant finding in our research was that of the high incidence of mental health problems in women who relinquished during this time.

How much of this was due to the fact of relinquishment is impossible to say but it was clear that parting with a child had a profound impact on the mental health of some birth mothers (Logan, 1996).

While the White Paper does acknowledge the position of birth parents, it fails to incorporate the recommendation of the Adoption Law Review that birth parents should be assigned their own worker, thus suggesting that the needs of contemporary birth parents will continue to be marginalised.

The complexity of openness and contact

To varying degrees, openness and contact have been considered good practice in adoption for some time now and the Government's proposal for more openness in the White Paper endorses this practice. There is a danger, however, in assuming openness to be a panacea for all. Research into openness and some elements of current practice could be criticised for their lack of clarity and precision about the definition of openness and contact – which can mean anything from indirect contact through letters and photographs to direct contact with the child.

When asked their views on these issues, the response from birth parents was highly complex. While all would have welcomed information about their child, many expressed ambivalence about the prospect of direct contact and, contrary to popular beliefs, the majority expressed a child-centred perspective – the interests of their child's security with the new family being paramount in their considerations (Hughes, 1995).

Many birth parents were, however, longing for information and actively seeking it. Some had had direct contact with their adopted child, now an adult. From their stories it was evident that such contact had profound implications, not only for themselves and their adopted child, but also for the families of each.

The implications associated with openness and contact must not be underestimated. The White Paper's directive that we plan into a child's adulthood means that we have to consider the long-term implications of any decisions about openness and contact. We need to be asking ourselves, whose needs are being met? Can any plans agreed be sustained throughout a child's life? What will be the impact on all concerned? Will circumstances change?

Clearly decisions about openness and contact have significant re-source implications, including the training and support of adoptive parents, ongoing support to birth parents and, most importantly, support for the child, whose needs will inevitably change throughout life. Detailed policy and practice guidelines will be needed to ensure that the complexity of the issues in judgements about contact and openness are fully understood.

Black and other minority ethnic groups

We have already referred to the fact that, where the information was available, our sample was entirely white British. This raises a number of issues in relation to the sensitivity and accessibility of post-adoption services to people from black and minority ethnic groups. How can we ensure that we reach them? How can we ensure that we provide services to birth parents from minority ethnic groups who are no doubt doubly affected by the impact of racism as well as the impact of relinquishment or losing a child through care. These parents will not only have lost their children but may have lost them into another culture through transracial placements.

The Government's response, both in the White Paper and in subse-quent debate, has been disappointing in relation to the issue of race. We now have to assume a 'common sense approach to adoption' in which issues of race and culture are considered alongside all other considera-tions. While we acknowledge the need to take account of other factors, not least the length of placement with current caretakers and the child's subsequent attachment, there is a danger that such a "dilution" of race will result in the needs of black children and their families not being met.

Post-adoption services

While adoption has a positive outcome for many children, it is also the case that loss is a central theme in adoption. For the birth mother, the loss of her child; for the child, the loss of the birth family; for the adopters, loss of the ability to have a child through birth; and for those who didn't adopt their child at birth, loss of their child's formative weeks, months or years.

The challenge posed by this "less than perfect" start means that difficulties may arise for any of the parties involved, at any time in the adoption or post-adoption process. Together with the themes identified in our study, this has far-reaching implications for service provision, and there is a need to develop flexible services which can respond to the differing and changing needs of all involved in the adoption triangle.

One final point: the fundamental principle behind the change in adoption law is to bring it in line with the Children Act 1989 and its central philosophies of maintaining children within their own families and, where this is not possible, to work in partnership. This poses major ideological challenges to those involved in adoption, not least because it questions traditional notions of adoption which were concerned with ownership, fresh start and the severing of links with birth families.

While the developments in adoption practice are welcomed, it is essential that the needs of all involved are taken seriously and that the help and support they need is acknowledged.

References

Department of Health, *Adoption: The future*, HMSO, 1993.

Hughes B, 'Openness and contact in adoption: a child-centred perspective', *British Journal of Social Work*, 25, pp 729–47, 1995.

Hughes B and Logan J, *Birth Parents: The hidden dimension*, School of Social Work, University of Manchester, 1993.

Logan J, 'Birth mothers and their mental health: unchartered territory', *British Journal of Social Work*, 26, pp 609–25, 1996.

20 Consumers' views of a post-placement support project

Janice McGhee

Janice McGhee in a lecturer in social work at the University of Edinburgh.

This paper was published in Adoption & Fostering, 19:1, 1995.

There has been increasing recognition of the need for continuing post-placement support for adoptive families beyond the initial adjustment period (Macaskill, 1985a; Yates, 1985; Rushton *et al*, 1993). This article reports on consumers' views on a particular model of support offered via a multidisciplinary consultancy service with a range of experience and knowledge in post-adoption support.

Set up by BAAF's Scottish Centre, the post-adoption consultancy service offered a one-off consultation to adoptive parents who were currently experiencing difficulties related to the adoption. The aim was to define and clarify problems and to look for solutions, including advice on linking with other resources if this was felt appropriate. Each session comprised an initial period to allow parents to outline their concerns and give consultants time for further exploration of relevant aspects. A short break ensued allowing consultants to formulate their response to parents followed by a session where the consultants and parents met together to discuss their views. The family afterwards received a written comment on the consultants' views of the problem and details of any advice or suggestions made.

The evaluation study aimed to explore with parents their experience of the consultancy service and any benefits received. Parents completed a questionnaire prior to the consultation, and a brief postal questionnaire approximately five to six weeks after. Twenty-seven out of 28 families who attended for consultation replied. Twelve families were interviewed using a semi-structured questionnaire.

Participants

Of the 28 families participating, 26 were adoptive parents and two were solely foster carers, although some of the adoptive parents were also foster carers.

There were three consultation sessions where the child participated (all adolescent or older children). The service in the main had an adult focus although there was some uncertainty as to whether children should attend. A number of parents had concerns as to the advisability of their child attending; others commented that this could have limited parental openness. It may be that a single session format involving children, especially younger children, is not helpful to parents.

The children for whom consultation was sought had been placed at a range of ages (see Table 1). This represents a wide range of adoption placements and may indicate that all groups of adopters continued to feel in need of post-placement support services at different stages in their lives.

Table 1

Age of child at placement

Age at placement	Number of children
Under one year	7
2–4 years	12
5–8 years	9
10–12 years	3

The age-range of the children was from two-and-a-half years to 23 years (see Table 2).

Table 2

The sex and age (in years) of children for whom consultation was sought

Under 5		5–11		12–15		16–18		over 18	
M	F	M	F	M	F	M	F	M	F
1	0	6	1	10	9	0	2	1	1

The children had been in placement for variable lengths of time: three for less than one year, six for between two and five years, ten for between six and nine years and a further ten between ten and 15 years, with two birth siblings who had been in placement for 16 or more years. Clearly the varied lengths of time partly reflected the age of the child, and again indicates a need for continued support.

Current difficulties

Parents sought consultation for a wide range of problems which reflected both the age and developmental stage of the children involved. Over half the parents (16) described both emotional and behavioural difficulties; ten described mainly behavioural problems; and two focused largely on emotional difficulties as the central aspect for consultation. A large number of behavioural problems were outlined, including school difficulties, oppositional behaviour, physical aggression, lying, stealing, verbal abuse and moral/sexual risks. These reflect the types of difficulties reported by parents in other studies of adopted children and their families (Howe, 1987; Howe and Hinings, 1987; Phillips, 1988; Rushton, 1989).

The emotional problems outlined by parents were also varied including: difficulties in peer relations; detachment from or lack of integration into the family; and problems in emotional relationships, both in expression of emotion and an emotional distance from family and friends.

Low self-esteem, insecurity, anxiety and self-injury were also reported. These difficulties are not unusual in children who have experienced separations and poor early care (Macaskill 1985a; Hill *et al*, 1988) which appeared to be a feature in the lives of some of these children. Of the 23 parents who responded, 19 located present difficulties as related to their child's past life experiences of separation, loss, poor early care and/or abuse.

A few families also identified difficulties related to the fact of adoption. Parents reported anger, a sense of abandonment, being asked direct questions about the circumstances of the adoption, and the child not wishing to acknowledge the fact of adoption, as examples of these concerns.

This broad picture of the most common difficulties parents brought to the consultation session conceals the often complex patterns and interactions of behavioural and emotional problems and the impact of these on families themselves. Some families were experiencing high levels of stress and strain within the family in response to these problems, including marital strain and effects upon siblings.

Contact with other agencies
Parents on the whole had been in contact and/or sought help from a wide range of agencies in relation to these difficulties. Social work help was the most common source of support, followed by teachers, educational psychologists and general practitioners.

Other supports
Some families received financial support, including adoption and fostering allowances and respite care. Most support to families came from relatives and/or friends, with church and contact with other adopters, either through self-help groups or on a more informal basis, the next most frequently identified forms of support. In the interview group a few families commented that relatives and friends sometimes had difficulty in appreciating the dimension of adoption and this may reflect the limitations of informal networks as found by Macaskill (1985a).

The consumers' experience and views of consultation
Drawing upon the interviews with parents alone it was possible to draw out some of the factors which prompted parents to attend for consultation. While this is limited it may give an impression of the complexity of families' experience. For many families there seems to have been a background of continuing or increasing difficulties; for some contact being precipitated by a crisis, for others an accumulation of circumstances and concerns. Sometimes the request for outside assistance was articulated as a need for expert, knowledgeable help in relation to the particular difficulties of adoption. Some families coupled this with a sense of isolation and a feeling that the problems they were experiencing were unique to themselves.

These families were not necessarily without social work or other supports, but a number felt that either the help they had received and/or the solutions they had tried were not working and that progress was not being made.

Another theme which emerged in discussion with some parents was their frequently high expectations of themselves as parents and a concern that in some way their parenting may be contributing towards the difficulties. As one parent said:

There's an added thing with adoption . . . you never know if you're doing the right thing. You're always wondering if there's something you're not doing right.

The concern that parental actions were contributing to difficulties could deter parents from seeking help. Finch and Jaques (1985) found that high expectations of parenting in adoptive families were not uncommon, which could make it harder for families to seek help. It may be that to open oneself to professional involvement could confirm a sense of failure. Alongside this was a concern expressed by two parents that the ensuing outcome could be the removal of the child.

I had a vision that if they called social services, X would be whipped into care.

This background of continuing difficulties, often experienced over a considerable time prior to seeking advice, was reflected in the wider sample.

Parents' views of consultation
Two-thirds of the families (18) felt their expectations had been met. Just under one-third felt that their expectations had not been met, with one family expressing ambivalence.

Positive themes
General reassurance and support seemed to be a major positive feature of the consultancy sessions. This was often a reassurance that parenting was adequate and this appeared to help to reduce any sense of self-blame for the difficulties being experienced. This sometimes appeared to be achieved by consultants focusing on the positives within the family situation. For a small group of parents reassurance also came through a

realisation that other adopters were struggling with the same problems.

However, a few parents who otherwise largely felt their expectations had been met commented on the limits of positive reassurance, a point also reflected by the families who felt their expectations had not been met. A focus on positives could result in a more limited exploration of the negatives within the family situation. The opportunity to discuss problems with a sympathetic and knowledgeable group and to have their distress understood was also seen as a positive feature. For a smaller group of parents the consultancy seemed to either offer fresh perspectives on the difficulties, or a sense of putting the problems into perspective.

The effect on difficulties

Parents were asked whether the consultation had affected the original difficulties for which they had sought consultation. It was not expected that any major change would have occurred in response to one session and the short time scale between consultation and follow-up. However, just under half of the 25 families who replied (12) reported that they felt the problems had reduced since consultation; 13 saw them as unchanged.

For those parents who felt there was a reduction in difficulties, this seemed to suggest a change in parental attitude towards or perception of the problem which then affected the way they dealt with difficulties. Five of the 12 families specifically reported feeling more confident in coping with the difficulties. The longer-term impact of the consultation was beyond the scope of the evaluation study.

Links to other resources

Part of the consultants' aims was to offer both a view of the problems and suggest ways to link with other resources. Parents identified suggestions they found particularly helpful and these revolved around three broad aspects:

- furthering an understanding or assessment of the child's needs and/or difficulties;
- offering specific suggestions and/or advice directed towards parental action or perceptions of the difficulties; and
- specific suggestions to link into other resources.

A range of resources – such as counselling and support groups – were suggested to families and seen as helpful. It was not possible within the time and resource limits of the evaluation to explore whether families gained access to the resources suggested. However, one family spoke of using the letter and recommendations of the consultancy group to negotiate and discuss their child's needs with another agency.

Negative themes

Eight families felt that their expectations had not been met and one family was ambivalent. All but one family were seeking consultation in relation to children aged 12 years or over. Apart from this there seemed to be no immediate and obvious similarities or consistent patterns between the families, but it appears that they did not receive either the specific advice and/or understanding they had expected from the consultation. Generally they considered that there had been no change in the original difficulties and tended to feel that the consultation had been able to offer them little as parents.

On the whole, these families had found it easy to participate and felt that the consultants had understood their difficulties, but said that there had been little help beyond reassurance and some minimal advice on specific actions. It is a very mixed picture and it is difficult to draw out a central thread.

Summary

Families' experience of and satisfaction with the consultation service presents a complex picture. For the majority of the families their expectations were fulfilled and a number of positive features can be drawn from the consultancy service within the limits of a one-off session. Reassurance, having the opportunity to discuss problems with a knowledgeable group and, to some extent, receive helpful suggestions were all identified as useful aspects. The process itself was valued by nearly all the families, who described it as easy to participate in, and had been fairly clearly explained by consultants. However, a smaller group of families (just under one-third) felt their expectations had not been met. While they were able to identify some of the positives commented on by the other families (in terms of participation and receiving some useful suggestions), they found that either their difficulties were not sufficiently addressed or that the session was not able to offer the specific under- standing or solutions they had been seeking. It would seem for a minority this format had a more limited value.

The training initiatives

A series of training initiatives was organised for both carers and pro- fessional workers addressing a range of topics, particularly focusing on the types of difficulty children and young people may bring to place- ment. The training courses were both knowledge and skill based in an attempt to increase understanding of the differing problems and to equip people with possible methods of approaching these issues. A broad range of topics relevant to post-placement issues was offered, including

* loss in adoption;
* caring for adolescents who have been sexually abused;
* adoptive fathers – parenting and support;
* adoption issues in adolescence;
* understanding and managing difficult behaviour; and
* parenting the child who has been sexually abused.

Overall the training series appears to have been successful in offering a range of well-organised and presented courses which were interesting and stimulating to participants. The courses offered to professional workers were seen by the majority of participants as having value to themselves as professional workers and for their work with parents and carers. The courses offered to adoptive parents and carers were also seen as helpful to them in their parental role, as well as offering the oppor- tunity to share experiences and similar concerns with other parents and carers. This may be a helpful way to offer support to parents and carers.

References

Argent H (ed), *Keeping the Doors Open: A review of post-adoption services,* BAAF, 1988.

Hill M, Lambert L and Triseliotis J, *Achieving Adoption with Love and Money,* National Children's Bureau, 1989.

Hill M, Hutton S and Easton S, 'Adoptive parenting plus and minus', *Adoption & Fostering*, 12:2, pp 17–23, 1988.

Howe D, 'Adopted children in care', *British Journal of Social Work*, 17, pp 493–505, 1987.

Howe D and Hinings D, 'Adopted children referred to a child and family centre', *Adoption and Fostering*, 11:3, pp 44–47, 1987.

Howe D, 'The consumers' view of the post-adoption centre', *Adoption & Fostering*, 14:2, pp 32–36, 1990.

Finch R and Jaques P, 'Use of a geneogram with adoptive families', *Adoption & Fostering*, 9:3, pp 35–41,1985.

Macaskill C, 'Post-adoption support: is it essential?', *Adoption & Fostering*, 9:1, pp 45–49, 1985a.

Macaskill C, 'Who should support after the adoption?', *Adoption & Fostering*, 9:2, pp 21–25, 1985b.

Phillips R, 'Post-adoption services – the views of adopters', *Adoption & Fostering*, 12:4, pp 24–28, 1988.

Rushton A, Quinton D and Treseder J, 'New parents for older children: support services during eight years of placement', *Adoption & Fostering*, 17:4, pp 39–45, 1993.

Rushton A, 'Post-placement services for foster and adoptive parents – support, counselling or therapy?', *Journal of Child Psychology and Psychiatry*, 30:2, pp 197–204, 1989.

Sawbridge P 'The Post-Adoption Centre – what are the users teaching us?', *Adoption & Fostering*, 12:1, pp 5–12, 1988.

Yates P, *Post-placement Support for Adoptive Families of Hard-to-place Children*, University of Edinburgh, unpublished MSc thesis, 1985.

21 Birth parents' experiences of contested adoption

Kathy Mason and Peter Selman

Kathy Mason is a Research Associate in the Department of Social Policy at the University of Newcastle. Peter Selman is Head of Department and Senior Lecturer in Social Policy at the same University.

This article was published in Adoption & Fostering, 21:1, 1997.

Contested adoptions in England and Wales

In the 1960s, when the number of non-relative adoptions in England and Wales was about 15–16,000 a year (Selman, 1976), it has been estimated that barely two per cent of such adoptions proceeded without the consent of the birth mother (Grey and Blunden, 1971). Twenty years later, when the total number of adoptions (OPCS, 1994) had fallen to below 8,000 a year (more than half of which were step-parent adoptions), estimates from the *Pathways to Adoption* study (Murch *et al*, 1993) indicated that 26 per cent of agency adoption applications and 75 per cent of freeing applications were contested. Applications without the agreement of the birth mother accounted for 28 per cent of non-relative adoption applications where there was no prior freeing order; for older children the proportion was substantially higher (Murch *et al*, 1993). This represents a fundamental shift in the nature of child adoption, the implications of which are only slowly being recognised (Ryburn, 1992; Ryan, 1994).

There is a growing amount of information about contested proceedings (Lambert, 1994), much of which is derived from wider studies of adoption in England and Wales (Murch, 1993) and Scotland (Lambert *et al*, 1990), but Ryburn (1992; 1994) has investigated contested adoptions as a separate group. Research on birth parents has also increased in recent years (Winkler and Van Keppel, 1984; Hughes and Logan, 1993; Wells, 1993; Tye, 1994), but few studies have focused on non-relinquishing parents.

The lifelong impact of voluntarily relinquishing children is now well recognised (Howe *et al*, 1992; Wells, 1993) and birth parents are gradually becoming a force in their own right in influencing social policy, for instance through the Natural Parents' Support Group. The voice of the non-relinquishing parents has not been heard although there is much to support the view of Ryan (1994) that 'contested adoptions cause considerable stress and pain for all involved'. In their study of birth mothers in contact with After Adoption in Manchester, Hughes and Logan (1993) looked briefly at the special issues raised by the minority of birth parents in their study who had lost a child through the care process and noted that it 'is a subject which merits further research'.

The needs of contesting birth parents have been noted in the Adoption Law Review. The 1992 Consultation Document (para 28.6) stated that

Information and counselling services should be available to birth parents whether or not they have agreed to the adoption of their child.

It is also recommended that:

. . . agencies should have a statutory duty to ensure that the parents of a child, whom it is proposed to place for adoption, are offered full opportunities to receive advice and counselling. This should be provided by a social worker who is not involved in the adoption plan if the birth parent so wishes.

This recommendation was not picked up in the White Paper, *Adoption: The future*, (DoH, 1993) which states only that they are '. . . entitled to expect sensible and objective counselling from adoption agencies'. There are no specific proposals on this issue in the draft Adoption Bill (DoH, 1996) although there have been suggestions that birth parents contesting adoptions should be referred to a Reporting Officer or guardian *ad litem* for independent advice.

However, section 2 of the Draft Bill does continue the commitment in section 1 of the Adoption Act 1976 to provide post-adoption services to 'persons who have been adopted' and to 'parents or guardians of such persons'. LAC (87) 8 Annex 3 makes it clear that services for birth parents include planning for future care, advice on the meaning of adoption, preparation for separation and 'providing . . . continuing counselling and support where it is needed after the child has been adopted', and that this may require referral to ' . . . specialist agencies where this is appropriate'. This aspect of post-adoption provision remains under-developed in respect of *all* birth parents, but particularly those who contest the adoption of their children.

In her report on the proceedings of two seminars organised by the Social Services Inspectorate to look at post-placement services for children and families, Hughes (1995) writes that:

Birth parents who have been involved in contested cases are not infrequently left with complex feelings with which they receive little help . . . It was reported that many birth parents in contested cases need post-placement support from an allocated social worker independent of those allocated to child and adoptive family, but such support is provided infrequently.

We endorse this view but would go further and argue, on the basis of findings described in this article, that the support needed should pre-ferably come from an independent organisation, as many parents find it difficult to accept or seek help from anyone associated with the agency which removed their child.

Parents Without Children: a service for non-relinquishing birth parents

Awareness of these issues led the Durham Diocesan Family Welfare Council to undertake a pilot study (Dunne, 1992), funded by Cleveland County Council, to explore the need for and feasibility of a service targeted at those birth parents whose children had been removed and placed for adoption against their wishes. The Council had extensive experience in the counselling of adult adopted persons, adoptive parents and birth mothers, although work with the latter had been confined largely to those who had relinquished their children voluntarily.

The pilot study established a clear unmet need for a service for non-relinquishing parents who felt that no-one in social services had any inter-est in them once their children had been removed so that most felt angry, guilty and useless. As a result, a proposal was drawn up for a three-year project and a request for funding made to the Tyne and Wear Foundation.

This was accepted and in 1992 funding was secured from Henry Smith's Charity for a project offering services, primarily within Cleveland, for birth parents who had contested the adoption of their children.

The project, managed and supervised by the Director of Durham Family Welfare Council, was to be known as "Parents Without Children" and employed two members of staff, one full-time and one part-time, who offered an independent, client-led service. Birth parents were to be given the opportunity to talk about their children's adoption from their point of view, with an offer of counselling if requested. In addition, they would be encouraged to compile and update information for their children and their new families. Initially the project sought to provide post-adoption support for non-relinquishing birth parents, but subsequently identified the need to offer advice and support to those presently contesting their child's adoption.

A study of non-relinquishing birth parents

The study involved 18 interviews carried out with a total of 21 birth parents: three couples, 13 women and two men. Their age range included nine birth parents in their 20s, six in their 30s, and four over the age of 40. The ages of one couple were not given. All but one birth parent were white British. A semi-structured interview schedule was used, with interviews taking place in a variety of settings including the birth parents' own home, the university and a room provided by a health advice shop. Each interview lasted between one and two hours.

Nine of the parents had first made contact with Parents Without Children after the legal adoption of their children. The remaining parents were still involved in adoption proceedings. However, three of these had seen their children adopted by the time of interview, with a fourth Adoption Order being due the following month.

Birth parents' experiences of losing their children

Earlier research on non-relinquishing birth parents suggested that those whose children had already been placed for adoption might have very deep problems. Hughes and Logan (1993) identified two particular features which characterised these (non-relinquishing) birth parents: anger and guilt, continuing long after the decision to place their children in new families; and the existence, in all, of significant mental health problems. The first feature reflected Ryburn's (1992) conclusion that the removal of children for adoption is 'a very public declaration that brings with it anger, shame, guilt and bitter recrimination'. Our research came to similar conclusions but showed clearly that the problems started long before any Order was made.

One of the most distressing points in the adoption process is when birth parents are faced with the decision whether to consent to their child's adoption. Several commented on pressures to sign forms for the adoption of their child:

> *I was told by the local authority solicitor and barrister that I was being selfish, as a mother and a parent, to my two children because I wouldn't sign the forms.*

One mother who had signed felt she had not understood what she was doing:

> *I am signing things and I don't want to because I don't know what I am signing. I just signed.*

Earlier in the process, attendance at case conferences and reviews had caused difficulties. Five birth parents had not attended any case conferences, one of these being informed that the agency did not have a policy of inviting parents. All the other respondents had attended, but some of these seemed to have little understanding about what was happening:

> *I didn't have a clue what they were on about. It was all foreign. I didn't know what they were on about. No-one explained it to me.*

> *Every time there was a different person heading the meeting. Not everyone turned up but they still carried on.*

Of the parents attending case conferences, four had gone alone with no-one to give them support. Others had taken either their mothers or their partners for support. Some of those going alone had not realised that they were allowed to take someone along with them:

> *I didn't know I could. They never even told me I could take anyone along with me.*

Others had been accompanied but found the experience so full of emotional turmoil that feelings of frustration had boiled over, making it difficult for both themselves and those in attendance:

> *I took my mother but she was asked to leave. I had a few rows. There was a policeman there and I had a verbal argument with him.*

Courts and the legal process

A major problem for several birth parents had been getting good legal representation, and many were unhappy with their solicitors. Most had chosen their own solicitor, either using someone previously employed for another purpose in the past or someone recommended to them by family or friends. Many of these solicitors had little experience of working with such types of cases and the parents felt their cases had not been presented in court as well as they might have been.

One of the most traumatic experiences for any parent contesting an adoption is the actual court appearance. The adversarial process means evidence has to be gathered by social workers for presentation in court to support their case for the adoption of the child against their parents' wishes. It is the selective nature of this evidence (Ryburn, 1994) which gives most concern to non-relinquishing birth parents, many of whom feel they are being blamed for everything. Some mothers complained that they had been publicly branded as bad parents:

> *They're saying you're no good; you can't look after your own children. I don't like that, I'm still bitter.*

> *All that social services did was to say how bad you were. There were a lot of good things that would have helped but it was the bad things they were saying.*

Respondents also felt that whatever they had to say would make no difference because no-one was listening and it was frustrating:

> *Knowing that you go to court and you are wasting your time because your voice is not going to be heard. They are not going to want to listen to what you want or what your expectations are.*

Support in times of need
Going to court and contesting an adoption can be a very isolating experience and we wanted to know who non-relinquishing birth parents turned
to for support during these difficult times. The majority said it had been
their families who had stood by them and that without them they would
have had no-one. However, there were respondents who felt there had
been no-one there to support them:

> *I haven't had no support off nobody, I have done it all on me own.
> Whatever happens at the end of the day I have got nobody to thank. I
> have done it all on me own.*

When asked whether they felt their social worker had kept them informed about what was happening to their children, the usual response
was that they had been told very little and had not been involved in any
way in the making of decisions about their children's future, which had
left many with a feeling of helplessness:

> *Once they have control, and believe me they have control, not only
> your kids' lives but your life gets turned upside down. One minute you
> have a family and the next you have got absolutely nothing.*

There was a general feeling that social workers were not working in the
best interests of the birth parents and seemed unable to appreciate the
trauma parents were experiencing. Many birth parents had not fully
appreciated that the social worker's focus had to be on the child, and
consequently found it difficult to understand the shift made by social
workers from one of support to "opponent" in the legal battle. (See
Ryburn, 1992; 1994.) However, criticism of social workers was not indiscriminate and several interviewees had positive comments to make about
individuals. Others had social workers who did keep them informed of
what was happening during the time their children were in care.

The impact of losing a child through adoption
The previous section has outlined some of the trauma experienced by
non-relinquishing birth parents. We also felt it important to try to
discover how respondents felt their lives had been affected by the
adoption of their children. We asked about the general, overall effect and

then about specific aspects of their lives, such as their ability to work, mental and physical health, and the possibility of having more children in the future.

The adoption of their children had a devastating and long-term effect on the lives of most of the parents, leaving them with feelings of isolation and emptiness. Some felt that their capacity to work had changed because their level of concentration had been affected. Thoughts of pending court cases or their children's whereabouts and welfare were always with them:

> It's not like I'm working all the time cause sometimes I wake up in the morning and all that's on my mind is me kids and then it gets me down.

> There are times when I have been to work but I have had to come home early because it is whizzing round in my head and it's best I come home.

Respondents felt there were aspects of both their mental and physical health which had been adversely affected by the adoption and in some cases said that their whole personality had changed because of their experiences:

> I am mentally ill. I turned violent. Before all this I never used to be violent.

> I'll never never ever feel right until I see him. I'll never be complete again, just like a jigsaw with some missing.

Losing a child through a contested adoption is inevitably traumatic and we asked our respondents what they found had helped them to cope. Some simply had to put on a brave face, while others had tried to get away:

> Well, there are times when I've been very stressed out. I've had to go out for a walk. Or there's times where I've had to go down and see me family.

One mother found that thinking of happy times with her baby helped most; by putting on records she used to play to the baby and recall happy memories. Finally, one mother used to just 'cry myself to sleep', while another just wanted 'loads of cuddles' from her husband and 'to sit on his knee and cry'.

Contact after contested adoption

Issues surrounding contact and levels of contact were the single biggest area of concern for the majority of birth parents in the study. They are issues which do not go away and are likely to be a major factor in any support offered, whether pre- or post-adoption.

Levels of contact and access to information varied greatly, with some parents being told nothing about the adoptive placement or about how their children were getting on, while others had been given masses of information. One birth mother was given files of three prospective adoptive families and encouraged to choose which she wanted her daughter to live with. She subsequently met her preferred family and was given a video of the house and the family's pet dog.

For other parents, contact had been minimal or completely denied. Many not only had no contact but had little idea about where in the country their children were. In contrast, one birth mother found her child had been placed with a family on the same housing estate but there was to be no contact. To make matters worse, it had been suggested the mother should not visit the local shops in case they bump into each other.

Several birth parents felt that contact had been unproblematic while their children were in foster care, but that once the Adoption Order had gone through it was seen as more appropriate to discontinue such access.

One area of concern is where contact has been discontinued for a period to allow a child to settle in their new home. As shown in other studies concerning the continuation of contact after care proceedings (Millham *et al*, 1986), it can often be difficult for birth parents to re-establish contact:

> *I have had contact with her, one contact with me daughter since she has been in care with this foster parent but otherwise no. Social services told me that I could see me bairn after she got settled in. She been there ten month and I have never seen her. I've never had contact with her.*

One or two birth mothers had problems with pre-adoption contact with their children because the foster carers did not want it:

One particular foster family didn't want anything to do with me. I mean they was dead set against me even seeing her.

It was difficult because she didn't like me going into her house where she was looking after him and that was why it stopped.

All parents were desperate for information about their children's welfare and would have liked more information about the adoptive placement. They wanted to know where their children were, to be able to meet the adoptive parents and to know how the children were getting on and whether they had settled with their new families.

Most felt that the best way of getting information about their children would be to have direct contact with them. There would be many advantages for both themselves and their children if this was made possible. One main advantage for the parents would be having the opportunity to explain why the adoption had taken place.

If visits were not felt to be appropriate, all respondents still wanted some form of information exchange so they were kept up to date about their children's well-being and also, it was felt to be important that the children knew what was happening to their birth family.

Hopes for contact in the future

Parents were asked who they would go to and who they would not go to for help, if in the future they wanted to contact their children. There was a mixture of responses, one or two being adamant that they would not go to social services for help but another accepting that they would have to contact social services because they were the ones who had handled their children's adoption. An example of good practice was noted by one respondent who had received a letter from social services advising where the adoption files were being kept, should information be needed.

Many parents were adamant that, despite admitted problems in parenting and often a loss of contact with their children, they continued to care about their children very deeply. While accepting that, for the present, they were being denied the chance to parent their child(ren) on

The impact on their physical and mental health was apparent and continued with them.

The issue of contact with their children was at the centre of the lives of all birth parents in this study. The fact that they had lost the battle to keep their children had not lessened the desire to have contact – or at least information and it became apparent that handling such issues would be a central feature of *any* service for non-relinquishing birth parents. The work done through Parents Without Children demonstrated both the extent of unmet need for support to this group and the possibility of providing a service that can do much towards meeting that need. It has also demonstrated that this need arises before the actual granting of an Order and that, at both pre- and post-adoption stages, the need is for support from someone who is clearly seen as independent of the agency involved in placing the children. The closure of the project has not removed their need for such help.

Most birth parents who have contested adoptions will not consider turning to social services for help and may be hesitant about going to *any* adoption agency There is an urgent need to ensure that such parents can be referred to an independent body which can offer non-judgemental support to parents who have lost their children through adoption. The value of such provision was endorsed, in response to a postal questionnaire, by many professionals working in child care, who saw social services as poorly placed to offer help to contesting birth parents (Mason and Selman, 1996). Failure to develop such provision will mean much personal suffering, but will also have repercussions on any children remaining in the family and could prove costly in terms of later treatment of birth parents for mental health problems.

References

Department of Health/Welsh Office, *Review of Adoption Law: A consultative document*, DoH, 1992.

Department of Health/Welsh Office, *Adoption: The future*, Cmnd. 2288, HMSO, 1993.

Department of Health/Welsh Office, *Adoption – A service for children*, DoH, 1996.

Dunne A, 'Parents Without Children' Project, DDFWC, 1992.

Grey E and Blunden R, *A Survey of Adoption in Great Britain*, HMSO, 1971.

Haimes E, Mason K and Stark C, 'What is a family?', in Humphrey R (ed), *Families Behind the Headlines*, University of Newcastle: Department of Social Policy, 1996.

Howe D, Sawbridge P and Hinings D, *Half a Million Women: Mothers who lose their children by adoption*, Penguin Books, 1992.

Hughes B, *Post-placement Services for Children and Families: Defining the need*, Social Services Inspectorate, DoH, 1995.

Hughes B and Logan J, *Birth Parents: The hidden dimension*, University of Manchester: Department of Social Policy and Social Work, 1993.

Lambert L, Buist M, Triseliotis J and Hill M, *Freeing Children for Adoption*, BAAF, 1990.

Lambert L, 'Contested proceedings: what the research tells us', in Ryburn M, *Contested Adoptions: Research, law, policy and practice*, Arena, 1994.

Mason K and Selman P, *Parents Without Children: Evaluation and research report*, University of Newcastle: Department of Social Policy, 1996.

Millham S, Bullock R, Hosie K and Haak M, *Lost in Care*, Gower, 1986.

Murch M, Lowe N, Borkowski M, Copner R and Griew K, *Pathways to Adoption*, HMSO, 1993.

Office of Population Censuses and Surveys, *Marriage and Divorce Statistics 1992*, Series FM2, HMSO, 1994.

Ryan M, 'Contested proceedings: justice and the law', in Ryburn M, *Contested Adoptions: Research, law, policy and practice*, Arena, 1994.

Ryburn M, 'Contested adoption proceedings', *Adoption & Fostering*, 16:4, pp 29–38, 1992.

Ryburn M, 'The effects of an adversarial process on adoption decisions', *Adoption & Fostering*, 17:3, pp 39–45, 1993.

Ryburn M, *Contested Adoptions: Research, law, policy and practice, op cit.*

Selman P, 'Patterns of adoption in England and Wales since 1959', *Social Work Today* 7:7, 1976.

Tye L, *Birth Parents Talk Back*, Cramlington: Birth Parents/Adoptees Support Group, 1994.

Wells S, 'What do birth mothers want?', *Adoption & Fostering* 17:4, pp 22–6, 1993.

Winkler R and van Keppel M, *Relinquishing Mothers in Adoption*, Melbourne: Institute for Family Studies, 1984, Australia.

Postscript

In recent years, adoptions in the UK have involved fewer children, yet there has been a diversification in the characteristics of the children, their birth family circumstances and their adoptive families. The heyday of adoption may well be past. The large numbers of infant adoptions which occurred up to the 1960s seem unlikely to return. The permanence movement of the 1980s enabled more children to be adopted from foster and residential care, but this tide has ebbed somewhat. The "backlog" of children in long-term care was largely dealt with. The current emphasis on partnership and family support means that all efforts should be made to sustain children in their birth families – or return them there. When this fails, the home difficulties or abuse have sometimes been so severe that it is hard for the children to accept or adapt to a new permanent substitute family.

Nevertheless virtually all the research evidence has demonstrated that adoption is a highly successful arrangement, especially though by no means exclusively for younger children. Each year the prospects of a few thousand children improve dramatically through adoption placements. The households created are more varied than they used to be. More older children, more of those with disabilities and siblings are placed than formerly; greater numbers of foster carers, families on low incomes and single individuals adopt than used to be the case. Since 1990 inter-country adoption has grown to become a significant part of the scene, though still much less important relatively than in countries like the Netherlands, Denmark and Sweden. Despite professional and legal discouragement, some step-families continue to find adoption attractive and they account for a high proportion of all adoptions.

At the same time, a growing trend has been evident towards maintaining some kind of openness, i.e. communication between the adoptive and birth families. As yet, this has mainly been indirect and infrequent, often with agencies acting as go-betweens. However, a small but increasing number of adoptions involve continuing direct communication and even face-to-face meetings. More and more, adopted adults brought up in so-called closed adoptions without such contacts are wanting to find out information about their birth relatives and in some cases to trace them.

Awareness has grown of the needs of birth mothers and sometimes other relatives for information and support. As yet the role and feelings of siblings, grandparents and other relatives in adoption remain unexplored.

While many adopters still wish to bring up their children without outside involvement, a number recognise the value to their children's identity and understanding of having some ongoing acquaintance with their birth families. Some adopters recognise that they need help in enabling children placed with them after infancy to form satisfactory relationships, overcome emotional difficulties and make educational progress. Thus in many ways the tasks for adopters and adoption agencies have grown more complex. As a result, a wider range of pre- and post-adoption services are required and, in some areas, have been provided. The legal duties for local authorities now recognise that needs for information, advice or help can arise at any stage in adoption and can concern any one of the main parties involved.

Many of the changes which have occurred have resulted from changing social patterns and practice beliefs. Altered attitudes have made it possible to recruit many more black workers and adopters, so that it has become more realistic as well as desirable for nearly all children to be placed with families of similar heritage. The law has influenced some developments (e.g. in relation to adoptees' rights of access to information). In other respects it has been the use of the law which has been significant. For example, in the 1980s local authorities decided to make more use of the existing powers to remove parental rights. They also applied for freeing orders mainly in contested cases rather than for adoptions with agreement, as originally envisaged. The legal position with respect to intercountry adoption has satisfied few but it has not been easy to secure reform. Other adjustments in the law may be needed as ideas about openness progress.

In the present situation, it would be rash rather than brave to predict the future direction of adoption policy and practice in the UK. Amid present and future debates and developments, it is a useful discipline periodically to pose the question: Who is adoption for? All will claim it should be for the benefit of the child but children are the least powerful of the interest groups involved and the outcome is by no means a foregone conclusion.

Malcolm Hill and Martin Shaw   **February 1998**

References

Archer, C, 'Families living with domestic violence', *Adoption & Fostering*, 20:4, 1996.

BAAF, *Intercountry Adoption*, BAAF, 1991.

Barn R, *Black Children in the Public Care System*, BAAF/Batsford, 1993.

Barn R, Sinclair R and Ferdinand D, *Acting on Principle*, BAAF, 1997.

Banks N, 'Children of Black mixed parentage and their placement', *Adoption & Fostering*, 19:2, 1995.

Barth R and Berry M, 'Outcomes of welfare services under permanency planning', *Social Service Review*, 61:1, pp 71–90, 1987.

Bebbington A R and Miles J, 'The background of children who enter local authority care', *British Journal of Social Work*, 19:5, pp 349–368, 1989.

Berridge D, 'Foster and residential care reassessed: A research perspective', *Children & Society*, 8:2, pp 132–150, 1994.

Borland M, 'Permanency planning in Lothian Region: the placements', *Adoption & Fostering*, 15:4, 1991.

Cooper D, *Through different eyes: The cultural identity of young Chinese people in Britain*, Avebury, 1995.

Dalen M and Saetersdal B, 'Transracial adoption in Norway', *Adoption & Fostering*, 9:2, 1987.

Dance C, *Focus on Adoption: A snapshot of adoption patterns in England – 1995*, BAAF, 1997.

Dickens J and Watts J, 'Developing alternatives to residential care in Romania', *Adoption & Fostering*, 20:3, 1996.

Fratter J, *Adoption with Contact: Implications for policy and practice*, BAAF, 1996.

Gill O and Jackson B, *Adoption and Race*, Batsford, 1983.

Goldstein J, Freud A and Solnit A J, *Beyond the Best Interests of the Child*, Free Press, 1973, USA.

Haimes E and Timms N, *Adoption, Identity and Social Policy*, Gower, 1985.

Harding L F, *Perspectives on Child Care Policy*, Longman, 1991.

Harper J, 'Counselling issues in intercountry adoption disruption', *Adoption & Fostering*, 18:2, 1994.

Harper J, 'Recapturing the past: alternative methods of life story work in adoption and fostering', *Adoption & Fostering*, 20:3, 1996.

Harvey P, 'Assessment and treatment of children with moderate learning difficulties with particular reference to effective communication', *Adoption & Fostering*, 20:3, 1996.

Hill M, Hutton S and Easton S, 'Adoptive parenting – plus and minus', *Adoption & Fostering*, 12:2, 1988.

Hill M, Lambert L and Triseliotis J, *Achieving Adoption with Love and Money*, National Children's Bureau, London, 1989.

Howe D, Sawbridge P and Hinings D, *Half a Million Women*, Penguin, 1992.

Hussell C and Monaghan B, 'Child care planning in Lambeth', *Adoption & Fostering*, 6:2, 1982.

Kadushin A and Martin J, *Child Welfare Services*, Macmillan, 1988, USA.

Kaniuk J, 'The use of relationship in the preparation and support of adopters' *Adoption & Fostering*, 16:2, 1992.

Katz L, 'Permanency action through concurrent planning', *Adoption & Fostering*, 20:2, 1996.

Kelly G, 'Patterns of care: the first twelve months', in Hudson J and Galaway B (eds), *The State as Parent*, Kluwer, 1989, The Netherlands.

Kelly G and Pinkerton J, 'The Children (Northern Ireland) Order 1995: Prospects for Progress?', in Hill M and Aldgate J (eds) *Child Welfare Services*, Jessica Kingsley, 1996.

Kelly G and Coulter J, 'The Children (Northern Ireland) Order 1995: a new era for fostering and adoption services?', *Adoption & Fostering*, 21:3, 1997.

Lambert L, Borland M, Hill M and Triseliotis J, 'Using contact registers in adoption searches', *Adoption & Fostering*, 16:2, 1992.

Lambert L, Buist M, Triseliotis J and Hill M, *Freeing Children for Adoption*, BAAF, 1990.

McKay M, 'Planning for permanent placement', *Adoption & Fostering*, 4:1, 1980.

McRoy R, 'American experience and research on openness' *Adoption & Fostering*, 15:4, 1991.

Magee S and Thoday R, 'How one local authority developed post-adoption services', *Adoption & Fostering*, 19:1, 1995.

Maluccio A, Fein E and Olmstead A, *Permanency Planning for Children*, Tavistock, 1986.

Murch M, Lowe N, Borkowski M, Copner R and Grew K, *Pathways to Adoption*, HMSO, 1993.

Nbabonziza D, 'Moral and political issues facing relinquishing countries', *Adoption & Fostering*, 15:4, 1991.

Phillips R and McWilliam E, *After Adoption: Working with adoptive families*, BAAF, 1996.

Reich D, 'Children of the nightmare', *Adoption & Fostering*, 14:3, 1990.

Rowe J and Lambert L, *Children Who Wait*, ABAA, 1973.

Rowe J, Hundleby M and Garnett L, *Child Care Now*, BAAF, 1989.

Rushton A and Minnis H, 'Transracial family placements', *Journal of Child Psychology and Psychiatry*, 38:2, pp 147–159, 1997.

Rushton A, Treseder J and Quinton D, 'Sibling groups in permenent placements', *Adoption & Fostering*, 13:4, 1989.

Ryburn M, *Contested Adoptions*, Gower, 1994.

Ryburn M, 'The uneven scales of justice', *Adoption & Fostering*, 21:2, 1997.

Scottish Office, *Adoption Applications in Scotland, 1993, 1994 & 1995*, Government Statistical Service, Edinburgh, 1997.

Selman P, 'Services for intercountry adoption in the UK: some lessons from Europe', *Adoption & Fostering*, 17:3, 1993.

Simon R J and Altstein H, *Adoption, Race, and Identity*, Praeger, 1992, USA.

Singh S, 'Assessing Asian families in Scotland: a discussion', *Adoption & Fostering*, 21:3, 1997.

Tisdall E K M and Plumtree A, 'The Children Act 1989 and the Children (Scotland) Act 1995: a comparative look', *Adoption & Fostering*, 21:3, 1997.

Thoburn J, *Child Placement: Principles and practice*, Avebury, 1994.

Thoburn J, 'Psychological parenting and child placement: 'But do we want to have our cake and eat it?', in Howe D (ed), *Attachment and Loss in Child and Family Social Work*, Avebury, 1996.

Thoburn J and Rowe J, 'A snapshot of permanent family placement', *Adoption & Fostering*, 12:3, 1988.

Tizard B, *Adoption: A Second Chance*, Open Books, 1977.

Tizard B, 'Intercountry adoption: A review of the evidence', *Journal of Child Psychology and Psychiatry*, 32:5, pp 743–756, 1991.

Triseliotis J, *In Search of Origins*, Routledge & Kegan Paul, 1983.

Triseliotis J, 'Foster care outcomes: a review of research findings', *Adoption & Fostering*, 13:23, 1989.

Triseliotis J, Shireman J and Hundleby M, *Adoption: Theory, policy and practice*, Cassell, 1997.

Verhulst F C, Althaus M and Versluis-den Biemen H J M, 'Damaging backgrounds: Later adjustments of international adoptees', *Journal of the American Academy of Child and Adolescent Psychiatry*, 31, pp 518–524, 1992, USA.